Who God Says You Are

Who God Says You Are

A Christian Understanding of Identity

Klyne R. Snodgrass

WILLIAM B. EERDMANS PUBLISHING COMPANY
GRAND RAPIDS, MICHIGAN

Wm. B. Eerdmans Publishing Co.
2140 Oak Industrial Drive NE, Grand Rapids, Michigan 49505
www.eerdmans.com

ISBN 978-0-8028-7518-1

Library of Congress Cataloging-in-Publication Data

Names: Snodgrass, Klyne, author.
Title: Who God says you are : a Christian understanding of identity / Klyne R.
    Snodgrass.
Description: Grand Rapids, Michigan : William B. Eerdmans Publishing Company,
    [2018] | Includes bibliographical references and index.
Identifiers: LCCN 2017031274 | ISBN 9780802875181 (pbk. : alk. paper)
Subjects: LCSH: Identity (Psychology)—Religious aspects—Christianity.
Classification: LCC BV4509.5 .S66 2018 | DDC 233—dc23
    LC record available at https://lccn.loc.gov/2017031274

To Ethan, Ryland, Caeden, and Gabriel and to their parents:
may they be wise enough to become who God says they are—
and especially to Phyllis, about whom Ryland may well have been right

And in memory of my brother Duane and my valued friend LeRoy Cox

Contents

Preface

This book is about the most fascinating subject in the world: you. What makes you—and me—who we are? I have been captivated for years by the subject of identity, a topic that has become a major focus in religious, philosophical, and sociological fields, and rightly so, for identity is foundational for all of life. This book is intended for anyone willing to wrestle with identity, especially Christians. In focusing on identity, this book offers a chance for each of us to consider who we really are, what makes us that way, and who we should become. Nothing is more important than dealing with our own identity. I write as a New Testament scholar, not as a psychologist, psychiatrist, or philosopher, and I am not consciously Freudian or part of any other school of thought. I have drawn deeply, though, from several fields treating identity. I deal with identity because I must and because I am convinced that is what the Bible is really about. It seeks to tell us who God says we are.

Quotations from Greek and Latin classical writers are from the Loeb Classical Library, unless otherwise stated. The translations of the Scripture passages are my own, and part of the material in the chapters treating factors 1, 2, and 4 is adapted from lectures I gave at Dallas Theological Seminary that were later published as three articles: "Introduction to a Hermeneutics of Identity," "Jesus and a Hermeneutics of Identity," and "Paul's Focus on Identity"—*Bibliotheca Sacra* 168 (January–March 2011): 3–19, (April–June 2011): 133–45, and (July–September 2011): 259–73, respectively. I thank the editors of *Bibliotheca Sacra* for permission to draw on this material.

PREFACE

Gratitude must also be expressed to several people who read part or all of the manuscript and provided reflection. They represent several arenas: social workers and sociologists, horse trainers, church leaders, pastors, theologians, editors, and seminary students. They include my daughter Valerie Luberecki, my brother Phil, Everett Anthony, Cathy Norman Peterson, Brian Tucker, Joel Johnson, Jenna Brand Frost, Peter Schwich, Stephen Spencer, Michael Emerson, and, most helpful of all, my wife Phyllis. No shortcoming of this book should be attributed to them, but such people have helped frame my own identity and in the process have made life extremely enjoyable. I am indebted to them.

I also want to express my appreciation to the good people at Eerdmans for showing interest in my work and for helping to bring it to publication, especially James Ernest, Michael Thomson, and Jenny Hoffman.

Who God Says You Are—and Should Be

In the social jungle of human existence, there is no feeling of being alive without a sense of identity.

—Erik Erikson, *Identity, Youth, and Crisis*

Identity and meaning in life go hand in glove. To have meaning is to have identity.

—Robert Brawley, "From Reflex to Reflection?"

There is only one question: Who are you? Everything else in life flows from that one question. That is true whether you are a person of faith or not; the identity question is *the* question. In fact, every religion, every denial of religion, and every philosophy or ideology seeks to tell people who they are, how they fit with the reality around them, and how they should then live. If your life has any meaning, it will be because you project—and have projected—a meaningful identity.

Who are you? Who gets to say? My answer is God, but that raises the question, Who speaks for God? My answer is Scripture, but that raises the question, Who gets to interpret Scripture? In the end, each person is responsible for interpreting, but that does not suggest some kind of naive individualism or that you can make a text mean what you want or that readers do not need to be taught. Interpretation should take place within a community of faith, one that includes the whole church past and present. We read together to understand together and hold each other accountable.

The purpose of any "scripture" is to answer the identity question, to tell people who God says they are. A text is only called "scripture" because someone believes that text has power to define and transform life. This is certainly the case with the Bible. The Bible seeks to tell us who we are, who God says we are—and should be—how we fit in God's purposes, and how we should live because of our identity.

At some level I have always known Scripture was about identity. Long ago I discovered a statement. I have lost the source, but the statement is lodged in my mind. It says, "People were always coming to Jesus and asking, 'What must I do?' and he in effect responded, 'Tell me who you are, and then you will know what you must do.'" Since discovering this statement, I have had an interest in identity, an interest that grew slowly at first but then became a compelling fascination. In more recent years I have begun to understand that all my work as a New Testament scholar and teacher seeks to explain identity.

The Bible is about identity. It explains God's identity or Christ's identity, but such explanations never have the purpose of giving us abstract knowledge about God. The identity of God or Christ is explained to show what humans created in God's image are to be. John Calvin put it this way: "Without knowledge of self there is no knowledge of God. Without knowledge of God there is no knowledge of self."[1] Theologians have often said something similar, but Plato had made the same point two thousand years earlier than Calvin.[2] You cannot know yourself without knowing the One in whose image you were created.

I am well aware that the word "identity" does not appear in most translations of the Bible and that there is no obvious corresponding Hebrew or Greek word. The English word "identity" appears late in the game, toward the end of the sixteenth century. Ancient people did speak of being and of self but had no word corresponding to our word "identity." While the

---

1. John Calvin, *Institutes of the Christian Religion*, ed. John T. McNeill, trans. Ford Lewis Battles, Library of Christian Classics, vol. 20 (Philadelphia: Westminster, 1960), 1.1.1 and 1.1.2.

2. Plato, *Alcibiades* 133C.

word may be recent, the thinking and theology are not. At some level, if you are human, you have to focus on identity, even though many try to avoid it. Life is about identity construction.

The famous maxim of Greek wisdom inscribed in Apollo's temple at Delphi, and often repeated, urged "Know yourself." The Greek philosopher Epictetus commented, "First learn who you are, and then, in light of that knowledge, adorn yourself. You are a human being."[3] The problem is that while philosophers urged "Know yourself," they did not effectively tell us how. Plutarch, another Greek philosopher, added, "Not much to say is 'Know thyself'; to do this, Zeus alone of gods doth understand."[4]

Can we and *should* we know ourselves? Goethe said, "I do not know myself, and God forbid that I should. Know yourself? If I knew myself, I'd run away."[5] G. K. Chesterton added, "One may understand the cosmos, but never the ego; the self is more distant than any star. Thou shalt love the Lord thy God; but thou shalt not know thyself. We are all under the same mental calamity; we have all forgotten our names. We have all forgotten what we really are."[6] We know things but not ourselves, and if we knew ourselves, we might not be pleased with what we saw.

There is another problem as well. On hearing of my interest in identity, a friend urged that I instead focus on vocation because focusing on identity might lead to self-centeredness, the last thing anyone needs. Yes, a concern for identity could lead to self-centeredness, and vocation and identity are intertwined. The problem is that vocation already assumes an identity, is less than identity, and can lead to self-centeredness as easily as identity can. Humans have the innate ability to distort any good into self-centeredness and an opportunity for self-promotion, even the reading of Scripture. If we are to understand who God says we are, it will not result from some naive self-centered reading of ourselves into the Bible.

3. Epictetus, *Discourses* 3.1.25.

4. Plutarch, *Moralia*, "A Letter of Condolence to Apollonius," 116C–D. Plutarch is quoting from a play of Euripides.

5. The English version of Goethe's comment is rather free. The original German is found in *Goethe's poetische und prosaische Werke in zwei Bänden*, ed. Johann Wolfgang von Goethe et al. (Stuttgart and Tübingen: J. G. Cotta'schen, 1845), 1.115. A less free translation would be, "Know yourself! What profit would I have? [Or: It's not worth my while.] If I knew myself, I would have to leave."

6. G. K. Chesterton, *Orthodoxy* (New York: John Lane, 1908), 97.

More problematic still are two misuses and distortions of the word "identity": one by the Christian identity movement and the other by modern identity politics. More audacious than imaginable, "Christian Identity" is a label hijacked by representatives of a white supremacist movement, some of whom even deny that non-Caucasian people have souls. "Identity politics" refers to political positions taken because of a focus upon identity features of social groups, particularly minority groups founded on race, class, gender, ideology, sexual orientation, cultural preferences, and the like. Such distortions and uses of "identity" are miles away from my concerns.

For all the difficulty, though, we must focus on identity. It is *the* most important question, and in some ways the only question. You *will* focus on identity. The question is whether you will focus on identity well or poorly.

Philosophers and theologians have always focused on identity, and in our postmodern[7] world identity is a hot topic. Technology has heightened the concerns about identity, for people can create an identity, even multiple identities, through social networking. Social media tend to distort identity, because they heighten self-centeredness. Much of this activity betrays a malignant narcissism, manifested especially in selfies and a desire to accumulate followers—"I am somebody if people know about me." At the same time, many in our society have lost any sense of a stable identity and have a gnawing anxiety about what it means to be a human. They have no idea who they really are or should be, and merely go through the motions of living. They give little explicit attention to their identity, and their identity is chameleon-like, shifting at a moment's notice when the people around them change or the subject changes. They are like the woman who, defining "homeostasis," the body's ability to maintain equilibrium and keep constant, said, "I don't have that. I don't have a constant self. I just fluctuate according to my environment."

Such people virtually do not own their own identity because they allow other people, especially the media, to define them. They spend

---

7. Postmodernism refers to the approach of many in current Western culture that promotes a radical pluralism, views truth as uncertain and contingent, and rejects the idea of an underlying foundational story by which truth is established.

considerable effort to avoid dealing with their own identity. They stay occupied with stimuli of any kind—games, smart phones, texting, the internet, TV—rather than actually thinking and dealing with their own being. The words of a country song both recognize the problem and express the futility: "You can run from yourself but you won't get far. No matter where you go, there you are."[8] It is as if our identity shadows us; we cannot escape and cannot hide.

If identity is so important, why do humans spend so little time actually focused on it? Recently my wife and I spent a month in a remote village in Alaska, without TV and mostly off the grid. It was wonderful, and we realized again the impact of the default settings of our society. The media, news, and entertainment did not get to bombard us every day. Our defaults reverted to more important items like community, people, relations, and important tasks—main factors in identity. Shouldn't we all be more conscious of identity construction and attentive to its processes than we are? Why do we permit identity merely to happen as a stream of consciousness without plan or forethought? Is it that the task of focusing on our identity is too overwhelming, too engaging, too mysterious, and requires more vulnerability than we are willing to give? Is it that we would have to face our failures more directly? Every escape from ourselves, however, comes at a cost to our own identity.

Identity theft is, of course, a huge concern, the fastest-growing crime in our society, but there is a bigger concern—identity counterfeiting. Our true identities are lost because of identity counterfeiting, which is a crime by the self against the self. God is not the only one telling us who we are. Family, friends, acquaintances, and society in general, especially the media and advertisers, tell us who we should be, what we should look like and act like, and what will be success for us—and we *buy* it. They offer us an identity, but mostly it is an illusion. Much of society's message is "You are what you possess and the status you have." Identity is based on what we can purchase and put on display, especially houses, clothes, cars, and unusual experiences, or it is based on our accomplishments and how busy we make ourselves look. It is all external image rather than internal and substantive

8. Clint Black's "Wherever You Go." The line quoted is also found elsewhere. The whole song is a revealing treatment of identity.

identity. Not all messages to us are negative, of course. Some can tell us legitimately who we are, and legitimate messages can be life forming, but too often the messages offer a distorted image and need to be resisted.

Image is not identity; image is what we project to others, what we put on display, and is an attempt to show how we would like to be seen, which may have little to do with who we really are. Our society spends billions on image and gives little real attention to identity. When tragedy comes and strips away possessions and appearances, who are we then? Or, who are we when we really face ourselves without our props?

A Greek philosopher was captured by pirates and put on the slave market. When a potential buyer asked what he could do, he replied, "Govern men."[9] Similarly, a man asked a Spartan woman being sold as a slave if she would be good if he bought her. She replied, "Yes, and if you do not buy me."[10] Both the philosopher and the woman knew their identity did not change just because they were stripped of possessions and placed in slavery. Who are you without your stuff and the pretenses?

I recall reading a news report about a twenty-four-year-old woman who was deeply in debt and in jail for fraud in accumulating designer clothes; she said, "I do not know who I am without my stuff." You are not your stuff. You are not your money, your clothes, your house, or the car you drive. You are not the group you belong to; you are not your political party, your country, your sports team, the celebrity you try to imitate, your job, or your entertainment. These may be factors in your identity or attempts to achieve identity, but they are not who you are and certainly not who God says you are.

Of course, peer pressure plays an enormous role in identity formation. We are driven both to be unique and to fit in; we want to be unique, just like everyone else. We buy into the descriptions others force on us, and our own identity is falsified. A young man said to me, "I'm not susceptible to peer pressure; I do what I want," but he never stopped to ask where he got his "wants." We assume that we define ourselves, but that is a delusion. Every day we are bombarded by messages attempting to tell us who we are. Being ourselves in a world that constantly seeks to make us someone

9. Diogenes Laertius, *Lives of Eminent Philosophers*, Diogenes 6.29.
10. Plutarch, "Sayings of Spartan Women" 242C.

else is a never-ending and arduous task. The task is made more difficult by our own self-deception, a common human ailment. Too frequently, because of concerns for self-defense and self-promotion, we *willingly* deceive ourselves. To quote Blaise Pascal, "Our own interest is again a marvelous instrument for nicely putting out our eyes."[11]

If ever people—especially Christians—needed to face the truth and resist the dictates of society, it is now. True identity has little to do with status, possessions, clothes, employment, entertainment, or honors. Christians by necessity must resist "herding," even when done by other Christians. Without question, other people influence us, but we must be sure that their influence does not take us away from our true selves.

No matter the dangers and problems in focusing on identity, we do not have a choice. All of life is lived out of a sense of identity, even if one's sense of identity is confused or unconscious. Therefore, we *must* give direct and frequent attention to identity. The Christian faith says not only that you can know yourself, at least at some level, but that you must know yourself, sin and all; that grace makes it possible to look honestly at yourself; and that you will know yourself and find your true self only by knowing the God revealed in Jesus Christ. With the conviction that Christ is the ultimate image of God, Blaise Pascal commented, "Not only do we know God through Jesus Christ alone; but we know ourselves only by Jesus Christ."[12]

As we will see, every reality of Christian existence is at bottom an issue of identity. As for self-centeredness, faith confronts and seeks to overcome self-centeredness, for conversion is about ego transformation and ego management.[13] Faith displaces the ego so that Christ is the primary determiner of the self. In other words, the Christian understanding of the self is found outside the self. Miroslav Volf correctly says that the apostle Paul "presumes a centered self, more precisely a *wrongly* centered self that needs to be de-centered by being nailed to the cross. . . . The self is never without a center; it is always engaged in the production of its own center."[14]

11. Blaise Pascal, *Pensées* (New York: Modern Library, 1941), no. 82.

12. Pascal, *Pensées*, no. 547.

13. "Ego" can be used less pejoratively of one's self-consciousness system, but I am using it of an inflated self-centeredness.

14. Miroslav Volf, *Exclusion and Embrace: An Exploration of Identity, Otherness, and Reconciliation* (Nashville: Abingdon, 1996), 69.

Displacement of the ego is not about a rejection of one's self—quite the contrary. With false humility, some reject the importance of their own self. Too often such effacement of the ego is a covert exercise of the ego. People say, "It is not about me; it is about God," but they spend the next forty minutes talking about "I, me, and my." Christianity does not seek the effacement of the ego, even when it focuses on humility or dying with Christ. It seeks the glory of God through the ego, as Irenaeus knew when he said, "The glory of God is a living [hu]man."[15]

If life and faith are about dealing with a wrongly centered self, identity formation is the primary task of the church. Church is the place people go to find their identity and declare their allegiances, and everyone goes to church somewhere. An actor was being interviewed in an empty theater; he looked around and said, "This is my church." Everyone goes somewhere to find their identity, assert their allegiances, and relate to others like themselves. Worship and instruction are about identity maintenance. In worship we remind ourselves who God is, who we are, and that the pseudo-reality around us does not give us the message we need. Evangelism and preaching are—or are supposed to be—articulations of a needed and new identity. As the Danish philosopher Søren Kierkegaard insisted, Christianity is not a doctrine but an existence-communication.[16] Church is also the place I go to make my protest: against the world, against Christians, and even against the church for its superficiality and for not doing justice to its own gospel.

Unfortunately, the church has often failed to communicate well what identity is about. Especially in societies like ours where many claim the label "Christian," what really makes a person a Christian? How tight or loose should the definition be? Lack of clarity renders the church ineffective. The gospel in our time is for many an unimportant item in their lives, as if it were a minor attachment, one that barely touches their identity. This is *not* the Christian faith.

15. Irenaeus, *Against Heresies* 4.20.7 (Ante-Nicene Fathers). An alternate and frequently used translation is "The glory of God is a human fully alive," but I have not been able to document the source of this translation.

16. *Søren Kierkegaard's Journals and Papers*, ed. and trans. Howard V. Hong and Edna H. Hong, 7 vols. (Bloomington: Indiana University Press, 1967–1978), 1:463 (nos. 1060 and 1061), but Kierkegaard makes this point repeatedly.

Christ is not an add-on to an existing identity; he seeks to remake your identity. Often conversion language is a gross exaggeration and implies that nothing of the old identity remains. Obviously much remains the same; you are still physically the same person with the same history and propensities in the same culture. What is changed is the old life of sin, the old being, and its *old orientation.* Even the things that do not change are seen from a new perspective. Christ is not an accessory to your identity, as if you were choosing an option for a car; he takes over identity so that everything else becomes an accessory, which is precisely what "Jesus is Lord" means.

We have been sold a cheap gospel without demand and without content, as if faith were a short transaction, a prayer, or a decision, to get security taken care of so we can go to heaven, but the New Testament is far less concerned with going to heaven than people think. In fact, as important as God's promises about the future are, the concern for going to heaven is one of the most distorting factors in evangelical Christianity. What counts is life with God and an identity shaped by God, both now and eternally.

What Is Identity?

Who are you? What seems like a simple question is not so simple, for identity is quite complex, as technical discussions among philosophers, psychologists, and theologians attest. In asking this question, I am less interested in the distinctions of self, selfhood, and the ego, or between the internal self "behind the mask" and the external self "in front of the mask."[17] Identity is the sum of everything that pertains to us and shapes us. Identity is that sense of being and self-understanding that frames our actions, communicates to others who we are, and sets the agenda for our acts. Identity drives life; it provides the energy and motivation for all else. It is the well from which life is directed and sustained. If you know who you are, you know what you must do, and if your identity is healthy, it

---

17. Psychologists use "mask" language because our word "person" derives from a word used of masks in ancient theater.

provides a confidence that enables action. We live out of a sense of identity. It may be unexpressed or even unconscious, but it still determines us. Who are you and what made you who you are? More importantly, who should you be and how does the Christian gospel redefine who you are?

Paul Ricoeur describes narrative identity—the story of who we are—as a function of permanence over time, established by self-constancy and perseverance of character.[18] There is continuity over a period of time, a coherence of being even though there is change. Ricoeur's statement presumes an ongoing story and an agent acting, being acted upon, and aging but still the same agent throughout. We are not passive subjects living out our identity.

I suggest there are nine major factors from which our identity is constructed. These nine factors are true of all persons regardless of their religion or lack thereof—Jews, Muslims, secularists, atheists, Christians, or whatever. Of most significance, as we will see, is that the Bible addresses all nine factors.

Before detailing these nine factors, a delusion needs to be addressed. We delude ourselves about how much *we* construct our own identity. Especially in our culture we assume that we as individuals are in control of our own identity and that we will be whoever we wish. That at best is partly true, and at times only marginally so. Much of our identity we do not choose, and we have little control over it; it is given to us. For all nine factors, to varying degrees, we have to say part is given and part is chosen.

The Nine Factors of Identity

Factor 1 is our physical and psychological characteristics, some given and some chosen: our gender, ethnicity, size, strength, abilities, tendencies toward shyness, aggressiveness, etc., all shape us. *You are your body.*[19] You are more than your body, but every other part of you is

18. Paul Ricoeur, *Oneself as Another*, trans. Kathleen Blamey (Chicago: University of Chicago Press, 1992), 113–39, especially 118–23.

19. Each of the nine factors in the book receives its own chapter. In our discussion of the factors in this chapter and the next, however, factor 4, "You Are Your Mind," is moved to the end of the discussion because it takes all the other factors into account and shapes

related to your body. Much is hardwired, but it is *not* necessarily determinative. We can learn, train, and even radically change some parts of our being, but clearly there are limits as to how much the body can be changed. To state the obvious, no matter how much desire and training are present, I will never play professional basketball, since I do not have the physical capacities required for the job—and never did. Further, we would do well to look in the mirror and ask what identity others assume on seeing us. For good or ill, people do make initial judgments based on appearance. They have no other option.

We are driven to become unique, but we already are. Uniqueness, which is at the center of identity, does not need to be created, for from our fingerprints to our toes, no two people have the same physical and psychological makeup. This physical uniqueness is foundational for identity, so the significance of the body for identity must not be underestimated. Identity is always embodied, and a person's body both shapes and expresses identity.

I have two friends, each of whom as a young overweight adult lost one-third or more of her body weight. The weight loss *required* a reframing of identity. They are still the same people, but they are not perceived or treated as the same people. Since they are not perceived the same way, they cannot perceive themselves the same way or relate in the same way to others. Their identity shifted.

Manipulations of physical appearance, such as hairstyle, clothes, body art, and jewelry, obviously shape and communicate aspects of identity. It is no accident that military academies, Nazi concentration camps, and various groups and companies have sought to control identity by shaving hair or regulating hairstyles and replacing personal clothes with uniforms. Appearance shapes identity.

Our physical and psychological characteristics include much more. Race and ethnicity shape us and place us in relation to other groups and cultures. Athletic and physical abilities create options, whereas their absence closes doors, which is true of numerous other innate capabilities such as creativity, verbal or conceptual skill, emotional competence, in-

---

identity. This affects the order in which the factors are discussed in these two chapters only; it does not affect the numbering of the factors.

terests, and more. Our identities are stamped from the beginning, but they are not predetermined. We still make choices and adapt our capabilities and are responsible for how they are used. *The self is a physical self.*

Factor 2 is our histories: *you are your history*, at least to some degree. We are what the past has made us, both our own history and the history into which we were born. Identity is a narrative construct, *a story*, part given and part chosen but all shaping us. Our experiences shape us. Soldiers returning from war are not the same people who left for war. We are shaped by our families of origin, opportunities, education, traumas, failures, successes, and celebrations. As one person put it, "People don't come preassembled but are glued together by life."[20]

Each person's story is unique. You partially write your own story. It is your story alone, but the story does not merely begin at birth. Each of us is born into a quite complex history—or histories. We are born into the history of our family, our community, our country, and, indeed, the human race. Alasdair MacIntyre is correct in saying, "I can only answer the question, 'What am I to do?' if I can answer the prior question 'Of what story or stories do I find myself a part?'"[21] Much of your story has already been written by other people. Worse, other people will continue to write your story, and you may not even notice. The early years of our personal history are under the control of parents and other authority figures, many specifically *given* the task of shaping us. We are acted upon by other people—like it or not—and we act on others. We have difficulties, successes, traumas, embarrassments, and knowledge-enhancing experiences. All these things shape our identity; they make us who we are. At some point we take over the task of writing our own story, but even then we only partially write our own story. Other people, wrongly or rightly, still take a hand in writing our story.

The first part of a person's story is the name given at birth. Names are markers of identity and may indicate gender, attachment within a family, place in a culture, desires of one's parents, or religious affiliation. Sometimes people seek to change their identity by changing their name.

20. Joseph E. LeDoux, *Synaptic Self: How Our Brains Become Who We Are* (New York: Penguin, 2006), 3.

21. Alasdair MacIntyre, *After Virtue: A Study in Moral Theory*, 3rd ed. (Notre Dame: University of Notre Dame Press, 2007), 216.

If a woman at marriage takes her husband's name, she may lose much of her identity; at least in most Western cultures her identity is changed radically to a degree the husband's is not.

No one chooses to be a self, but each of us has the responsibility of *making* our self within the larger stories of which we are a part. Selfhood is an achievement, something one must become, a point emphasized by Søren Kierkegaard.[22] We live into an identity given to us partly at birth. *To some degree* we do indeed make ourselves what we are, and we must take responsibility for what we become. All we do and think contributes to our identity within our larger stories and helps shape those stories. *The self is a narrative self.* How will we manage this construction of our own self as we write our own history in a larger story?

Factor 3 is about relationships: to some degree *you are your relations.* Life is relational, and relations determine identity. One of the few ways we have of explaining ourselves is by pointing to our relations, to our parents, to a spouse if we have one, to other family members, or to groups to which we belong, such as community, church, school, military unit, team, or club. We tend to think identity is an individual matter. It is not. In fact, the very idea of an individual is questionable, for no one exists—or is formed—in isolation. Identity is not an individual affair; it is a social construct. We are not who we are by ourselves. An African proverb asserts, "A person is a person through another person." A Mexican proverb adds, "Tell me who you are with and I will tell you who you are." "Who are you?" is not a question you answer alone, a fact to which we will return.

Sometimes scholars contrast group and individual societies, often suggesting that ancient societies were dyadic (i.e., relational, a person needs another person to know himself or herself) and ours is individualistic. But this contrast is at best an exaggeration, if not an illusion. For all that our society thinks it is individualistic, we are not mere individuals but persons in groups and categories. We do not even know how to be an individual without looking at others and determining how we want to be similar or dissimilar. The motives driving our choices are communally determined. Groups have value systems that shape us. Even the language

22. See C. Stephen Evans, *Kierkegaard on Faith and the Self: Collected Essays* (Waco: Baylor University Press, 2006), 265–66.

we use to boast of being an individual is given to us by other people. Some societies are indeed more communally driven than others, but none is really individualistic.

Especially important is one's family of origin and what happens with relations during childhood and adolescence. Obviously important too are the friends one chooses and the people with whom one is thrown together in neighborhood, school, and work. Being in relation with other people inevitably means we expect specific things of them: good will, safety, fairness, honesty, assistance, and contribution to life. Whether those expectations are met or not shapes us, sometimes tragically so when boundaries are abused. Another shaping aspect stems from what we perceive that others expect from us and whether we accept, reject, rebel against, or modify those expectations; this too is an issue to which we will return.

We are never so aware that we are our relations until the death of someone close. The death of a family member caused a woman to say, "It is discouraging not being able to be yourself," and "It is difficult to learn how to be a new self." Another woman said she felt her identity stopped after the death of her sister and mother. She was stuck, not knowing who she was without them and their voices in her life, even though sometimes the voices were negative. *The self is a relational self.*

Factor 4 is discussed at the end of the list because it incorporates all the other factors to do its job. We will hold it until then.

Factor 5 deals with commitments: *you are your commitments*, and commitments cover a broad spectrum of life. Ben Meyer, a New Testament scholar, said, "'Identity' is what the core of one's allegiance makes one to be,"[23] which is scary, for many give no serious thought to the core of their allegiance, and as a result their identity, like their commitments, is mush. Identity is gained and expressed by where we give our attention, by what we care about and value with regard to relations, place, activities, and attitudes. We commit ourselves to what we *think* is good and valuable, whether it is or not. Our commitment to a location is crucial; we are defined to some degree by the place we live, especially in growing

---

23. Ben F. Meyer, *The Early Christians: Their World Mission and Self-Discovery* (Wilmington, DE: Michael Glazier, 1986), 174.

up. Commitment to a geography also involves commitment to a language. To some extent *geography is identity*. I am an East Tennessean and I am marked by that, even though I have spent three-fourths of my life elsewhere. My speech betrays my origin, and I assume the land should have mountains. One of the first questions we ask people is, "Where are you from?" We sense that if we understand origin we begin to understand identity.

Our commitments to investments of interest, time, and money shape us. That to which you assign value assigns value to you and defines you. A commercial for baseball has a young man say, "I live for this game!" Really? It is sad if that is the extent of his life. Of course, it is just a commercial, but it seeks to persuade us to give maximal attention to and be defined by baseball. Tell me how you spend your time and money, and I will tell you who you are. To some degree you become what you give your attention to.

Similarly, what you oppose, hate, and fight shapes your agenda and shapes who you are. Identity is determined by differences and oppositions. We stake out an identity by not being like others, regardless of the motivation for difference. This is one reason our society has become so antagonistic. No matter what the other side is doing, people oppose it because it is the other side. In the process we allow the very thing we oppose to define us, sometimes in directions we would not otherwise go. Too often we become like the very thing we fight. Be careful what you hate and oppose, for your opposition will shape you.

Our commitments to attitudes, perceptions, opinions, likes, and dislikes also define us. Beliefs and attitudes held are not merely thoughts we hold but realities that shape identity. For example, attitudes about sexuality, violence, materialism, and what is important and valuable shape us. Our true "theology" is those beliefs we give defining force for ourselves, not the ideas in books with which we agree.

Commitments to the icons, "heroes," and people we seek to impress also define us. We are shaped by what or whom we admire and identify with. Plato asked, "Or do you think it possible not to imitate the things to which anyone attaches himself with admiration?"[24] Why do we give

24. Plato, *Republic* 500C.

such defining power to media stars or sports figures? A singer reportedly charges eight hundred dollars to have a picture taken with her. Why do we think that a picture with a famous person, or even seeing a famous person, contributes in some way to our own identity? It does not.

That to which you assign value assigns value to you—or devalues you—and defines you. Obviously, we should be careful in deciding which commitments are worth our time and attention, for commitments determine identity. *The self is a committed self.*

Factor 6 deals with our actions: *you are what you do.* Related to commitments, actions we are assigned or choose, especially our jobs, are huge determiners of identity. There is no such thing as an identity that does not act. The self is a self because it is an agent; it decides and acts to achieve a goal. As we grow we develop the ability to act and, hopefully at least, the freedom to act. The self looks for and chooses things to do, and it is evaluated in terms of its competence to act and the value of the choices. Implied in the ability to act is the responsibility to act well and to be held accountable for one's actions both by oneself and by others. To be human is to have a sense of responsibility, and such a sense produces action, or at least the awareness that one should act.

You are what you repeatedly do is a point as old as Aristotle. People sometimes believe their thoughts and actions are not necessarily related, as if they could believe one thing and act differently. Humans by nature are good at tearing the act of thinking from the act of being. The result is a separation of head and heart, of thinking, doing, and being, and of faith and works. Hypocrisy is the result. What we do, however, shows what we *really* think. A focus on identity allows us to put being, thinking, and doing back together. There is no being without doing. We are what we do, no matter what we say.[25] Nor is there a necessary sequence from being or thinking to doing. There is a reciprocal action. Sometimes we learn first and then do; at other times—and in fact maybe most times—we do first and then learn. *The self is an acting self.*

Because boundaries determine identity, **factor 7** is: *You are your*

---

25. I am well aware that some people are placed in circumstances where they have no freedom and are forced into actions they would not otherwise commit. I deal with this briefly in the chapter on actions.

boundaries. Being is a process of recognizing boundaries, putting down some boundaries, and removing others. Life is about discovering where our boundaries are. An infant learns to differentiate itself from its mother. Children are taught not to violate the boundaries of others: don't hit people, don't take their property, mind your own business. Boundaries are placed to avoid danger and to prevent harm. We create boundaries to prevent violation of our identity.

People need to and will differentiate themselves from others. If they do not find good ways, they will choose bad ones. We are both separate from and bound to other people. Our very separateness establishes identity, and clearly identity has to do with opposition, which is most evident in teenagers trying to distinguish themselves from parents and friends. Every factor about identity is in opposition to or distinction from something else.

The first and most obvious boundary is our skin, which separates us from others. Our ethnic identity also distinguishes us and places us in one group rather than another, and belonging to a group establishes boundaries, like it or not. Our geography separates us from others as well. We live in one locale, belong to it, and are determined by it, not some other place. Our geography may be the limit of our horizon or the choice to be or not be in certain places. Again, geography is identity, and clearly limited boundaries make us narrow.

Boundaries are created by our associations: to be part of a group—a political party, a church, a soccer team, or whatever—is to set down a boundary between you and those who do not belong to that group, even if you do not want such a boundary. Marriage is a boundary marker; in fact, in marriage a couple agrees to merge boundaries *partially.* Those boundaries do not become coextensive, but no one else is permitted within the boundary created by marriage in the same way the two married persons are.

Among the most important boundaries are ethical boundaries, places where we have—or should have—drawn a line and said, "I will not violate this boundary." Evil—sin—is largely about the violation of legitimate, even holy, boundaries and the construction of illegitimate boundaries between people or between us and God. Known theft and slander, for example, create boundaries so that people do not speak. Forgiveness is necessary for the removal of illegitimate boundaries. Boundaries are also created by our ethical decisions, so that we have boundaries of concern and boundaries to actions. We care about some things because of ethical commitments, and certain actions are precluded by who we think we are.

We need boundaries around the good, and around what should be, so as not to settle for something less. Boundaries should be permeable for the good but resistant to evil. How solid are our ethical boundaries? Are they boundaries of convenience easily violated, or do they actually constrain and shape our actions?

Boundaries can be factors of identity or causes of division. Who gets inside our definitional boundaries, and how easily? How do we negotiate boundaries? Border control is not merely an issue for countries. How and where do we do boundary maintenance legitimately for our own being?

Sometimes people think they live or would like to live without boundaries. It cannot be done. Boundaries exist whether we are aware of them or not, and they are necessary for healthy living. As one young woman put it, "I feel the most free when I know exactly what my boundaries are." *The self is a boundaried self.*

Because identity is not static and is always in process, **factor 8** is: *You are an ongoing process of change.* Identities will be lived and must be lived into. Identity is flexible, in process, and never an accomplished fact until death. We continually change physically as we age, and we change in other ways as we have new experiences, new learning, new relations, new commitments, etc. We are constantly constructing our identities, although we are usually oblivious to the whole process.

Change is coming; it always does. You are more than you presently are. You are in reality more than you grasp, at least potentially, and you also are in a process of loss. As we age, we encounter loss, and we also lose memories, relations, and commitments of various types as life progresses. But who are you in the midst of change? Is your identity strong enough to carry you through? Will change radically alter your identity? Will your identity grow in a good direction, or is it frozen in an unhealthy place? We want life settled and constant. It never is. That is why the Scriptures emphasize that only God is the same—faithful, constant, and never changing. But what happens when your god has to change, when you have had an idol, or at least a distorted view of God—which all of us do at times?

If identity is a process of ongoing change, to what degree are we passive in letting change happen, and to what degree do we take responsibility for the change, knowing that there is much we do not control? We *can* control investment in learning, maintaining proper relations and boundaries, and other aspects of identity maintenance, but clearly we cannot define ourselves without attention to who we are becoming. *The self is a changing self.*

Identity includes some sense of the future, some sense of where we are going and what will happen next, for from our identity we project a future. This leads us to **factor 9**: *You are your future.* If a young person says, "I am a high school senior," the obvious question is, "What will you do next year?" It is not merely high school seniors for whom such questions are relevant. For all of us, to say who we are is to invite the question what we will be next and in the future. Identity casts a shadow forward. Futures cannot be controlled, but they can be anticipated, tentatively planned, and cared for. If our futures seem to have us on hold, who are we while we are waiting?

Even if one is unaware of it, one has some sense of a goal—or *the* goal—of life. It may be our definition of success, retirement, or something more substantive, such as life with God. Whatever it is, our concept of the future pulls us and shapes us. Knowing we do not measure up to the anticipated goal creates anxiety and guilt, even if unacknowledged. *The self is an anticipated self.*

But we still do not have an identity. An identity is the result of internal thinking that organizes, prioritizes, values, and interprets all the other eight factors, and here things get complex—but fun! The final factor in our discussion is factor 4, which we have delayed treating until now: *You are the result of your mind—your internal self-interpreting, self-directing memory.* Something internal gathers all other factors, filters them, interprets them, and uses them to direct life. Humans are the only self-interpreting animal, and identity is very much about memory. Without memory there would be no identity. But it is not just memory; identity is an internal ordering and synthesizing process framed by memory, and this internal ordering even chooses in part what will be remembered.

Identity is not comprised just of all the boundaries, relations, and commitments; it is the result of our ability to *think about ourselves*, to be self-aware and to analyze our own thoughts and actions. At bottom identity is the internal me censoring, filtering, valuing, synthesizing, and interpreting how I stand with regard to all the realities of my life. What gets in, what gets valued as good, what is given importance and attached to, what receives commitment, what gets rejected or denied—even if true—and what has such force it cannot be ignored? What do I really care about, like, and dislike, and why? Identity is the result of the thinking me that interprets and concentrates my life and character. It says, "This is how I will—or must—understand and present myself."

Identity has been defined philosophically as the unity with oneself, that stable core of defining factors where a voice says, "This is the real me." Postmodernists tend to reject the idea of a unified identity—more about that later—but the less people have a stable core, the more they are diagnosed with personality disorders or institutionalized. We assume some kind of persistent sameness within a person and a persistent sharing of some kind of essential character with others.

Real identity, then, is who you are in the dark, when you think no one is watching, not the image you project because of what you want people to think. *The real you is the internal you.* Part of this internal self-interpreting aspect has to do with accountability, responsibility, esteem, and self-awareness. How do I see myself in relation to other people and to reality? To whom am I accountable, and how do I view myself for the way I have handled my responsibilities? *I am accountable first of all to myself, and I, like every person, seek a positive self-evaluation—or at least an explanation as to why a positive self-evaluation is not possible and a negative self-evaluation is not my fault.*

We cannot avoid the complexity of this internal self-interpreting, self-directing memory, nor should we. Attention to this internal process enables life. This internal process involves first a *moral* discussion about values and the good to which we seek to attach ourselves and to which we give allegiance. We do seek to attach ourselves to the good, or at least the perceived good; we have to, since we seek a positive self-evaluation. But who gets to say what is good? What language will we use to speak of the good and valuable, and who will teach us this language or tell us what is good and valuable? Values are learned. Who teaches values in our culture? What should we care about? Most of our society has lost all basis for evaluating what is good and chooses relativism. Choose any value you want! But what will make the good so clear and desirable that we will not settle for something less? Our sense of self-respect and self-worth is at stake. By giving ultimate value to that which does not deserve it, we diminish ourselves. Where is honor, and who determines what is honorable? The self-interpreting memory is largely, even if unconsciously, about honor, honor derived from the values perceived in the other identity factors.

Since it is about the good, values, and honor, this self-interpreting memory is an *ethical* concern. It is a decision about how you understand the significance of an event, an idea, your reaction, or your looks. It is a decision about how you will defend yourself against what someone said or what happened to you.

But there are problems. Our interpretation of ourselves is compromised by our self-deception, part of the work of sin. The self is both the deceiver and the deceived. The very instrument in charge of framing identity is not worthy of trust because it is too self-centered, too self-defensive, and too willing to cheat. Sin also contributes to fragmentation because sin makes humans contradict who they are and should be in God's purposes. If our inner being, our heart, is key for the internal self-interpreting memory, how do we get it to be honest and just, not defensive, and willing to obey? How do we get in there to work internally on ourselves?

Especially in the postmodern world, some people doubt whether there is such a thing as a unified being at all. They argue that no real unity of being exists, that we have multiple voices within us, multiple selves, and that we are fragmented. How should we react to the postmodern claim?

If the problem is some idea of a fixed identity independent of history, culture, and relations, obviously such an idea of identity will not work. If the claim stems from the multiple contexts in which we all find ourselves and the multiple roles we have and ways we present ourselves, again postmodernists are correct. We have multiple manifestations of our identity, depending on various contexts. We are a hierarchy of nested identities, but certain aspects of our being are not variable. We adjust to context, but our integrity depends on our being the same person in all contexts. Hypocrisy is the attempt to present an image that is not real, and we all sneer at hypocrisy and do not want to be guilty of it. But are the pluralities within us connected and in dialogue, or are they strangers to each other? All of us know a "me" that is not "me"; or, stated differently, the mind has a mind of its own.

The biblical text is well aware of the fragmentation of our being. Paul's lament in Romans 7 that the very thing he wants to do he does not do and his discussions of old being and new being are evidence, as are the complaint about double-minded people in James 1:8 and the psalmist's concern for the integrity of a pure heart (Ps. 24:4).

Freud and numerous others also recognized the fragmentation. Freud said, "The ego is not master in its own house."[26] Such expressions as "Jekyll and Hyde" and "the force and the dark side" express the fragmentation too. If postmodernism denies any concept of a unified self, does not Christianity both acknowledge the problem and offer a solution? Surely one of the goals of saying "Jesus is Lord" is a unity of being—or at least a coherence of being—even in the diversity of experience.

However, even if we reject the idea of a unified self, there is *still* something internal that experiences and narrates all that happens. The people who emphasize pluralities of self are the very people who discuss identity crises and speak of the fragmentation and meaninglessness people experience. An awareness of the multiple ways we present ourselves does not require the conclusion that there is no larger sense of self, and that larger sense of self is, or at least determines, our identity. The real issue is how we view what *it* is that experiences and narrates all these factors and modes of existence. There is an internal self-interpreting, self-directing memory, even if it is not wholly unified. Researchers of identity speak of "an ideal executive self," a sense of self that orders a hierarchy of selves, regulates the tensions of multiple voices, and establishes a sense of a unified self. The purpose of every religion is to create an executive self,[27] and Christianity seeks this very goal in naming Christ as Lord.

To what degree is the fragmentation of the self a result of the failure

26. Sigmund Freud, "Fixation to Traumas—the Unconscious," in *The Standard Edition of the Complete Psychological Works of Sigmund Freud*, trans. James Strachey (London: Hogarth, 1966), 16:285.

27. Patrick McNamara, *The Neuroscience of Religious Experience* (Cambridge: Cambridge University Press, 2009), 30–31, 40, 246, et al.

to attain the good that we ourselves value? There is the good we affirm that summons us to a higher level than we attain. We know we should be more than we are, and we give meaning to life when we attempt to live up to our own ideals. Ben Meyer speaks of "the compelling phenomenon of one's summoning self—a self strangely, disconcertingly more me than my already given, long since familiar self—yet, not me, not yet me, not yet wholly real," and says this *summoning self* confronts one's merely given self.[28] This *ideal*, unrealized self is a basis for hope and possibility, if we do not content ourselves with the actual (or given) self. God seeks to put us on a path to this ideal self, the self God intended with creation.

We must also know that this *internal process of identity construction involves two conversations*. First, identity is partly an *internal conversation* whereby we address ourselves and which reveals the fragmentation within ourselves. We are both the subject analyzing and interpreting, and the object being analyzed and interpreted. Language such as "Then I said to myself" is revealing, but who is addressing whom? Clearly the conversation is partly between the ideal self and the actual self as in Romans 7, but it may reflect as well dialogue about multiple roles in which we find ourselves.

Second, this internal self-interpreting, self-directing memory is not merely the individual making assessments. Identity is even more a result of a *conversation* between the individual and the external community. Identity is assigned and mediated to us largely from the outside. I was trying to explain the self-interpreting memory in a church, and a wise woman told me I was missing something. A severely cognitively impaired girl was regularly brought to that church by her family. The woman pointed out to me that this girl has an identity even if she does not have a self-interpreting memory. She has an identity given her by her family and her church. The same is true for a person with Alzheimer's or an infant; each has an identity, one assigned by others and based on memory or hope respectively. *This assigning of identity from the outside is true of all of us.*

---

28. Meyer, *The Early Christians*, 27–28. C. S. Lewis had earlier written in reference to heaven, "The thing you long for summons you away from the self." See *The Problem of Pain* (New York: Macmillan, 1962), 149.

Our identity is assigned to each of us by significant others in our lives and is also something we assign to ourselves in response to a community's assignment of identity to us. Identity is then an interaction of self-description and communal description. We internalize what others say about us. *You are who you think other people say you are and how you react to that message,* at least to some degree or unless you know the perception is wrong and resist it. We judge ourselves in light of how we think other people judge us. Protests that we are independent and wholly determine ourselves are illusions.

I am a New Testament scholar partly because other people say I am and allow me to be in institutions, organizations, and activities appropriate to the role. Most people seek the approval of some group of people, and that seeking and the interpretation of the success of that seeking are identity-shaping factors. With teenagers this is most obvious, but it is a factor throughout life. The more the internal and external assessments are in agreement, the stronger the sense of identity that results. Neither assessment is necessarily correct, and as difficult as it may be, one can reject a community's description. But an external assessment can be disproven only by performance.

Most of us have seen the YouTube video of Susan Boyle trying out for *Britain's Got Talent,* a British TV show very similar to *American Idol.* This frumpy-looking woman, merely because of her looks, was in effect told she was not a singer by the judges and the audience, but she refused that description and asserted a different identity by her stunning performance. The same thing happened later with a duet by Charlotte and Jonathan, with Simon Cowell, one of the judges and creator of the show, muttering when he first saw Jonathan, an oversized seventeen-year-old, "Just when you thought it could not get worse." But after a stunning performance, Cowell was comparing Jonathan to Pavarotti. You can prove who you really are only by performance. To what degree do we individually and collectively have to reject a community's description of us? What happens when a person is assigned a label such as stupid, alcoholic, or useless?

With all this assessment, memory, and self-interpretation, clearly a priority must be placed on our minds. Pascal said, "Thought constitutes the greatness of a [human. A human] is but a reed, the most feeble thing in nature; but he [or she] is a thinking reed. . . . All our dignity consists, then, in thought."[29] We might reject saying *all* our dignity consists in thought, but Pascal is correct in saying thought constitutes the greatness of humans. If the thinking process is so important in identity construction, we cannot afford to be oblivious to decisions we make, but by what standard shall we judge and direct our own decisions?

Those are the nine factors. The result in all nine factors is that much about our identity we did not choose. With all of identity part is given and part is chosen, and each part contributes to our individual uniqueness. We did not choose our families, our language, or our country. We were born into a place, a society, a culture, a worldview, and an ideology or religion. However, what we do with what we are given is largely up to us. How we relate to the givens in our life is not set in stone. We choose whether we will continue in each, some more so than others. I may decide not to live in Tennessee or even to evade its impact, possibly even intentionally changing my accent (which I do not), but I cannot evade that I am a Tennessean by birth and origin, that I am an American, that my mother tongue is English, that I was born into and participate in a certain history—all items not my choice but a result of the particularities of my birth. *The issue is what we do with our given identities.* We may be limited by the horizon of our vision, but *life is not predetermined.* Just as virtue has to be learned, possibilities for life have to be learned as well, and *one of the purposes of Christianity is to give you a vision of what is possible and what should be, to give you a vision of who God says you are.*

Another point is clear. The statement "Geography is identity" involves more than merely our location. In fact, it relates to all the factors of existence. Part of my geography is my own body, part is where I live, part is the limit of my horizon. I live in a physical place, in a culture, in a community, a society, a family. Who I am is determined by the geography of my life, relations, commitments, and future. There is good reason that the first question in Scripture is God asking, "Where are you?" (Gen. 3:9).

With all these factors shaping our identity, why do we give so little conscious attention to the process by which identity is being formed? Why do we not evaluate the internal and external messages we encounter? Why do we not test the truth and validity of the messages and make

29. Pascal, *Penseés*, nos. 346–47.

wise decisions about the way we want to establish a worthwhile identity? Why do we not focus on learning what is important? Are the problems of pride and laziness, which some see as the origin of all sin, too much in play? Granted, life often overwhelms us with demands, but still, why are we not much more careful with regard to our own identity?

Sin, of course, distorts and derails the whole process. Sin, the propensity to self-centeredness and worse, is not a tenth factor of identity but a reality that pervades all our identity—all nine previously mentioned factors, especially the internal, self-interpreting memory that organizes and values the rest of life. The destructive fragmentation and fracture we know in our relations and in ourselves are the direct result of sin. This creates another kind of internal dialogue. Shall we do wrong or right? Shall we be honest with ourselves or hide in self-deception? A theological and practical problem is obvious. The very part of us organizing, valuing, and interpreting life is already disoriented by sin. Sin is part of our identity, but sin does not get the last word, as we will see.

So, who are you? It is worth stopping at this point and contemplating your own identity and how each of the nine factors functions specifically for you:

> your physical and psychological makeup
> your history
> your relations
> your commitments
> your actions
> your boundaries
> the ongoing process of change in your life
> your future
> your internal self-interpreting, self-directing memory

Remember though: identity is not solely an individual affair. It is part of a conversation between the individual and the external community. Who do others say you are? Who has the right ultimately to say who you are? Who you are, of course, is not a settled answer. There is still that ideal self, the summoning self, that God intends you to be and that is in front of you calling you.

Wendell Berry wrote, "We could say that the human race is a great coauthorship in which we are collaborating with God and nature in the making of ourselves and one another. From this there is no escape. We may collaborate either well or poorly or we may refuse to collaborate, but even to refuse to collaborate is to exert an influence and to affect the quality of the product. This is only a way of saying that by ourselves we have no meaning and no dignity; by ourselves we are outside the human definition, outside our identity."[30]

If I could offer you the opportunity to coauthor a book with the world's best author, you would likely jump at the chance. God invites you to coauthor your story with God. That, in effect, is what the Bible offers.

From here we will see how Scripture addresses all nine factors to tell you who God says you are. *The crucial point is that you must not be passive in claiming and forming the identity God says is yours.*

---

30. Wendell Berry, "Men and Women in Search of Common Ground," in *The Art of the Commonplace: The Agrarian Essays of Wendell Berry*, ed. Norman Wirzba (Washington, DC: Counterpoint, 2002), 137.

Faith Transforms Identity

Our vocation is not simply to be, but to work together with God in the creation of our own life, our own identity, our own destiny. . . . We are even called to share with God the work of creating the truth of our identity. . . . To work out our own identity in God. . . . The secret of my full identity is hidden in Him.

—Thomas Merton, *New Seeds of Contemplation*[1]

Identity is a fundamental component of spirituality. A truly spiritual life can only be lived by one who knows who he is and knows himself, accepts and comes to terms with himself as he is. . . . Identity is the object of a ceaseless arduous quest whose stakes are life and death. The search for identity becomes a task which inspires the whole life of man.

—Pierre Bühler, "Christian Identity: Between Objectivity and Subjectivity" [The same is true for a woman]

---

1. Compare Brennan Manning's statement "Our identity rests in God's relentless tenderness for us revealed in Jesus Christ" (*Abba's Child: The Cry of the Heart for Intimate Belonging* [Colorado Springs: NavPress, 1994], 51).

Many years ago I heard a sermon—actually, a parable—entitled "Joe the Foolish Screwdriver." It was about a power drill who thought he was a screwdriver until someone convinced him he really was a drill, plugged him in, and set him to work. The point of the parable was that people often mistakenly assume their identity is one thing when it is really something else. The Christian message asserts that our identity is different from what we think, and it sets aside false understandings and explains our true identity—the one God says is truly ours—calls us to that identity, plugs us into life with God, and gives us good work to do.

Most of us know we are not what we should be. One of my students, talking about his former unhealthy lifestyle, said an almost audible voice kept reminding him, "This is not who you are." A drug addict in the midst of his confusion lamented, "I have no idea who I am." We prefer to ignore and stifle such thoughts, but all of us know something inside us encouraging us to live better than we do. The pervasiveness of the question "Who am I?" indicates that something is wrong,[2] that we are adrift and need reorientation and coherence.

Christianity insists that humans cannot be who they really are apart from God. As Robert Wilken puts it, "Because human beings were made in the image of God our lives will be fully human only as our face is turned toward God and our actions formed by his love. . . . We know ourselves as we transcend ourselves, and we find ourselves as we find fellowship with God."[3]

The idea of transcending ourselves points to the image of an ideal self, the summoning self, and is part of the claim of God on our lives. Unfortunately we are more likely to hold others accountable to our ideal self than ourselves. We are more like the man Seneca, a first-century philosopher, tells of, who after arguing for ethics said, "You have no right to make me live up to my own standard."[4] We are all guilty of abdicating from responsible selfhood. We strike a deal with

2. Phillipe (Flip) Theron, "Devastating Grace: Justificatio IMPH and I-dentity," in *Christian Identity*, ed. Eduardus Van der Borght, Studies in Reformed Theology 16 (Leiden: Brill, 2008), 33–49, here 34.

3. Robert Louis Wilken, *The Spirit of Early Christian Thought: Seeking the Face of God* (New Haven: Yale University Press, 2005), 153–54.

4. Seneca, *On the Happy Life* 24.4.

ourselves and choose something less; the church has been excessively guilty of this.

One of the aches of my life has been watching the failure of Christians to understand their own message, their viewing Christianity as so superficial as to be irrelevant, and their failure to capture the depth of commitment and transformation that faith involves. Christianity is seen as a minor attachment to their well-guarded identities rather than the ground-shaking transformation of identity it really is. No wonder the American church is declining and has less and less influence in people's lives, especially young people's lives. Many "believe all the right things" but have a gnawing sense that there is no reality to their faith. But faith is not about believing stuff; I *insist* that biblical faith is about being attached to Christ, bound to him, and *participating* in life with Christ and having your identity transformed by that participation. The same ideas of attachment and participation are true of Old Testament faith, as Deuteronomy 30:19b–20a shows: "Now choose life, so that you and your children may live, so that you love the LORD your God, obey his voice, and are *attached* to him. For he is your life." Paul says something similar in Philippians 1:21: "For me to live is Christ." By necessity, being bound by faith with the God revealed in Jesus Christ transforms identity. How could it be otherwise if *he is your life*? If transformation of identity has not occurred, the faith cannot be real.

The early church knew the impact of faith on identity. The gospel gave early Christians a heightened sense of identity, which is evident in their explanations of the difference being in Christ made. The Letter to Diognetus, a second-century defense of Christianity, in arguing that there is something extraordinary about the lives of Christians, is evidence of their focus on the identity of believers. The letter describes Christians this way:

> They live in their native countries, but only as outsiders. They participate in everything like citizens and tolerate all things as foreigners. Every foreign place is their homeland, and every homeland is foreign. Like other people, they marry and have children. But they do not expose their young. They provide a common meal but not a common bed. They happen to be in the flesh, but do not live according to the

flesh. They spend time on earth, but their citizenship is in heaven. They obey the fixed laws, and their lifestyle rises above the laws. They love everyone, and are persecuted by all. They are misunderstood, and are condemned. They are put to death, and are made alive. They are poor, and enrich many; they lack all things, and prosper in everything. They are dishonored, and are glorified in their dishonors; they are slandered, and they are acquitted. They are disparaged, and they bless; they are insulted, and they offer respect. When doing good, they are punished as evil; when being punished, they rejoice as people being brought to life. They are attacked as foreigners by Jews, and they are persecuted by Greeks. And those who hate them cannot explain the reason for their hostility. (5.5–17)[5]

Further evidence of early Christian focus on identity is obvious with Augustine, to whom some even trace the beginnings of the modern understanding of personality, especially because of his *Confessions*.

Christians today need to be aware of how the identity described by Scripture interacts with their own identity, confronting, changing, and shaping to bring about new life in Christ through the work of the Holy Spirit. Such an approach presupposes a willingness to find one's identity in Scripture.

God calls us to know him, but that cannot happen unless we know ourselves. The most important spiritual journey and act of discipleship is in shaping our own identity in response to the call of God to be who we are supposed to be, someone created in God's image. It is a call not to settle for what we are or to be thrown off course by what happens to us, but to shape life in response to God.

People often focus on salvation as the central concern of Christianity. Salvation is obviously important,[6] but I am convinced that, in focusing on salvation, we have often missed the *more foundational* focus on identity. Everything else flows from identity. In fact, rightly understood, salvation is about identity, for salvation belongs to those who through God's Spirit

---

5. *The Epistle to Diognetus (with the Fragment of Quadratus): Introduction, Text, and Commentary*, ed. Clayton N. Jefford (Oxford: Oxford University Press, 2013), 145.

6. We should recognize, though, that specific language about being saved is *not* all that frequent in Scripture.

have adopted a Christ identity. Atonement is much less about theories of satisfaction and much more about being one with Christ and taking our identity from him. If life and faith are to have meaning, it will be because we understand and live our identity. The gospel is about identity, not going to heaven, and is way more than believing certain ideas, as important as the ideas may be. Who is the gospel trying to make you? If you are not going to be who you really are and were intended to be, of what value are you? If salt has lost its saltiness, it is good for nothing (Matt. 5:13).

Who are you? What has happened to you and through you? Where are you? Where are you going? Who is going with you? What do you do because of who you are? Tell me and I will know your identity. The degree that Christ is involved in the answers corresponds to the degree that you are actually a Christian. Do not balk at the word "degree," for being a Christian, like identity, is a process, not a mere event. If Christ is not involved in the answers to those questions, can you even confess to being a Christian? But should the focus be on finding ourselves or on finding God? Those are not unrelated questions. We will never find who we really are without in the process finding God. We know ourselves in knowing God, and we know God in knowing who we really are. A focus on identity is not about a self-centered self-realization; it is about knowing who we are in relation to God and other people. Self-knowledge is and must be an act of discipleship.[7]

The nine factors of identity and the comments on sin treated in the previous chapter do not require Christian presuppositions. They are true of all humans, but all factors shaping our identity must be reconsidered from a Christian perspective. *All nine factors have to do with God.* The Christian faith and its Bible are about identity, and they seek to move us toward that ideal self that God intends. *Faith transforms identity, or else it is not faith.*

If anyone understood the significance of identity, it was the apostle Paul. Philip Esler even describes Paul as an entrepreneur of identity,[8] but

7. Mark Husbands, "Reconciliation as the Dogmatic Location of Humanity: 'Your Life Is Hidden with Christ in God,'" in *Women, Ministry, and the Gospel: Exploring New Paradigms*, ed. Mark Husbands and Timothy Larsen (Downers Grove: InterVarsity, 2007), 132.

8. Philip F. Esler, *Conflict and Identity in Romans: The Social Setting of Paul's Letter* (Minneapolis: Fortress, 2003), 109.

this description fits all the biblical writers to some degree. Further, every Christian leader today should be an entrepreneur of identity, someone in the business of identity formation. To do that leaders will have to embody and model the characteristics of this Christ identity and be able to communicate it to others and assist them in taking it on. They will be agents of identity transformation.

The discussion of Christian identity does not suggest that we engage in some superspiritual task; it urges that we engage in the task of becoming human. Are we not human already? At one level, yes, but being human is both a reality and a process, *both a gift of God and a responsibility*, a task to be performed with God, for we cannot be fully human apart from relation with God. Identity is a "God thing," and it must be lived. Identity and identity seeking are about discipleship.

Our society does not like responsibility. We prefer to sue someone rather than take responsibility for our action, or to take a pill to avoid responsibility for sexual relations or how much we eat. Being human is entirely a gift of grace, but with grace comes responsibility, and the primary responsibility is to become human. The purpose of the gospel is to make us *fully* human. Jesus came to reveal the character of God, yes, but just as much he reveals to us the character of being human.

The gospel seeks to make us fully human, the humans God intended us to be. This does not suggest that a focus on identity is about self-help, nor does it assume or require any particular theory of psychology or theological system. Scripture is not about theology; at most it implies a theology. Scripture is about identity. Therefore, identity is not merely a topic of theology. It is a human topic, one that precedes theology. The complaint "I don't know who I am" is a thoroughly common human complaint, and it is this failure the gospel seeks to overcome. We will not know who we are until we know our God who created us and seeks relation with us, and we cannot live differently until we see ourselves differently. Theology *results* from identity because theology seeks to work out the implications of identity.

Scripture seeks to tell us who God says we are, and in doing so offers a new means of existence in a culture of death. At birth we are given an identity into which we must live. Similarly, with the gospel, at baptism we are given an identity into which we must live. The gospel is about identity transformation, and evangelism is helping people understand who they really are and assisting them to become that.

However, we have a problem, and the problem is the church itself. One of my students returned from a church internship thoroughly discouraged about ministry because of the superficial commitment of Christians. Her experience is too common. Churches have so diluted and distorted the Christian message that for many any understanding of Christian identity has been lost. A visit to many churches reveals quickly that people do not want a new identity; they want to feel good about themselves, to be comfortable and entertained, and to know they are "good" people who will go to heaven someday. Christian faith is reduced to believing certain ideas or engaging in certain minimal rituals such as baptism and going to church. None of this does justice to a biblical understanding of faith. The concern is not about going to heaven, as important as eternal life with God is; it is about life with God now *and* in the future. Believing certain ideas, being baptized (regardless of timing and mode), and attending Christian services do not make you a Christian. Having a Christian identity makes you a Christian.

My comments are not intended to diminish the importance of the church. Quite the contrary, they are a challenge for the church to recover and embody its own message.

Faith, true faith, reframes identity. Faith means living out the identity God says you have, the identity given you in Christ. For example, Jesus said: "As you have the light, believe in the light that you may become children of light" (John 12:36). The expression "children of" (or the singular "child of"/"son of"/"daughter of") has a Hebrew origin and means "characterized by." To be a child of light means to be characterized by the light. To paraphrase Jesus's words, we might say, "As you receive God's revelation, believe in that revelation in order that you might be characterized by—shaped by—what God says." Faith is a set of choices, commitments, and relations in line with God's intent that enable being and, by their very nature, transform identity.

Not surprisingly, then, text after text specifically asserts the identity of Christians. As obvious examples, note the following:

"You are the salt of the earth. . . . You are the light of the world." (Matt. 5:13–14)

Therefore you are no longer strangers and travelers, but you are fellow citizens of God's people and members of God's family. (Eph. 2:19— Ephesians is primarily a document about identity formation)

You are an elect race, a royal priesthood, a holy nation, a people belonging to God. (1 Pet. 2:9)

You are not in the flesh but in the Spirit since the Spirit of God dwells in you. (Rom. 8:9)

Do you not know that you are the temple of God and the Spirit of God dwells in you? (1 Cor. 3:16)

Such texts could be multiplied easily, but not all of the Bible is so explicit. Often Scripture's concern for identity is implicit. While some psalms and the wisdom literature (books like Job, Proverbs, and Ecclesiastes) focus on the individual, the Old Testament is primarily about the identity of Israel, the people of God, and less on the identity of the individual. Why is so much attention given to the story of Israel? So that people will know God's story of commissioning Israel to bless all nations and in the process know who they are and how they fit in God's story. History reveals identity. Also, to speak of the identity of the nation implies what individuals should be. The covenant with God and its assumptions, such as the Ten Commandments, determine the identity and character of both the nation and the individual.

The New Testament is more explicitly concerned with the identity of the individual, but even there the individual is never viewed separately, apart from the community, which is an indictment of the individualistic understanding of many Christians. Christian faith is not merely about me and Jesus.

No matter what the purpose of a biblical book or the problem it seeks to solve, in the end each book of the Bible contributes to who God says we are. For example, Paul wrote Galatians to deal with the problem of Jewish Christians forcing Jewish legal observances on gentiles, and he does so by describing their identity, by reminding the Galatians who they are in Christ: "For you are all children of God through the faithfulness of Christ Jesus" (or "the faith in Christ Jesus," Gal. 3:26).

Judaizers had come to Galatia and said, in effect, "Your identity is not good enough. You need to have a more Jewish identity to be a Christian." Galatians as an identity document answers the questions, Who are the true children of Abraham? and How does one become a child of Abraham? The Galatians were told they were inferior and that the law was the way to gain status as children of Abraham and of God. Paul would have none of it. They did not need to become Jews to be Christians. Their identity as Christians—and ours—is based in *participation* in the life of Christ, not in keeping Jewish regulations. Being baptized into Christ strips dependence on our own accomplishments and clothes us with Christ. There is no reason for an inferiority complex, for no one is superior in Christ and all are bound together in unity. Galatians is about the identity, origin, *and* resulting behavior these gentiles have in Christ.

We often miss the focus on identity, for we ask questions about theology or seek answers to our own concerns. We seek answers to questions the text is not asking or answering. I am concerned about the identity the text seeks to communicate to its readers. The Bible has theological implications, but it is not theology, and its concerns are often different from ours. The Bible is about identity formation, and *we should read it to understand who God says we are. Identity is the goal of interpretation.* In the end, the whole debate about the authority of Scripture is about identity. Do we—and how do we—allow Scripture to tell us who we are and who we are to be, or do we give that authority to something else?

Since the Bible seeks to tell us who God says we are, each of the nine identity factors in the previous chapter must be reconsidered. Scripture treats all nine factors to show us who God says we are and how each identity factor should be understood and lived out. Each of the identity factors must be reframed biblically. At this point I will provide a quick overview of how each factor is reframed by faith; later I will discuss each in more detail.

The Nine Identity Factors Reframed by Faith

Factor 1: our physical and psychological characteristics. Surely *the* defining reality is the fact that *we are created in the image of God*, a point made on the first page of most Bibles. *The image of God is the most important fact about us. Our physical and psychological makeups derive ultimately (not directly) from God, are to reflect God, and give us certain abilities and responsibilities.* If the theological component of our identity is missing, we have no idea who in the world we are. If we are created in God's image, there is nowhere else to go to know who we are, even though God is the last place many people want to look. Suddenly our bodies take on value; the physical—created by God and declared good—is not negative. Another fact results: Our bodies are not our own. They belong to Christ (1 Cor. 6:19–20). Further, we are mortal but not limited to mortality. We are a people with a hope, and ultimately a resurrection people.

Factor 2: our personal histories. Our histories and our experiences have shaped us, but Christians by faith have adopted a history not our own to be our own. Our true history is the history of Christ into which we are grafted. His history, within which and to which our personal history is subsumed, is our defining history. Conversion is the acceptance of a new identity, of deriving our identity from someone else's story, of transferring defining power from our personal history and self-presence to Christ's history and his presence. While we cannot change our histories, we do not have to live them or give them ultimate defining force. Our histories do define us, but they are subordinated to the defining history of Christ. *The question concerning to what a person gives ultimate defining force in life is the key identity question.* To what do you really give ultimate defining force?

Factor 3: our relations. The primary relation for Christians is our relation to God in Christ, and that has ultimate defining force. The idea of being *in* Christ may seem strange to us, but it is at the heart of Christianity, especially in Paul's writings. For Paul, the body of Christ is the fundamental metaphor, and Christians are part of that body. Being in Christ determines us, but in addition to setting us in relation to Christ, it also sets us in relation to all others in him and to all of humanity. Our true family, as much as we may love our historical families, is the family of God (Mark 3:31–35 and Eph. 2:19–22). *Christianity is not an individual affair,* even though we are responsible as individuals and must make individual choices. Others belong to us and we belong to them. Life is relational; it is dialogically constructed. That much of the Bible focuses on how relations with others should be lived is no surprise. Other people have derivative defining force, but Christ is the ultimate definer and defines all other relations.

As in the previous chapter, we will hold treatment of **factor 4**, the mind—that internal self-interpreting, self-directing memory—until the others have been considered.

Factor 5: our commitments. Our commitments are all redefined as well. Since we are defined to some degree by our commitment—willingly or unwillingly—to a location, Christians must know their true location is in Christ. *Geographically we belong in Christ and are defined by him; he is our environment.* He is the sphere of influence within which we live, and that is why the language describing faith as participation is so powerful. No part of Christianity is more compelling and transforming than the idea of life in Christ. We also live in a specific physical place, and our relation to that place changes because of our relation to Christ; we will return to this issue.

We are defined by investments of interest, time, and money since that to which we assign value assigns value to us. Jesus underscored this by saying, "Where your treasure is, there will be your heart" (Matt. 6:21/Luke 12:34), that is, there will be the controlling center of your being, which is what "heart" in Scripture usually refers to. Christianity offers a conversion of our values. If our values have not been converted, we have not been converted. Valuing what God values shapes us and directs us. In naming Christ as Lord we honor ourselves. As a second-century Christian put it, "Whatever you honor most will rule you. Honor what is best that you may be governed by what is best."[9] People render themselves worthless by investing their lives in worthless things.

The negative counterpoint to what we value is what we oppose: what a person hates and fights shapes life's agenda and shapes identity. Some realities we must oppose. When we pick an opponent that needs to be opposed and fight that opponent, we are still to be defined by Christ. To fight evil without becoming evil is the task of all Christians—and a fundamental human problem.

9. *The Sentences of Sextus,* ed. and trans. Richard A. Edwards and Robert A. Wild, Texts and Translations 22, Early Christian Literature Series 5 (Chico, CA: Scholars, 1981), 41–42.

Commitments to attitudes, ideas, and opinions shape us, and this is the reason the Bible places so much emphasis on the mind. There is a commitment to having the mind shaped by the mind of Christ (2 Cor. 10:5). *Identity is a mind thing.*

If people shape themselves by their commitments to their "heroes" or icons, Christians know *there is only one icon worthy of our commitment, Jesus Christ.* Similarly with regard to people we seek to impress, there is only one we should be seeking to impress—God. Note Jesus's complaint in John 5:44 (cf. 12:43) that people cannot believe because they seek the honor that comes from humans rather than that which comes from God.

Factor 6: our actions. If actions we are assigned or choose shape us, surely with Christ all our *actions are reoriented.* When Paul in Ephesians began to address the ethical implications of the gospel, he told people "to live worthy of the calling with which you were called" (Eph. 4:1). He might as well have said, "Live worthy of your identity": he spent the rest of the letter, the next three chapters, explaining how this new identity is lived out. Christians are no longer merely to act out of self-interest; rather they are to live with a new orientation based in unity with Christ and with his people. Some actions are prohibited and others are required. Christians are expected to be productive in life. Suddenly worship, entertainment, and work become crucial to identity. Some Christians have implied that people can act in ways totally separate from what they believe and know. No, we cannot. We are what we do. Being Christian assumes a *commitment to do the will of God, and such a commitment defines us.* Suddenly it is clear why worship, Christian rituals, and obedience are so important. Actions define us. When this is understood, there is no antithesis between faith and works. Humans cannot live without acting. Identity assumes an agent acting and being held responsible. You will work. The question is whether you work in accord with faith or unbelief, in accord with your Christ identity or as though your identity were elsewhere. When faith is understood as identity in Christ, then works are not separable actions but the necessary living out of that identity.

Factor 7: our boundaries. *Boundaries* involve nearly all aspects of Christian living. If identity is a process of recognizing, establishing, and negotiating boundaries, how could it be otherwise? Much of the Bible is about boundaries—a boundary around one tree in Eden, a boundary around Mount Sinai, boundaries in the tabernacle and temple, to note a few examples. Ethics are about boundaries. The Ten Commandments put down boundaries to mark identity. God says, in effect, this is who I am and who you will be, a one-God people who do not make idols or violate God's being, who know how important boundaries of time and family are, who do not violate boundaries of person, property, truth, or relations.

Christianity is about the maintenance of some boundaries and the removal of others. It is about drawing boundaries that neither violate nor exclude and that defile neither neighbor nor self. Boundaries marking off sin are retained, while boundaries between humans and God and between various groups of humans are redefined or removed and prohibited.

Factor 8: our process of change. *Regarding identity as an ongoing process of change*, Christianity emphasizes that life with Christ is a life of growth, a walk with God, a continual renewal, a process of continually being changed from one stage of "glory" to another (2 Cor. 3:18; 4:16; Eph. 4:22–24; Col. 3:9–11). Conversion, contrary to what many assume, is a process, not an event. Saying this does not diminish the importance of decision—or decisions. Since conversion is a process, identity maintenance is of major importance, which is the church's task in worship and education. Worship and learning are about identity maintenance, but too many Christians own a frozen identity. For some their new birth was a stillbirth and changed nothing. For others their Christian identity is frozen at some juvenile stage not worthy of mature living.

Factor 9: our future. *If identity includes some sense of the future*, Christians are shaped by and motivated by their hope in the promises of God. The gospel includes an eschatology, some sense of the end and goal, or we do not have a gospel. Conviction about future life with God shapes identity both in the present and in the future.[10] Christians live out of a sense of God's promises about the future, promises that are already in effect in the present. We live into God's future. Earlier when speaking of identity in general, I said that identity is in process until death, but for Christians death is not the end of identity, for judgment and openness to God's future continue to define. Why else could Paul in 1 Corinthians

---

10. Note Esler's comment (*Conflict and Identity*, 337): "All this means that groups tell themselves who they are in part by imagining where they are going."

13:13 speak of faith, hope, and love remaining always? In eternity we will still trust in God, hope in God's ongoing work, and live in love.

And now, with the other factors before us, we can treat that all-important **factor 4: our mind—our internal self-interpreting, self-directing memory.** Christian existence is an *internal, reflective adventure, both remembering and interpreting who we are*—and then living it out. Identity is an affair of the mind, which is why all of Scripture has a heavy focus on the mind and on establishing a sense of what has value and the goodness for which we should strive. Much of our identity is fractured, so that we are opposed to our true selves. Scripture describes the division in our being, most notably in Romans 7, which describes the struggle in doing precisely the opposite of what we wish. If the purpose of any religion is to create an "executive self," one that suppresses inappropriate desires and unifies one's being—at least to some extent—in pursuit of the good,[11] that is precisely what the Christian gospel seeks and what is accomplished in the affirmation "Jesus is Lord." God seeks to unify us within ourselves, not centered on ourselves. Christianity, far from being anti-intellectual, orders the mind and directs it toward continual learning about life, value, and the good. Such learning is not merely about "religious things"; it is about all knowledge and all of life. This opens the way, and even is a call, for Christians to make real contributions in all areas of life. Therefore, Christians should be the most analytical and discerning people anywhere.

Correspondingly, this is the reason for the biblical focus on the heart and on faithfulness—the continuity of identity. "Cleansing" of the heart is a way to focus and direct the controlling center of one's being, the executive self. The role of prayer, worship, and meditation becomes clearer; they are avenues for our minds to remember and interpret and to be reformed with the identity God seeks for us. The role of memory in worship at Passover and in the Lord's Supper and baptism becomes clear. With these acts memory is an act of participation in which events—especially Christ's death and resurrection—are called forth in the soul.[12] We remember,

11. Patrick McNamara, *The Neuroscience of Religious Experience* (Cambridge: Cambridge University Press, 2009), 30–40.

12. See Nils Dahl, "Anamnesis," in Dahl, *Jesus in the Memory of the Early Church: Essays* (Minneapolis: Augsburg, 1976), 11–29. Cf. Deut. 5:3 and Mishnah Pesahim 10:5.

affirm, and engage the realities of God's acts in Christ. The Lord's Supper and baptism are identity-shaping acts based in identification with a crucified and risen Lord. Issues of self-esteem, accountability, and responsibility take on even more significance. The internal conversation and the conversation between the individual and the external community and the interaction of self-description and community description are enhanced. The internal conversation is guided by an understanding of the pattern revealed in Jesus Christ and is—or should be—overseen by God's Spirit. The conversation of the individual and the external community becomes more complex, for it involves conversation *with God*, with other Christians, and with society in general. Even more important is the addition of God's description of us. What really counts is who God says we are. For Christians identity is founded on what God says, and it is affirmed and tested by the interaction of self and community.

Identity is the most important subject for all of us, and not merely for selfish reasons. God's intent and purpose are to establish identity in us by the work of Christ and the activity of the Spirit. The purpose of the Christian gospel is identity formation, to move people to be who God intended humans to be all along.

If this is the case, we should read biblical texts looking for identity. For years I have advocated a hermeneutics of identity. Hermeneutics is the process by which one understands and appropriates communication, and for our concerns it is about understanding and appropriating Scripture. A hermeneutics of identity is a process of interpretation that consciously probes for information on identity. To illustrate the process, in the next section we will treat a few Gospel texts to show how much identity is the focus of the teaching of Jesus.

Jesus and Identity

Jesus clearly sought and still seeks to change identity, as is especially evident in the Sermon on the Mount, which is largely an identity document showing what it means to be a disciple. People often fear the Sermon on the Mount because it seems so stringent. They fear it might lead to works righteousness, the attempt to save ourselves by our own efforts at obedience. Nothing could be further from the intent of the sermon. The Beatitudes and the sermon as a whole are not law, but, as W. D. Davies said, they are the bright light of the gospel.[13] They both show the nature of the kingdom of God and are an invitation to the kingdom.

Still, the history of the interpretation of the Sermon on the Mount is depressing. People spend more time arguing why we should not or cannot keep the sermon than they do seeking to understand it and live it.[14] The sermon is not legalism and does not just convict people of their sins, although it does do that. It holds up an expectation, a vision, of what should be and calls people to it. The sermon tells people who they are to be and what they are to do. Jesus and Matthew both thought this was what your identity should be and how you should live. The sermon informs and beckons our summoning self.

The Beatitudes are *identity* markers of those shaped by the kingdom.[15] They are almost a table of contents for Matthew's Gospel, for Matthew develops their themes throughout his Gospel, which shows just how seriously he meant them. The Beatitudes relate especially to the internal self-interpreting memory, which Scripture often refers to with the word "heart." Blessed are the poor in spirit, the meek, those hungering and thirsting for righteousness, the merciful, the pure with respect to the heart, and the peacemakers. All these point to the controlling, valuing, and organizing part of our identity.

The Beatitudes are followed by identity statements: "*You are* the salt of the earth. . . . *You are* the light of the world." These statements are not hyperbole or wishful thinking; they are descriptions of the result of the disciples' relation to Jesus. The descriptions call and enlist disciples into this identity.

The rest of the Sermon on the Mount focuses on a righteousness that goes to the core of your being. Specifically, in Matthew 5 it deals with

13. W. D. Davies, *The Setting of the Sermon on the Mount* (Cambridge: Cambridge University Press, 1966), 437.

14. See Clarence Bauman, *The Sermon on the Mount: The Modern Quest for Its Meaning* (Macon, GA: Mercer University Press, 1985).

15. See Philip F. Esler, "Group Norms and Prototypes in Matthew 5:3–12: A Social Identity Interpretation of the Matthean Beatitudes," in *T. & T. Clark Handbook to Social Identity in the New Testament*, ed. J. Brian Tucker and Coleman A. Baker (London: Bloomsbury, 2014), 147–71.

anger and the way you treat people, sexual integrity, marital fidelity, honesty, retaliation, and love of enemies. Jesus cares very much how you treat people. Chapter 6 deals with authenticity of religious acts and the direction of one's life. Chapter 7 gives further commentary on relations with others and then focuses on obedience. The sermon is largely about obedience to the will of God and taking your character from your God.

Jesus describes the identity people should have, what God intended from the beginning. The assumption is that if people see that identity, they will want to choose and *could* choose that identity. Yes, we all feel nailed by the Sermon on the Mount, and rightly so, but its purpose is not to make us feel that this ideal is impossible. It is to hold this model up for appropriation, to say this is the model you should choose.

Is such a life too hard? Is the sermon an impossible ideal, too hard for mere humans? What is hard is a life of sin. Too many people, Christians included, think that a life of sin is easy and a righteous life is impossible. The Roman philosopher Seneca, like other philosophers, asserted, "The road to the happy life is an easy one . . . the maintenance of all the virtues is easy, but it is costly to cultivate the vices."[16] If a Roman philosopher could understand that living right was easy and beneficial, surely Christians have better reasons to come to the same conclusion. Jesus holds up the ethical qualities he does because they embody what life should be and enable true living. The sermon offers a good life and is not too hard. This is not to ignore the cost of following Christ or that life is often difficult, but following Christ is much less costly than choosing and cultivating sin.

Imagine a community where the Sermon on the Mount was lived, a community where people not only did not murder but also controlled their feelings toward others, where men not only did not commit adultery but also did not lust after women or treat them merely as sexual objects (and where women were not guilty of such sins), where people kept their marriage vows, told the truth, did not retaliate, and even loved their enemies, just like their God does. Imagine a community where people did not use religion as a means of self-promotion and were not controlled by desire for money, a community where people lived with integrity. We would

16. Seneca, *On Anger* 2.13.2.

all love to live in such a community, but that is precisely what Christians and the church are to be. When one finds a community marked by these characteristics, which is indeed possible, life really is joyous.

Both Matthew and Jesus not only agree that such communities are possible but think this is precisely what you need to know about discipleship, what God wants, and what you can do, which is the reason Matthew placed it as the first recorded teaching of Jesus in his Gospel. Matthew thought that if you understood this ethical call, you would want to follow Jesus and you would understand the rest of the story more easily.

There is nothing here about earning salvation from your own effort, something neither Matthew nor Jesus worried about. The life described is a life patterned on God's character and lived in relation to Christ, drawing life from Christ. The theology at work is that humans are to take their character from their God, which is the consistent teaching of Scripture. If your heavenly Father loves his enemies, can you do less? To be a "child of" means to be "characterized by"; to be a child of God means one is *characterized by God!* God's people are to take their identity from their God. Humans were created in the image of God. How could it be otherwise? But this involves action. Performance and identity cannot be separated. You cannot be without doing, which is underscored by the parable of the two builders at the end of the sermon (Matt. 7:24–27). The wise person hears and does; the foolish person hears and does not do. Identity is shown by action or by failure to act. By obedience we live into an identity we have from God. This is not performance on our own; it is performance as God's children. Doing demonstrates identity.

Another text where Jesus obviously focuses on identity is the parable of the two sons and the compassionate father, more commonly known as the parable of the prodigal. If identity is comprised, among other things, of relations, commitments, and boundaries, this parable in Luke 15:11–32, which mirrors God's forgiveness and challenges attitudes of the "righteous," is especially about identity.[17] The parable starts with identities in relation and assumes the freedom of those identities to make choices, even bad ones, but choices have consequences. The prodigal, like most

17. See my discussion in *Stories with Intent: A Comprehensive Guide to the Parables of Jesus* (Grand Rapids: Eerdmans, 2008), 117–43.

humans, thought identity was enhanced by possessions and life without boundaries. As Miroslav Volf says, the prodigal attempted to unson himself.[18] He wanted to change his geography, his commitments, his actions, his relations, and his boundaries. After losing all his possessions, he found himself in a far country where he did not belong. He made alliances that did not fit his identity and performed degrading acts. This was not who he was. Then, in one of the most striking and insightful comments ever, the text says, "He came to *himself*" (v. 17). Sin here is understood as the inability or the refusal to live in accord with one's true identity. Sin is fracture and fragmentation, including fragmentation from ourselves and within ourselves. All of us are fractured—bifurcated—by the refusal to affirm the reality of our true identity. The prodigal finally was made to understand his true identity—a son. Truth allows us to come to ourselves; only with truth do we know who we are. But, caught with the realization of his inadequacy, the prodigal thought he was unworthy of his own identity and wanted to settle for being a hired hand (v. 19). The father insisted on his identity as a son, embraced him, and acted to reinstate that identity as son. Grace lets you be who you are supposed to be even though you do not deserve it. *Grace enables truth.*

God's identity is also mirrored in the text. God is the gracious one, always compassionate and receptive. His identity and relation to humans then determine their identity.

Issues of identity also drive the second stage of the parable. The elder brother showed himself as suspicious of joy, jealous, and judgmental. He rejected the identity of his brother, calling him "this son of yours," and sought to exclude relation with him, but the father insisted that the prodigal was "this brother of yours." Further, the elder brother misinterpreted his own identity. He viewed himself as a mistreated slave, but the father insisted that he too was a son, a privileged one at that.

Another compelling text on identity is the account in Luke 7:36–50 with its short parable of the two debtors. The narrative describes a meal at the home of Simon, a Pharisee, a person recognized as righteous and concerned with purity issues, especially regarding meals. During the meal

18. Miroslav Volf, *Exclusion and Embrace: An Exploration of Identity, Otherness, and Reconciliation* (Nashville: Abingdon, 1996), 158.

the men would have been lying on cushions with their feet angled away from the food, and others (neighbors, servants, or women) who wanted to hear would have gathered at the perimeter. A woman recognized as a sinner was present; probably but not necessarily she was a prostitute.[19] She performed acts that, if not obscene, at least in the first century had to be viewed as socially completely inappropriate. She anointed Jesus's feet with costly perfume, kissed his feet, and let her hair down to dry his feet. Letting her hair down in public would have been especially offensive.[20]

Questions of identity dominate the narrative. The identities of Jesus, the woman, and the Pharisee are all at stake. The Pharisee had at least entertained notions that Jesus was a prophet, but in his mind Jesus's tolerance of the woman's actions proved otherwise. If he were a prophet, Jesus should have perceived what sort of woman she was and rejected her, but the narrative shows that Jesus is a prophet and much more. He perceived what was in the heart of Simon, and he was also the one who announced forgiveness of sins. Jesus then told a simple parable about two debtors, both forgiven their debt. In the exchange that follows, the text is strikingly odd, for it says Jesus *turned to the woman* and *said to Simon*, "Do you see this woman?" Simon had been *looking* at her the whole meal, but he had not *seen her*. Perhaps the greatest ability any human can develop is the ability actually to see other people as individuals who require recognition, respect, and truth. Surely this is a major goal in being human, for meaning in life is about relations. Simon assumed the woman was a sinner, but Jesus identified her as a forgiven sinner. An implicit question in the narrative is, Who is righteous?[21] Simon was assumed by the community—and probably by himself—to be righteous, but Jesus said the sinner woman was more righteous than Simon because of her actions and her receiving forgiveness. The identity maps have all been redrawn.

Text after text in Scripture majors on identity, as we will see. We too

---

19. See Barbara E. Reid, "'Do You See This Woman?' Luke 7:36–50 as a Paradigm for Feminist Hermeneutics," *Biblical Research* 40 (1995): 37–49.

20. Mishnah Ketubbot 7:6 says a woman is not to go outdoors with her head uncovered. If she does, it is grounds for divorce. For more evidence on this and other cultural issues in this parable, see my *Stories with Intent*, 82–83.

21. This is a theme elsewhere in Luke, especially in the contrast between the tax collector and the Pharisee in Luke 18:9–14.

need our identity maps redrawn; that is what conversion is about. You cannot be better than you are, act better than you do, or think better than you do until you see yourself differently. Scripture gives us an alternate vision as a foundation for life. It tells us who God says we really are.

Identity really is the most important topic, and identity formation is the most important work we can do. Make no mistake. To focus on who God says you are does not mean you become this new reality just because God says it. No, who God says you are points to your real identity and who you are supposed to be. But you can still choose to live a lesser or even a false identity. Who God says you are is an invitation, a call to engage with God, to participate with God, and to become who you are supposed to be. It will not merely happen. It is work, discipleship work, but it is good work, and you will never be really satisfied with anything less.

In the following chapters, all nine factors of identity will be examined more fully. In my description of identity factors the self-interpreting, self-directing internal memory was treated last, for it gathers and interprets the other eight. But we will be at a disadvantage if the more detailed discussion of each factor treats this topic only at the end. We will discuss it earlier, in the chapter entitled "Factor 4: You Are Your Mind," to provide a theological basis that will enhance discussion of the other items.

FACTOR 1

You Are Your Body

===

A person is known by his appearance, and a sensible person is known when first met, face to face. A person's attire and hearty laughter, and the way he walks, show what he is.

—Sirach 19:29–30

A powerful bodily experience—the "body-self"—has a far stronger purchase on one's sense of who and what [one] is than do any social roles.

—Jouette M. Bassler, "The Problem of Self-Definition"[1]

To say "You are your body" may seem obvious, but this is not merely to say "You are your meat and bones." The body is more than physical stuff and includes all that we assume with human existence, for your mind, hardwiring and all, is part of your body. Or is it? Some would argue that the body is merely a vehicle in which the mind, the self, is housed. That will need discussion, but you are still your body.

We may give our bodies lots of attention, but we do not *think* much

---

1. Bassler here is adapting a comment from Robert F. Murphy, *The Body Silent* (New York: Norton, 1990), 105. A similar comment by Ludwig Wittgenstein bears reflection: "The human body is the best picture of the human soul." See his *Philosophical Investigations*, trans. G. E. M. Anscombe (New York: Macmillan, 1953), 178.

49

about how our bodies determine us. We just assume our bodies. But do not underestimate the importance of the body for identity. Our body is a huge determiner of our identity, for most people *the* greatest determiner of all. Our bodies determine so much about us: gender, size, race, attractiveness, vulnerability, health, metabolism, opportunities, proclivities toward communication, attitudes such as anger or passivity or aggression, drive, and a host of other factors. Our reactions to the benefits and liabilities of our bodies also shape us.

Sometimes people think of the body as if it were an isolated material entity, but nothing is further from the truth. Our bodies are always connected both literally and metaphorically to others and other realities. They never are in isolation. Our bodies were formed while connected to a womb. Our bodies were born connected to parents and family. As we grew, gained experiences, and made commitments, the connections of our bodies multiplied exponentially in relations and actions that define us. Our bodies become connected to habits, to responsibilities, to sin, to inadequacies, possibly to addiction, to sickness and death, to a host of other options, and hopefully to Christ. To what will you consciously connect your body? None of the realities of our bodies is conceived in isolation. They all are grasped in relation with family and community and in the way societies value and interpret them. Two people with the same physical characteristics in two different cultures will not have the same identity. You are your body, but even that is understood communally.

Physical abilities and gifts are particularly determinative, and especially the degree to which one is *satisfied or dissatisfied* with one's own body. If you have uncommon or even common abilities, it is part of your identity and will shape you. Attractiveness, like it or not, will open doors that would otherwise be closed. Mental capacities, hardwired in the brain, likewise open or close doors. The more one is dissatisfied with physical appearance and ability, the more negative are the results for positive identity construction. If damage is done to the body physically or psychologically, the impact, even with healing, may not go away. The scars and the diminishing are always there, even if to varying degrees.

You are not going anywhere in this life your body does not take you. Your identity is fused to your body. Many parents tell children, "You can be anything you want," but that is a lie. They cannot be what their bodies do not allow. No matter how much desire and training are present, few will be professional athletes or rocket scientists.

You both are and have a body. You use your body and are accountable for it and vulnerable to it. You own it, and it owns you. You are conscious of it at least partially. It is both the subject analyzing and the object being analyzed. You do nothing apart from your body; no, not even prayer.[2] Thinking and language do not happen apart from your body.

Your body is the means by which other people determine who you are, so recognition is a big factor in identity. We read bodies, and we do it quickly. Within seconds even small children discern whether another person is safe and an opportunity for enjoyment or is a threat. Sameness of body, even in the process of change, makes identity possible. Your body is the place you relate to other people.

Your body is also the physical substance through which you perceive reality. You encounter the world and the world encounters you only through your body. You have no other choice. Your body is the means of expression and communication, of experiencing pleasure and pain, and the means by which you express happiness or grief. The experiencing body is the self. If your body suffers, all of your being suffers, and you experience all of life in a field of suffering. You do nothing in this life apart from your body. "Geography is identity," and part of your geography is your own body. There is no external point from which any of us may view existence, even though we act like there is.

But let's not overstate the case at the outset. Yes, you are your body, but you are not *merely* your body. There are *nine* major factors that make up your identity, and all must be given their due. Your body may be foundational, but *all the other factors are intertwined* with the body, and Christianity transforms how the body is viewed in relation to them. Your body is born into a history and into a set of relations and is part of your boundaries. Your body is engaged in the conversation between the individual and the external community. Your body makes you recognizable

2. 1 Cor. 14:14–15 says, "If I pray in a tongue, my spirit prays but my mind is unproductive. What then? I will pray with my spirit, but I will also pray with my mind." The statement seems to point to two different kinds of activities in the brain, one less conscious than the other and less valuable than the unified activity of spirit and mind.

to others, and you have an identity only in relation to others.[3] The body is the means by which you make commitments and perform actions. The body is always changing and will die, so identity is always changing, but does identity die? You are more than your body, for so many other things go into making up your identity. Although your body is a major factor determining your identity, there is no one-to-one relation between your body and your identity so that the body expresses all of identity. Still, this body is significant! One New Testament scholar even says—rightly—that the body is "the earliest gift of our Creator to us."[4] But what if the gift is unsatisfactory to us or even "defective"? You cannot take the gift back for a refund or exchange it for another.

With all nine factors of identity, part is given and part is chosen. None of us chose the body or mental structure that we have, but at some level we must accept what our bodies are and decide how we will use them most effectively. We do choose what we will do with our physical and psychological makeup. We are all created with certain tendencies and abilities, each contributing to our uniqueness. At the same time, those tendencies, abilities, and inabilities are not merely accepted as givens. They must be schooled and augmented, and some inabilities will have to be overcome for us to function well in life. Some tendencies, such as self-centeredness, aggression, anger, and timidity, will have to be changed, controlled, redirected, or eliminated so that our actions and attitudes fall within a legitimate range of what it means to mirror the character of God. Sometimes we must choose not to be who we are, if we are to become who we should be. Our identity in Christ is in front of us calling us. Even our physical and psychological makeup must be filtered through the character of Christ.

There are huge theological issues here. How good and valuable is human nature, and how destructive and incapacitating is sin for our bodies? All sin is "constitutional"; it is in the fabric of our being. It is part of our hardwiring, and we are not all wired the same way. This raises major questions about free will and responsibility, but even so, sin is part of who

3. Halvor Moxnes, "Asceticism and Christian Identity in Antiquity: A Dialogue with Foucault and Paul," *Journal for the Study of the New Testament* 26 (2003): 3–29, here 19–23.
4. Ernst Käsemann, "Primitive Christian Apocalyptic," in Käsemann, *New Testament Questions of Today* (London: SCM, 1969), 135.

we are and the way we are oriented to ourselves. Negative tendencies that are part of our nature will have to be corrected and controlled. We often say, "That is just the way I am," but that is a confession, not an excuse, and it is a platform for repentance and change. Note how the virtue lists like Galatians 5:19–23 disallow tendencies such as envy and anger and require positive virtues such as love and self-control. We are not bound to our tendencies, even if they are not easily set aside.

You did not get to choose your body, and hardly anyone is completely satisfied with his or her body. If a few people are, they will not be for long, for aging is relentless and destructive. And yes, you have to be you. There is no other choice. You cannot make yourself taller or shorter or of a different race. You cannot absent yourself from your physical and mental makeup,[5] but nor are you merely a victim of your body.

You do choose to some degree how your body will present itself. Clearly there are limits, but you can shape your body somewhat, or if you have a lot of money and are obsessed, perhaps you can shape it a lot. The amount of money spent on cosmetics, weight loss, and plastic surgery is ridiculous and unconscionable, which suggests that many people are not satisfied with their bodies at all. In fact, many hate their bodies, but does that merely suggest that we idolize attractiveness, which is rather easy to do? In any case, the body you have is the only one you will get, so how can you accept your body positively, regardless of your dissatisfaction, and live positively? How can you find a foundation for living that is more substantive and enduring than appearance? To what degree will you have to reject the way your body defines you? Certainly people with serious physical disabilities must reject any supposed devaluation of their being.

It is worth stopping to reflect on how our physical and psychological makeup is presented to others. We convey messages about how we want to be identified. Through cultural signals such as clothing, hair style, jewelry, and a variety of other "markings" we communicate realities like gender, marital status, sexual interest, modesty, rebellion, class, desire to fit specific occasions, and attitudes toward ourselves. Often we buy

5. "We're all of us sentenced to solitary confinement inside our own skins, for life" (Tennessee Williams, *Orpheus Descending*, act 2, scene 1).

into cultural expectations without thinking, but, if we take our being in God's image seriously, we will need to be much more thoughtful. Is the presentation of our body an attempt to identify with the culture or rebel against it? Are we merely tired of ourselves? What actually honors both our bodies and God?

Much of this, of course, is a facade, and there is a huge difference between form and true identity. We spend too much time on form and pay little attention to what really counts, identity. Humans look at appearance, but God looks at the heart (1 Sam. 16:7). This contrast argues that there is something much more substantive than appearance. This is not to say that appearance is unimportant. The Old Testament in particular often shows an appreciation for beauty, not least in the Song of Songs (see also 2 Sam. 14:25, 27). Appearance is not negative, but it is no sufficient foundation for life and relations. If there is not something more substantive than appearance, one's identity is an illusion.

So, what does God say about our body? The creation story stresses that God created humans in his own image, gave them responsibility, and then judged his creation, including human bodies, as *very good*. The Bible does not offer a negative evaluation of the body and the material realm.

The Image of God

The most important thing that can be said about humans is that we are created in the image of God.[6] This is an all-consuming assertion about the origin of the body and the source of identity, and is a foundation for all theology. If we are created in the image of God, we are not the origin of our own existence, we cannot explain ourselves, and we are not the ultimate source of our own identity. We are the result of action by Another; our identity is a gift of grace; and we mirror and point to Another. If this is true, the oft-repeated comment from theologians is obvious: we can never know ourselves without knowing the God in whose image we

---

6. Note Pope Francis's comment, "We are living a moment of annihilation of man as image of God" (*USA Today*, August 2, 2016, online), which, if true, means we live in a time of crisis.

are made. I underscore again what John Calvin said at the beginning of his *Institutes of the Christian Religion*: "Without knowledge of self there is no knowledge of God. Without knowledge of God there is no knowledge of self."[7]

With the universe as enormous as it is—billions of light-years across— where is dignity to be found for mere humans on a seemingly insignificant planet?

Louie Zamperini was an Olympic distance runner who survived capture and torture by the Japanese in World War Two. Laura Hillenbrand, in writing the story of his life, wrote about prisoners subjected to dehumanization: "Without dignity, identity is erased. In its absence, men are defined not by themselves, but by their captors and the circumstances in which they are forced to live. . . . Dignity is as essential to human life as water, food, and oxygen."[8] She argued that dignity—that sense of self-respect and self-worth that is the innermost armament of the soul—lies at the heart of humanness.[9] Without dignity Zamperini would have died. The point is underscored by John Kilner in his *Dignity and Destiny: Humanity in the Image of God*. Dignity determines destiny. This is especially important. "Images or standards according to which one lives have power to shape identity. False images can foster false identities."[10] What you think is the basis of your identity, even if only unconsciously grasped; it shapes you, directs you, values you or devalues you, and controls what you do. A conviction of being created in the image of God gives us dignity and enables worthwhile identity because it orients us to a valid destiny. Humans have dignity because God gives it to them.

You have dignity and value because God says you do. God has founded your identity as something important because you were created for relation with God and to mirror God's character. There are many ways in which you are not like God. You are human, limited in numerous ways by

---

7. John Calvin, *Institutes of the Christian Religion*, ed. John T. McNeill, trans. Ford Lewis Battles, Library of Christian Classics, vol. 20 (Philadelphia: Westminster, 1960), 1.1.1 and 1.1.2.

8. Laura Hillenbrand, *Unbroken: A World War II Story of Survival, Resilience, and Redemption* (New York: Random House, 2010), 183.

9. Hillenbrand, *Unbroken*, 182.

10. John F. Kilner, *Dignity and Destiny: Humanity in the Image of God* (Grand Rapids: Eerdmans, 2015), 259. Kilner's book provides a good treatment of the issues.

definition: finite in every respect, sinful, and inadequate for independent existence, but you were never intended for independent existence. You were created for life with God.

Regardless of what you feel, you were created in God's image, and even though finite and vulnerable, you are still capable and possess power. A second-century Christian, reflecting on humanity in the image of God, commented, "Live therefore as one who is next in rank after God," and added, "You will not live well without God."[11] This presupposes, of course, creation with a purpose, not as an anomaly, but then, it is hard to take your identity from an anomaly.

If being in the image of God is so crucial, what does it mean? Stunningly, for all its importance, the Scriptures do not explain "image of God" and only mention it explicitly seven times (Gen. 1:26–27;[12] 5:1; 9:6; 1 Cor. 11:7; *2 Cor. 4:4; Col. 1:15*; James 3:9) and allude to it only a few other times.[13] Two of the explicit references, the ones in italics, refer to Christ. It is Christ who is truly the image of God, but accordingly also the image of what humans are to be.

Obviously there are many ways in which humans are not like God, and the difference between God and humans must be emphasized. Being in the image of God does not mean being like God without qualification. For good reason Scripture stresses that God is not like humans and transcends all they are (e.g., Job 38–41; Isa. 40:12–26; 44:6–8; and a host of other texts). Clearly the image of God does not have anything to do with God having a body.[14] God is spirit and is invisible.

Then what is "image of God" about? People usually point to *human* capabilities: the ability to reason, a moral self-consciousness, having dominion over creation, relational existence, and especially the power to communicate.[15] All these are important, but a number of recent discussions argue that this focus on *attributes of humans* distorts and misleads and is not what image of God means. Some animals share these char-

---

11. *Sentences of Sextus* 34 and 215.

12. The two words "image" and "likeness" do not refer to different ideas. They are Hebrew parallelism and point to one idea.

13. Rom. 8:29; Col. 3:10/Eph. 4:24; Heb. 1:3; and possibly 1 Cor. 15:49.

14. This is to take nothing from the incarnation, but that is a different subject.

15. See Kilner, *Dignity and Destiny*, 18.

acteristics to a limited degree, and if some people have less reasoning or relational power, does that mean they are less in the image of God? Is "lesser in the image" even conceivable? Is someone with Alzheimer's disease still in the image of God and still valued as such? People do not have value because they are useful or have potential but because they are humans. Humans have value, period.[16] Because they have value, people can, if not debilitated, learn to be useful. Further, Scripture texts on the image of God mention only dominion and possibly allude to relation, so much more caution is needed. Also, can the image of God be lost, or damaged by sin? Clearly most of humanity has not lived up to any idea of the image of God, especially if the focus is on attributes. Does the image still exist?

Such questions were heavily debated in the church's history, and no doubt will continue to be, but one thing is clear. It is Christ who is truly the image of God (2 Cor. 4:4; Col. 1:15). In him we see both a revelation of who God is and a revelation of what humanity is to be in terms of the character we are to have. It is dangerous to view the image of God as certain attributes found in humans. There is a long history of demeaning and mistreating those who were viewed as less—or not at all—in the image. Leaders like Oliver Wendell Holmes Sr. justified killing Native Americans because they thought such people were "less in the image."[17] The human attributes listed above are important, but they are subsidiary to, or attendant factors of, what the image of God actually is. The most important word in the expression "image of God" is "God." The expression should convey that God is the source and determiner of human existence. "Image of God" is primarily intended to convey that humans are *connected to God*, were *created for relation to God*, *point to God*, *represent God*, and are *accountable* to God. The image is about *participation with God* and *vocation given by God*.

Strikingly, the Hebrew word for image (*tselem*) of God is also used for idols as illegitimate images. We can easily point in the wrong direction, as idolatry always does, but the failure to be who we are degrades us.

---

16. This is not to deny the tragedy of Alzheimer's and the diminishing of life or the theological questions that get raised.

17. See Kilner, *Dignity and Destiny*, 8–37, for this and other shocking incidents of mistreatment of people thought not to be in the image of God.

Idolatry corrupts identity.[18] This is the reason idolatry is always rejected. It is an affront to God and a failure to be what humans are supposed to be. It is a failure of our own identity. No other image of God is allowed but the one God created for the task—humans. By giving ultimate value to that which does not deserve it, we diminish ourselves. We are to be representatives pointing to God, but we divert our attention and point to illegitimate idols instead. This is precisely what the "mark of the beast" is about in Revelation 14:9. It is a metaphor for taking one's identity from a godless culture rather than God. Opposed to this are texts like Revelation 14:1, which speaks of the name of God on the forehead of God's people. This is metaphorical language for people whose identity is found in the character of God.

Image of God is not merely about pointing to God, though. It is also about connection to God, living in relation to and participating with God. Also, the image is not merely an individual thing; we are not in the image of God by ourselves. The image of God is *communal* and involves our relations with God and with each other in ways that reflect the being of God. It is about humanity as a whole as well as about individuals. Additionally, the image of God involves male and female together, a point emphasized in Genesis 1:27 and 5:2. The emphasis on male and female together is not mentioned with the creation of animals.[19] In the interaction of male and female we reveal—or distort—the image of God. Male and female together in community reflect the image of God, and not merely in marriage. Suddenly human sexuality takes on an enormous significance, for how we relate sexually has to do with mirroring God!

Clearly none of us lives up to the idea of the image of God. Does that mean the image is lost or distorted by sin? Sin has distorted all humans, and although these questions are debated, we must insist that the image remains. Scripture, even after the fall of humanity, never suggests that the image is lost. Still, though Scripture presents Christ as the true image of God, an image into which Christians are being transformed, the image of God is not a static concept of the past but an *anticipation* of an end-time

18. See Anthony Thiselton, *The First Epistle to the Corinthians*, New International Greek Testament Commentary (Grand Rapids: Eerdmans, 2000), 446.

19. The only other places the exact Hebrew expression is rendered as "male and female" are in the flood narrative in reference to animals (Gen. 6:19; 7:3, 9, and 16).

goal. "We will be like him, for we will see him as he is" (1 John 3:2; see also Rom. 8:29 and 2 Cor. 3:18). The image of God is something that pulls us toward the goal and for which we will be held accountable.

The image of God, then, is an *identity* given to us by God at creation. It is an act of grace, a result of the love of God, but it does not just happen. It is a foundational identity that must be lived into so that a complete identity is forged by life with God. Our bodies and our lives are not our own, as if we were independent of creation and masters of our own lives. We belong to God and to Christ (1 Cor. 6:19–20). We are at most secondary owners of our bodies.

Why is the image of God so important? One crucial result of humanity created in the image of God is the *value* assigned to humanity, and value is a prime determiner of identity. You are valuable because God says so, no matter what else. What will you do with your value?

Without a sense of value life is meaningless, and people often devalue themselves, forgetting that they are the image of God. Such self-denigration is destructive. Henri Nouwen said, "Self-rejection is the greatest enemy of the spiritual life because it contradicts the sacred voice that calls us the 'Beloved.' Being the Beloved constitutes the core truth of our existence."[20] Being in the image of God is a foundation for living, even if we are dissatisfied with our physical appearance. Appearance cannot be the basis for living, for it does not last. God by grace gives us value for all of life, and this valuing becomes the lens by which we view other people as well. The image of God is about the dignity and value of all people. The ability to relate to God and each other, to mirror God's character and concerns, and to understand and care for all people and all of creation indicates the ultimate value inserted into every human life. Humans have supreme value because they are created in God's image. If God is not in the picture, humans are seriously devalued and life is without meaning.

Jesus deals with attention to the body and, somewhat amusingly, its value in Matthew 6:25–33. You should not be worrying about the body and what you will wear, for the body is more than clothes. God provides for the birds of the air, and you are much more valuable than birds. If

20. Henri J. M. Nouwen, *Life of the Beloved: Spiritual Living in a Secular World* (New York: Crossroad, 1992), 33.

God clothes the grass of the field, will he not clothe you? The focus is not the body but what the body should do. The real task of the body is to seek the kingdom and God's righteousness. This is merely another way to emphasize that humans were created for relation with God, bear his image, and are engaged in his work.

The image of God is not about me and my kind. It is a recognition that all humans of whatever race bear the image of God. This awareness requires that we see other people for who God says they are, no matter how different or deficient we might think they are.

What Is the Body and What Is a Human?

To be human is to be in the image of God, body and all, even if image is not about body. But what does God, according to the Christian tradition, say about our bodies? Defining "body" is a theological task. Are we just bodies, or is there more? If there is more, what is the relation of material and immaterial? Is there a soul, a spirit, or both in addition to the physical, and how do the physical specifics of hardwiring in the brain determine and relate to the "nonmaterial" part of our being? What is the relation of brain and mind—the relation of the physical organ and self-consciousness and thinking? Is the material body negative and the immaterial mind positive? How indeed should we understand our own makeup?

The issues are quite complex—some beyond final answers. This was perhaps the hardest chapter to write, and I confess that I delayed it until last. My bewilderment has good company, for church fathers often felt it, as evidenced in Augustine's saying, "I find my own self hard to grasp."[21] Conclusions here are foundational for identity and all of life. Certainty

21. Saint Augustine, *Confessions*, trans. Henry Chadwick (Oxford: Oxford University Press, 1991), 10.16.25 (see also 10.5.7). See Robert Louis Wilken, "Biblical Humanism: The Patristic Convictions," in *Personal Identity in Theological Perspective*, ed. Richard Lints, Michael S. Horton, and Mark R. Talbot (Grand Rapids: Eerdmans, 2006), 13–28, here 18, who quotes Basil as saying, "We are more likely to understand the heavens than ourselves" (*Hexaemeron* 10.2), and Gregory of Nyssa, "Because our mind is made in the likeness of the one who created us, it escapes our knowledge" (*On the Making of Man* 2).

about the relation of material and immaterial may be elusive, but clearly some wrong answers, really wrong ones, will destroy both life and meaning. An understanding of our nature is the foundation from which we live.

Christians have always insisted that human life cannot be reduced to that which is merely material. Many people naively assume that a human being is made up of two parts, a body and an immortal soul, with the soul being "Who I really am." Others, equally naively, assume on the basis of one text (1 Thess. 5:23) that humans consist of three parts—body, soul, and spirit—but this text is not giving an analysis of human components. Other texts will not allow such a tripartite division or such a literalistic reading.[22] The biblical witness is not uniform, and recent discussions, often involving neuroscience, have raised serious questions about either a body-soul or a body-soul-spirit division.

Further, the case can be made easily that the immortality of the soul is an idea that stems from Greek philosophy and does not fit comfortably with Christian thinking. Only God is immortal, and the Christian focus is on resurrection. Some ancient Greeks presumed the immortality of the soul, and some of them took a negative view of the body. The proverb *sōma sēma*—"The body is a tomb"—summarized the thinking. Christians cannot take such an approach, but statements like the Greek proverb raise questions about the relation of mind and body. What is the relation of spirit, soul, mind, will, body, conscience, and heart? How many parts of a human are there? What do the various words in Scripture really point to?

This is not the place for a full treatment, but we can say that the biblical language is neither technical and scientific nor uniform. The relevant words have a range of possible meanings and are used differently in different contexts. Translations often mislead, especially with the word "soul," and suggest a precision that is not there. The Hebrew word *nephesh*, often translated as "soul," is so broad it can refer to the throat (Isa. 5:14), to life (Gen. 1:20), to a living being (2 Sam. 14:14), to the inner being parallel to "spirit" (Isa. 26:9), and even to a corpse (Num. 6:6). The relevant Greek word *psychē* can refer to the self, to the inner being, to life, or merely to a

22. See, for example, Phil. 1:27 (". . . that you stand in one spirit, with one soul contending for the faith of the gospel"); 1 Cor. 7:34 (". . . that she may be holy both in body and in spirit"); and 2 Cor. 7:1 ("Let us cleanse ourselves from every defilement of the flesh and the spirit"), to say nothing of texts that speak of heart, mind, conscience, and other such terms.

person. In Luke 12:19 the rich fool says, "I will say to myself (*psychē*), 'Self (*psychē*), you have many good things,'" and in verse 20 God says, "Fool, this night your life (*psychē*) will be asked of you." In verses 22–23 Jesus says, "Don't worry about your *life* (*psychē*) regarding what you will eat nor about your body regarding what you will wear. Your life (*psychē*) is more than food and your body than clothing." *Psychē* here is definitely not "soul," since the soul does not need food. Acts 2:43 says, "Fear came upon every person (*psychē*)," and 15:24 uses *psychē* of the mind ("troubling your minds"). Sometimes, though, *psychē* does refer to the immaterial part of one's being, obviously so in Jesus's statement "Do not fear those who kill the body but cannot kill the soul (*psychē*). Rather, fear the one who can destroy both soul and body in gehenna" (Matt. 10:28). For Paul *psychē* is rather unimportant; it occurs only thirteen times in his writings, with only two or three of them referring to the inner being. Making precise distinctions is difficult when one notices texts such as Philippians 1:27, where "soul" (*psychē*) and "spirit" (*pneuma*) are used as parallels: "that you stand in one spirit, with one soul contending for the faith of the gospel."

Rather than thinking of components of humans, both Testaments assume that humans are psychosomatic wholes—mind-body wholes. We are thinking organisms, material beings, created for relation to God. There are several ways to speak of humans functionally, but the Bible is not describing components. A person is a psychosomatic whole. There is no thought of compartmentalization or overemphasis on any one aspect. There is a looseness in usage of terms that defies scientific categorization. The inner being does not exist without the body. The suggestion that your body is a garment you wear is naive in the extreme. Those who argue "I am not my body" use the body to make the assertion.

I am definitely not suggesting that the material is all there is. Yet we must not think of the inner being as some independent existence, and we must not think human nature can be compartmentalized. Scripture does speak of an inner and an outer being (2 Cor. 4:16), and clearly both Jesus and Paul can think of body and soul/spirit as separate after death.[23] Some speak of a duality without dualism, but that is confusing language.

23. See Matt. 10:28; Phil. 1:21–24; 2 Cor. 5:1–10; and 12:2–3.

Just as clearly, the death of the body is not the end of existence, or texts about resurrection and being with Christ and God make no sense.[24] But what should we call this essence of being that survives death, and how should we explain it? Although other terms are used, Paul would probably choose the word "spirit," and it may be most useful for us. Paul viewed spirit as referring to the depth and center of one's true inner being and the channel for communication with God, but not something separate from the body.[25] Paul served God with his spirit (Rom. 1:9), and the Spirit witnesses to our spirits that we are God's children (Rom. 8:16); the spirit is what is saved in the day of the Lord (1 Cor. 5:5); we are to cleanse ourselves of all defilement of the flesh and the spirit (2 Cor. 7:1); and Paul prayed for people that grace would be with their spirit (Phil. 4:23). The human spirit is the place for the transforming work of the Holy Spirit. This inner being results from being embodied in the image of God, and it involves a self-awareness and a high-level mental and relational capability that enables self-interpretation, high moral reasoning, and relation with God.

Still, even with an emphasis on humans as psychosomatic wholes, there is tension between the mind and the body. The body often desires what the mind rejects, and the mind itself—our self—is fractured. A psychosomatic whole does not mean unity or a unity of direction, for tension and fracture characterize our very being. Augustine commented that the mind commands the body and is presently obeyed, but the mind commands itself and is resisted.[26] Why do we resist our own minds and do what we know is wrong? Our identity is very much tied to the way we handle the fractures and tensions in our being. Handle them well, and you are wise and mature. Handle them poorly, and be labeled a fool.

Your body is a thinking, relating, connecting, performing organism, especially in relation to God. How it does those things determines who you are. The body is certainly *not* inherently negative. It is part of God's good creation. The body may well be a moral battlefield, but the body

24. Resurrection texts are, of course, frequent; see as examples Luke 23:42–43; John 11:25–26; 14:1–6; 1 John 3:1–3; and Rev. 6:9.

25. When Paul says something like "If I am absent from you in the flesh, I am with you in spirit" (Col. 2:5), he is speaking of his influence, not literally of his disembodied presence with them.

26. Augustine, *Confessions* 8.9. Augustine decided that there are two wills.

is not the real culprit. Sin is, but sin is an illegitimate intruder, which is Paul's point in Romans 7:17–24. The body was created for life with God and can be and is to be used by God. First Corinthians 6:13 says, as we might expect, "The body is not for sexual sin but for the Lord," but strikingly it adds, "And *the Lord is for the body.*" There is no negative view of the body here! The Lord is for the body, committed to it, and seeks its good. What an example of grace! The body is joined to Christ, is the temple of God, and is a means of bringing honor to God. We are to present our *bodies* to God, consecrate them to God, and submit them to his control, and therefore to discipline them as God's Spirit engages our own spirit. Future redemption/salvation is specifically the redemption of our bodies.[27]

It is true that "flesh" often does carry a negative connotation. However, while sometimes "flesh" appears to be equivalent to "body" and can refer literally to physical existence,[28] the majority of biblical occurrences are referring to a *way of life, not merely the body.* It is a term pointing to weakness and temporality, that which is merely human and not God, that which is dominated by natural, earthbound tendencies and leaves God out of the picture. It can refer to that which is morally deficient, one's unregenerate nature, or even hostility to God.[29] Usually "flesh" is not the same thing as "body," and translations routinely paraphrase the word. There is nothing inherently negative about the body except its mortality. Although "fearfully and wonderfully made," the body ages and one day will be a dead body.

One of the key results of a positive view of the body as a psychosomatic whole is the rejection of a head-heart distinction. "Heart" in Scripture usually refers to the controlling center of one's being, which we know is actually the brain. There is not one part of me that thinks and another that feels. Emotions, deriving from our brains, are *felt* deep in our bodies, but the heart is merely a pump. Reason and emotions *cannot be separated.* The same brain produces both, and reason and emotions are always intertwined and require each other, even when they display

27. For these ideas see 1 Cor. 6:15–20; 9:27; Phil. 1:20; 3:21; Rom. 8:23; and 12:1.

28. For example, 2 Cor. 7:1; Gal. 2:20; Phil. 1:22–24.

29. Cf. Pss. 56:4 (NIV: "mortals"); 78:39; Isa. 40:6; Matt. 16:17; John 1:13 (NIV: "human decision"); Rom. 8:3–9; Gal. 5:13–24.

the fracture in our own being. Both reason and emotions are *embodied.* They are produced bodily in the brain, and at the same time, because of the continual shaping of the brain, they help structure the brain. We are indeed "fearfully and wonderfully made."

Sexual Identity

Obviously our bodies and brains and the way they shape identity are enormously complex, much beyond what can be treated here, but because of the perversion in our culture something must be said about sexual identity. Does physical hardwiring predetermine sexual identity, an identity that one should "live into"? Living into an identity may be appropriate in some regards, but it will hardly work with regard to sexual matters. All of us are bent and twisted when it comes to sexuality. Sexuality is a large and positive—or at least potentially so—part of our identity, but, despite the idolizing of sexuality in our culture, Christians must not view it as an unbridled determiner of identity.

You are your body, but you are not merely your sex organs, attractions, and desires. Life and the body are much more than sexual desire or expression. Humans seem to be the only animals that have to decide whether and how they will use their sexuality. The females of some species of animals do make choices about which male will be allowed to mate, and mating has to do with relationships in some animals, but with many other species neither is true. With such animals sexuality is not about relations or seeking enjoyment, and it is not about self-understanding and self-worth. Horses do not decide whether or how they will be sexual. They just are; the females come in heat, and the males are driven to oblige. With humans sexuality is about relations, enjoyment, self-understanding in community, self-worth, security, and much more. If sexual relations are for humans the one place where pride, power, and pleasure come together, pleasure may well be the *least* important of the three. Pride is such a factor because of issues of self-worth, an understanding of identity and value. The sense of being valued sexually leads to self-worth and pride. Power is a huge factor because sexual performance shows capability and strength, indicates control over others, and yields again a sense of value, self-worth, and pride. Sexual relations enable a person to say I am worth something because someone else found me valuable and I am capable and skilled because of what I persuaded—or forced—the other person to do. But is this focus on pride, power, and pleasure merely the way our society views sexuality? What happened to love and giving oneself to another completely and enduringly? Scripture offers something much more intimate, powerful, and satisfying with its view of proper sexual relations. A question is worth pondering: Do we love loving or being loved?

Sexual identity is not merely about whether one is attracted to the opposite or the same sex. Sexual identity involves a very complex process of evaluating sexual attractiveness and deciding how we will *use* our sexuality. "Use" is not a negative word unless one decides to use sexuality in a negative way. Each of us decides—or allows others to dictate to us—how gender and sexual tendencies will be manifested and implemented, so we might as well be intentional about it in order to be wise. Within what boundaries is sexual intercourse permissible? You cannot say "within the boundaries of love" for a host of reasons, not the least of which is that love is itself so easily misconstrued and distorted. Are sexual relations and sexual intimacy *rights* or *responsibilities*? Is everything one feels acceptable? How should Christians deal with singleness? The answers determine the outcome for the rest of the questions, but there are still numerous issues to decide. What will you wear and how will you wear it? What will you think and plan, and how will you implement your plan—or failure to plan? How you use sexuality is directly tied to all the other categories. If you are attractive, options, possibilities, and burdens may be yours that are not factors for someone not so attractive. Being not so attractive may lead to efforts to force attraction by giving sexual relations.

Sexual orientation is not the same as sexual identity, and orientation is influenced by numerous factors, including hardwiring, parental impact, and abuse. Many people dis-identify with an orientation, and an orientation is not an identity until it is embraced and acted upon. Even then it is not necessarily permanent. Clearly all of us are affected by the hardwiring of our brains, but we are not predetermined. We choose whether to follow an orientation and what we will do with our attractions. Nor are we dealing with an either-or choice, for the plasticity of our brains means that our *choices and experiences structure the brain—*

for good or ill—and choices made at one point may be reversed later—for good or ill.

The real issue always is what we allow to be the primary determiner of identity. For Christians, if the answer is not the character of Jesus the Christ, then the affirmation "Jesus is Lord" makes no sense. Sexual ideas and practices are and always have been a primary arena for expression of identity, for our bodies are sexual. The evidence from Scripture is focused against the misuse of sexuality. The vice lists usually list sexual sins first, sometimes with three different words (e.g., Gal. 5:19–21), because that is precisely the place where people are most likely to go off the rails. Neither the loose heterosexual nor the homosexual practices our society condones fit with a Christian identity. *The issue is not orientation but action.*

The Body and the Body of Christ

We think of our body in individual terms, and fair enough, for one's body is uniquely one's own. Still, for Christians we cannot think merely in individual terms, for faith means being in Christ and part of *his* body, his church. Identity is never merely an individual affair, especially so in Christ, and the primary determiner of our identity is that our bodies belong to the body of Christ, in which there are many other and various kinds of bodies. Conversion includes conversion of our bodies, not merely our minds, and sets our bodies in new relations. More attention will be given to this later, but for Christians one's body is joined to Christ and to all those in Christ (1 Cor. 6:15; 12:13–27; Rom. 12:5). We may be our bodies, and our body is ours, but it does not belong to us (1 Cor. 6:19). It belongs to Christ and functions alongside others who are part of his body. Our body is not Lord, Christ is.

To say Christ is Lord of the body is no simplistic matter. The person in that body still has to decide how to relate to his or her own body and what to do with that body. Here the marvelously complex interplay of God's initiative and human response is at work, but regardless of what else is said, if the human does not act, nothing happens.[30] God does not manip-

---

30. A good number of people deny the reality of choice. They make a choice in doing

ulate us, even when seeking us. We will give our bodies to something, and Scripture urges us to give them to God: "Do not present yourselves . . . to sin, but present yourselves to God" (Rom. 6:13); "Present your bodies as a living sacrifice" (Rom. 12:1).

This requires that we control and steward our bodies. The body demands attention, and when we ignore the body, we are more easily victimized by it.[31] The body can take you over, or you can take over your body. Will your body be your master or an opportunity to be human as God intended? The body is to be subservient and is to be brought under control. Paul even speaks metaphorically of striking and enslaving his body (1 Cor. 9:27). But to what is the body subservient? Stewarding the body is not merely about exercise and weight control, it is also about stewarding the mind and shaping the spirit. It includes the rejection of idolatries, addictive pleasures, compulsive habits, and inattention to the substantive matters of life. In a society where many view not recycling as more immoral than using pornography,[32] stewarding our bodies and minds is crucial and allows us to overcome the fracture in our being so that we know how to follow God and do so. It is about learning and being shaped by God's Spirit. That does not happen without investment and attention.

At some point, even if your body is as healthy as possible, it *will* master you as it ages, fails, and refuses to do what you desire, but that is not the end. There is still the expectation of resurrection and the redemption of the body. Our bodies are destined for the future. The purpose of the gospel is to make us fully human, but that requires explanation. Being fully human is the opposite of being merely human, human without God in the picture. Being fully human means living and stewarding our bodies in relation to God and in keeping with God's intent. The Lord is for the body, the body is good, and it is to be used for good in God's purposes,

so and cheapen life. Much of life is determined, but choices still remain. An addict may not have the choice not to be an addict, but he or she can choose to get help and to initiate change. The same is true with regard to sin.

31. Milan Kundera, *The Unbearable Lightness of Being*, trans. Michael Henry Heim (New York: HarperCollins, 1984), 39.

32. See "Porn in the Digital Age: New Research Reveals 10 Trends," Barna, April 6, 2016, https://www.barna.org/research/culture-media/research-release /porn-in-the-digital-age-new-research-reveals-10-trends#.

even though existence is temporary. Despite death, the body is still good and will be raised and transformed to God's intent.

I have asserted without hesitation that you are your body. However, I cannot tell a specific person—you—what that means for understanding your own identity, for every person's body is different. I *can* urge you to be conscious of your body and how you are shaped by it. I *can* urge you to reflect on the value of your body and what you should do to honor your body and honor God with your body. I *can* urge you to reflect on the value of other and very different bodies and what you should do to honor those bodies. I *can* urge you to realize that your body belongs to God as much as the rest of you does. Your body is not yours, even though you are responsible for it. Value your body highly. It is the place for your relation to God.

FACTOR 2

You Are Your History

Everything has a past. Everything—a person, an object, a word, everything. If you don't know the past, you can't understand the present and plan properly for the future.

—Chaim Potok, *Davita's Harp*

It's like everyone tells a story about themselves inside their own head. Always. All the time. That story makes you what you are. We build ourselves out of that story.

—Patrick Rothfuss, *The Name of the Wind*

The narrative self supports the self-concept I have of myself. It is the story I tell myself about the ways in which my memories are linked together to form the person that I am.

—Patrick McNamara, *The Cognitive Neuropsychiatry of Parkinson's Disease*

History reveals identity. "We are . . . what the past has made us."[1] Our histories shape us, but much of our own history we do not write. We do

---

1. See Alasdair MacIntyre, *After Virtue: A Study in Moral Theory*, 3rd ed. (Notre Dame: University of Notre Dame Press, 2007), 130.

not come into the world clean and unattached. We are born into histories—the histories of our families, our region, and our country—and our histories affect us in ways we do not notice. History is mediated through other people who explain who we are. Our parents, grandparents, and family stories shape us even when we are unaware of them; those stories become part of our preunderstanding, assumptions we accept as true.

Why do Greek and Turkish Christians on Cyprus, or Irish Protestant and Catholic Christians, have such a hard time relating to each other? Why do people hate Germans who had nothing to do with Nazism eighty years ago? These people are born into a history of hand-me-down hate and are unwilling to give up the past and take their identity from somewhere other than their perception of their own history and culture. They are lost in their own histories. For many, history is a treasured possession of one's identity, even if it does not deserve to be.

Each of us also has his or her individual history of experiences, choices, and acts, and these memories form a story that shapes our self-understanding. As we mature we become the one interpreting and explaining what has happened to us. Our lives are not a series of unconnected events, and something within us longs—is even forced—to create a connected story that makes sense of the pieces and moves us in a successful direction. We create our story from the events and circumstances life hands us, even if we do not do it well. We have a narrative identity.

Our Past Shapes Our Present

Our histories, like other aspects of identity, can both enable and disable taking our identity from Christ. Some people are embarrassed about their histories and seek to hide them; others are proud of their histories, sometimes to the point of arrogance. Although I do not look like it, I am one-sixteenth Cherokee and proud of it. That heritage shapes my self-understanding, even if in fanciful ways. Few are aware of this history, and no one relates to me on this basis, but it is still part of who I am.

All your experiences and choices contribute to your history. Some you chose, and some you did not. Events are not mere items from the past; they are the fabric from which our lives are woven. Some think "What happens in Vegas stays in Vegas," but not on your life. *You* know what happened in "Vegas," good or bad, and it comes home with you, whether you admit it or not. You cannot change your history, and you ignore it to your peril. How you handle your history will enable or disable your ability to live. If you do not handle it well, you will be like Lucy in the *Peanuts* cartoon, who explained to Charlie Brown why she did not catch a fly ball: "The past got in my eyes."

We know inherently that our history shapes our identity. As my colleague Jim Bruckner puts it, "Identity is lost when the roots come loose."[2] This is one reason we are interested in genealogy and in learning the history of our own families. The history of a particular family may not be important in the grand scheme of things, but if it is *our* own family, suddenly it becomes very important because that history gives us place and hopefully mentors and equips us for moving forward. But it is not just our families. Our history, especially if it is positive, provides anchors for our identity, and all of us need such anchors, whether they be in our family, our good experiences, or in relation to God. Christians have—and need—such anchors in conversion and meaningful worship and experiences in life with God. One has only to think of the frequency with which Paul points back to God's confronting and redirecting his life on the way to Damascus and other times that God encountered him and led him, or to his positive experiences with specific churches, which encouraged him and strengthened him. With us as well, history provides points of stability that our identity needs and to which we point for some sense of coherence.

However, our understanding of our own history is always incomplete. Our memory is selective and sometimes misinformed. At times people create memories to enhance their past or to avoid facing negative results of the truth about their past. We will address this more later, but obviously relying on a false memory is a poor foundation for identity.

History, or at least the history we retain, is not merely something about the past. Since we retain it in memory—even if inaccurately—it is a factor of our present life. Tragedy, divorce, success, or whatever is not merely the past. We carry our past with us. I am the one who wrecked a car,

2. Private conversation.

studied abroad, and had medical experiences about which I wish I knew nothing, but having had them, I live differently. The past always shapes our present. We call it experience and value such knowledge highly, but it is not just about being smarter. All our experiences shape us, even if, or especially if, we do not handle or remember our experiences well.

Our own histories are not the only determining factor. Often we are dealing with histories in which we were not directly involved, but they still shape us—for good or ill. Being born into family, communal, and national histories can give shame or honor; can provide a basis for establishing a strong identity; or can be an obstacle that must be overcome. Some things will disappear and be forgotten, but others will be an enabling or a plague, like children bearing the names of fathers and grandfathers who were Nazi killers. With our history we inherit an identity, but an inherited identity cannot be lived—nor can an inherited faith. They can be lived into, or if necessary, rejected and changed.

Perhaps nowhere is the effect of history so obvious as with race relations in the United States. The sins of the treatment of Native Americans and slavery, the Civil War, segregation, and attempts to move past the divisions in the civil rights movements have all shaped our identities. For most of this history none of the people involved are still alive. Our ancestors did things or suffered things in which we were not involved. Yet, this history shapes our present life as we and others try to account for the past, ignore it, make amends for it, or interpret it. It is easy to see why Scripture speaks of sin being visited on the third and fourth generation (e.g., Exod. 20:5), but we are not confined to our histories and their divisions. You are your history, but history is not the only factor of identity. Histories too must be evaluated as to what legitimately goes into identity construction and what must be lamented and rejected or praised. Sometimes this is no easy process, especially when people have been damaged by their histories. Will they seek revenge? Will they live in humiliation? Or will they remember that, no matter what, they are still the image of God?

Christ Defines Our True History

The Bible places a huge emphasis on the importance of history for identity and points to a larger history, the history of God's effort to have a people, into which we are born. More specifically, the New Testament stresses that Christians by faith have adopted someone else's story to be determinative of our own. *Our true history is the history of Christ into which we are grafted. His history, within which and to which our personal history is subsumed, is our defining history.* That is what faith, baptism, and the Lord's Supper are about. Christians lay the story of their lives—damage and all—in the hands of God, confess that parts of their story are not good, affirm that they do not direct their own story, and ask that their story be taken into and conformed to the narrative of what God is doing in Christ. Obviously Christ's history is a long story and includes both the history of Israel and the history of the church. To be embedded in Christ's history includes being involved with the history of his people. No Christian can think, as Henry Ford did, that history is bunk. Being a Christian means having a focus on history.

The importance of history for our identities is clear with worship—and remember, worship is about identity construction and maintenance. Much about worship is focused on history, on remembering and naming what God has done in the past and banking life on the significance of those past events, but also lamenting events in the past and present to remind ourselves what we should and should not do and that this world is not as it should be. Praise is a narration of God's character demonstrated in his past acts. With praise we give thanks, remind ourselves of God's identity, and frame our lives on the revealed character of God. Ritual in worship is intended to call forth history for the purpose of identity formation. The rituals of Judaism and the early church were not dead rituals; they were identity-enhancing practices. In reliving Passover, Tabernacles, and Pentecost, Jews were not merely remembering the past; rather they observed these acts of worship to remind themselves, as the Mishnah puts it, "that they too had come out of Egypt" (Pesahim 10:5). The observance is a kind of actualization, an owning of the history, and the same is true of Christian rituals like the Lord's Supper. We do more than remember Jesus's death and resurrection; we "share in" or "participate in" his body and death. For example, 1 Corinthians 10:16 asks, "Is not the cup of blessing which we bless a participation (Greek: *koinōnia*) in the blood of Christ? Is not the bread we break a participation (Greek: *koinōnia*) in his body?" Observing the Lord's Supper is an act of taking his history as our own.

Conversion is the acceptance of a new identity, a new self-understanding, and it means we derive our identity from someone else's story. We transfer defining power from our story to Christ's story, especially his resurrection. In other words, as others have noted, conversion is an autobiographical revision to place oneself in a new master story.

It may seem strange to think of the gospel as a rewriting of our own histories, but that is exactly what Paul thought happens with faith. He told the Colossians, "Since *you* died with Christ" (2:20); "Since *you* have been raised with Christ to the right hand of the Father" (3:1); "For *you* died, and *your* life has been hidden with Christ in God" (3:3). Death and resurrection are realities of *our* history and of *our* living, and conversion is about our own death and resurrection.

Even so, our personal histories are *not* changeable, but histories are to be remembered and processed for truth and learning, *not* lived in or given ultimate defining force. *What a person gives ultimate defining force is the key identity question, and for Christians only Christ is given ultimate defining force.* Giving something else ultimate defining force is idolatry, and inevitably leads to sin. Think, for example, how tribal identity with Rwandan Christians trumped Christian identity and led to genocidal slaughter. All of us have our tribal identities and sinful pasts that do not deserve, and must not be given, ultimate defining force.

No one knew more than the apostle Paul, a person with a wretched history of persecuting God's people, that only Christ deserves ultimate defining force. God stopped him in his tracks with a powerful and sudden revelation of the risen Christ. Paul knew he did not deserve to be involved with communicating the gospel. He viewed himself as the least of the apostles, not sufficient to be called an apostle. But *no one's history is useless*, and Paul would not let his history have defining force. Instead, he gave defining force to the risen Christ and to the call and working of God in his life.

Paul tells about this process most clearly in 1 Corinthians 15:8–10, an extremely important identity text, as he discusses the resurrection and those to whom Jesus appeared alive: "Last of all, as to someone of an untimely birth, he appeared also to me. For I am the least of the apostles. I am not worthy to be called an apostle because I persecuted the church of God. But by the grace of God I am what I am, and his grace to me was not useless. Rather, I labored more than all of them—not I but the grace of God with me." When Paul said, *"By the grace of God I am what I am,"* he made the most freeing statement in all the world. This is not a statement of arrogance or distance from others. Paul is not saying, "This is just who I am, and leave me alone." It is not a statement of one who takes grace lightly or does not know the significance of Christian faith. It is a statement describing the experience of one whose life has been turned around, reordered, and given responsibility he did not deserve. Paul is saying in effect, "By his grace God has taken the deadness of my history and created life and value, and he has engaged me in his own work." This should be the witness of all Christians, but you are not permitted to say "By the grace of God I am what I am" *unless* you can also point to that grace being a transforming power that has put you to work for God.

Earlier in the same letter Paul had pointed out that grace destroys arrogance. He asked the Corinthian Christians, "What do you have that you did not receive, and if you received it, why are you boasting as if you did not?" (1 Cor. 4:7). All that we are and have is a gift of grace. If all is a gift of grace, no one has any ground for thinking he or she is better than someone else.

"Grace" is not just a feel-good word. My best definition of "grace" is this: grace is not something God gives us, but God giving us himself. That is what changes our identity. You cannot have the gift apart from the Giver. You cannot have the gift of God's salvation and love apart from the presence of God continually at work in your life. To receive the Giver is to be energized by his power and grace. It is no surprise then that Paul says this grace was not useless to him, without effect. It put him to work. Grace is a power that energizes and has effect. "Cheap grace," for all its value as an expression, is a misnomer. Grace that does not change and energize is not cheap grace; it is grace never known. If work does not result, grace has not been experienced. Grace—and faith—lead to doing *by necessity.*

Think of the words in 1 Corinthians 15:8–10 in connection with the identity-shaping factors. Paul's self-understanding and arrogance were reframed. By rights he should have been blackballed because he persecuted the church, but his history was subverted and transformed by the history of Christ. His commitments and loyalties were reframed. His relations with God and Jesus were reoriented, and all his human relations were transformed, especially with gentiles, but also with the church and with other Jews. All these people, most of whom he looked down upon before, were important to him after his conversion, and he served them. His relation with the Torah was changed. The Torah was no longer the center of gravity and no longer the ultimate defining force; Christ was. Paul's boundaries had been redrawn. The boundaries between people were obliterated; imagine what that meant for a scrupulous Jew. His internal life, his self-interpreting memory, had been reordered as well, as the self-reflexive nuances of these verses attest.

God is in the business of restructuring identities for all willing to be changed. Our histories are not like Paul's. Some of us may be worse; some of us—maybe many of us—are more victims than victimizers. Regardless, we are not predetermined by our histories. We are never so separated from God by our histories that we are precluded from our real selves, from being who we should be. Paul attests to God's restructuring twisted histories to create new identities in 1 Corinthians 6:9–11: "Do you not know that unjust people will not inherit the kingdom of God? Don't be deceived. Neither the sexually immoral nor idolaters nor adulterers nor men who have sex with men nor thieves nor greedy people nor drunkards nor abusive people nor swindlers will inherit the kingdom of God. And that is what some of you were. But you were washed, you were sanctified, you were acquitted in the name of the Lord Jesus Christ and by the Spirit of our God."

This transformation of histories is the focus of Ephesians, an identity-formation document if there ever was one. The letter is structured around five "formerly-now" statements that describe what Christians used to be with their history of sin and alienation and what they now are in Christ (2:1–10; 2:11–13, 19–22; 4:17–24; and 5:8; see also the implicit contrasts at 3:5 and 4:28). These "formerly-now" contrasts offer a painful but realistic assessment of life without God, but they also give compelling descriptions of conversion and its effect.[3] These portrayals of life before Christ and then with Christ are designed to keep people from living like everyone around them and to call them to mirror their relation with Christ in their daily lives. They contain narratives about change in geography, attitudes, values, commitments, and relations. The most striking of these contrasts, the one in 5:8, functions as a summary of much of the letter: "*For once you were darkness, but now you are light in the Lord. Live as children of light.*" Conversion is about God redirecting histories and thereby changing identities.

This obvious identity text contains words few of us would be willing to say, as Paul did, to people we have not met: "You once were darkness but now you are light in the Lord." We might be willing to say, "You are part light and part darkness," or "Try to be light," but not "You are light in the Lord." Paul's assumption is that if people are in the Lord, they will be transformed by his character. Earlier the text had focused on what was proper and what was fitting for Christians (vv. 3–4). Clearly identity and a lifestyle that fits with a Christlike identity are in view.

Again, note that the former history is not the determining history. You once were darkness, but that is not who you are now. Old characteristics have been set aside, and a new identity has been granted. Note the participation language. You are only light *in the Lord*, that is, to the degree your identity is housed in and defined by his, that sense of a new geography. "Geography is identity" is a truth evident more in Ephesians than anywhere.[4]

Note also the blend between the indicative and the imperative, which is characteristic of much of the New Testament. The grace statement of identity comes first, but then you are called to live out that identity. Belief is the act of living out the identity God says you have by grace. The imperative is a necessary component. Unless the identity is lived out, it is not

---

3. Note the comment by Gerd Theissen, "Paul has a deep anthropological pessimism with a strong affirmation of life. Paul advanced neither a holistic nor a dualistic anthropology but a transformative one." See his "*Sarx, Soma,* and the Transformative *Pneuma*: Personal Identity Endangered and Regained in Pauline Anthropology," in *The Depth of the Human Person: A Multidisciplinary Approach*, ed. Michael Welker (Grand Rapids: Eerdmans, 2014), 166–85, here 169.

4. Rom. 5:2 describes grace not merely as the entrance to the faith, but as the sphere in which we live, another instance of geography being identity.

real. The fruit of the light is in all goodness, righteousness, and truth (Eph. 5:9). The necessity of doing is a given. Doing emerges from an identity, and once this is understood, the faith-works dichotomy collapses. Some Christians have implied that you can believe without it impacting the way you live, which is absurd and only reveals that people neither understand faith nor really believe. There is no antithesis between faith and works. Everywhere Scripture compels doing in accordance with the identity God gives. You will work. The question is whether you will work in accordance with faith or unbelief, in accordance with your Christ identity or from some other identity.

Note too the focus in 5:10, 15, and 17 on the mind and the process of discerning what fits with the Lord and is pleasing to the Lord. Christian identity is an internal mind exercise, that internal self-interpreting memory, lived out in obedience to the Lord it seeks to understand.

One of the really odd things about the early Christians, especially Paul, is the way they talked about gentiles being grafted into the history of Israel and the history of Christ. They repeatedly used Old Testament language of Israel to describe gentile Christians. For example, 1 Peter 2:9–10 says Christians are a chosen race, a royal priesthood, a holy nation, God's own possession, ones formerly not God's people who now are God's people, and *all* these descriptions are taken from Old Testament texts about Israel. They are descriptions of God making people his own and giving value to them. At the same time, New Testament writers were insistent that gentiles did not need to—and must not—become Jews in order to become Christians. As William Campbell points out, Paul sought to relate gentile followers of Christ to the traditions of Israel but at the same time to prevent them from becoming proselytes to Judaism.[5] They belonged in Israel, but they did not belong to Judaism. For example, in Galatians 3–4 and in Romans 4 Paul wants his gentile readers to know that they are children of Abraham but that they did not get that way by keeping works of law, and they must not think they now should keep works of law.

The New Testament's description of the former way of life underscores that we cannot be cavalier about our histories. We have all done

---

5. William S. Campbell, *Paul and the Creation of Christian Identity*, Library of New Testament Studies 322 (London: T. & T. Clark, 2008), 54.

wrong, and wrong has been done to us. Whether we have been victims or victimizers, no identity will be restructured while a person seeks to deny the truth of history. The attempts to abolish history have their own long history, but it cannot be done. Nations attempt to deny their past atrocities, but everyone still knows the truth. For both groups and individuals, history must be evaluated in truth and processed so that we learn how to live.

Trauma Shapes Us, but Grace Shapes Us Even More

Telling the truth—naming and facing reality—is *the* essential ingredient for identity transformation. We cannot be changed if we are trying to deny the reality of what needs to be changed. You will never know who you are or become who you should be by denying the truth of the past, but grace—the very presence of God *for us*—makes facing the truth possible. God's grace comes first and is always the foundational reality. Time may be required to deal with the damage caused or experienced, but the crucial fact is that our histories do not deserve ultimate defining force. To give something other than our past ultimate defining force is the first step to healing. Only God revealed in Christ merits being the ultimate defining force of our lives.

This is not to deny the difficulty of dealing with our histories. The worse the history, the harder it is to deal with it. Trauma does shape us, sometimes tragically so, so much that people may feel their identity has collapsed. A parent who has suffered the death of a child or a woman who has been raped cannot just ignore the reality and get over it. A person guilty of wrong cannot blithely ignore the damage done to others.

A woman who was raped while intoxicated described wrestling with her degraded identity:

After a few hours of this [being probed and photographed], they let me shower. I stood there examining my body beneath the stream of water and decided, I don't want my body anymore. I was terrified of it, I didn't know what had been in it, if it had been contaminated, who had touched it. I wanted to take off my body like a jacket and leave it at the hospital with everything else. . . . [To the rapist she said] You took away my worth, my privacy, my energy, my time, my safety, my intimacy, my confidence, my own voice, until today. . . . I had to force myself to relearn my real name, my identity. To relearn that this is not all that I am. . . . I am a human being who has been irreversibly hurt, who waited a year to figure out if I was worth something. . . . I didn't want anyone's pity and am still learning to accept victim as part of my identity. . . . He is a lifetime sex registrant. That doesn't expire. Just like what he did to me doesn't expire. . . . It stays with me, it's part of my identity, it has forever changed the way I carry myself, the way I live the rest of my life.[6]

She cannot change this history, and the trauma will always be there, but she does not have to let the trauma define the rest of her life. We may grieve about the past and carry it with us, but we do not live our past. Our identity in Christ must be shaped by Christ more than—way more than—anything else, including past trauma.

People say, "Forgive and forget." You cannot forget; you *can* refuse to give the past defining force. In the Genesis story Joseph was sold into slavery by his brothers and then wrongly imprisoned for over two years. Joseph named his firstborn son Manasseh, which means "causing to forget," because God caused him to forget his troubles (Gen. 41:51). Joseph did not want his past to determine his life and his future relations with his brothers. In truth, though, in naming his son Manasseh he was not forgetting. Instead, the son would be a constant reminder of the past, but this was Joseph's way of asserting his refusal to let the damage of the past define him. He could have used Paul's words "By the grace of God I am what I am," and almost did when he said, "God sent me before you to preserve life" (Gen. 45:5). We do not forgive and forget; we forgive and forgo vengeance, even while we insist on truth being told and responsibility for wrong being dealt with.

6. This is part of a letter the victim read at the sentencing of her rapist, a Stanford University swimmer. The quotation can be found in an article written by Katie J. M. Baker, "Here Is the Powerful Letter the Stanford Victim Read Aloud to Her Attacker," BuzzFeed, June 3, 2016, https://www.buzzfeed.com/katiejmbaker/heres-the-powerful-letter-the -stanford-victim-read-to-her-ra?utm_term=.bweL78wgQ#.joKgJo1r5.

If we are the victimizer instead of the victim, we have a tendency to deny or avoid the truth. Often we do not want to admit to ourselves our sins or take responsibility for what we have done. Deep down, however, we still know the truth, and we will never be healthy until we face reality, seek forgiveness, and make restitution if possible. Confession is still a key ingredient in Christian living. Facing the pain we have caused creates even more pain, but it is the only way to wholeness. Failure is giving up on change and accepting what we have let ourselves become. There is a better way. We do not have to live manipulated by a negative history.

All the experiences in our story shape us. While trauma shapes us, even if we do not want it to, grace shapes us even more, especially grace from God, but also from humans. The popularity of the story and the musical *Les Misérables* attests to this fact. As another example, a friend tells of a white racist soldier left for dead in the hot sun who was rescued by an African American and given a drink from the African American's canteen. The racist could no longer be a racist; in fact, he became an ardent opponent of racism. Grace forced reconstruction of his identity and priorities. The same is true with the transforming grace of God, but grace must not be presumed upon so that people avoid dealing with the truth. Grace enables facing the truth but is not a substitute for it.

We are called past our histories—not out of them—to live in Christ. We cannot get out of our histories, and our histories do define us, but they are subordinated to the defining history of Christ. Paul witnesses to this reality again in Philippians 3:4–11. Here he lists factors from his history that were matters of pride—his family heritage and blameless legal obedience especially—but he considered it all loss to gain Christ. The facts were still true, but they received no defining force.

Each of us has to be who we are, and we will carry our history with us, but we do not have to be stuck in who we are. You are not *merely* your history. Even God cannot call us out of some place other than where we are and who we are. We are not called out of culture, but culture too is deprived of its central defining force. Culture is a necessary ingredient but not determinative. In fact, culture has to be assessed on the basis of the gospel as to whether it must be resisted or can be used. Despite its importance, culture in the end is irrelevant, as Paul implies in 1 Corinthians 9:19–23. In this text Paul says he became as a Jew to the Jews, which is amazing. He *was* a Jew and was proud of being Jewish (cf. Rom. 3:1–2; 11:1; and 2 Cor. 11:22), as long as someone did not try to make ethnic heritage and customs a ground of superiority or salvation. First Corinthians 9:19–23 also says that he just as easily became as a non-Jew (those without the law) and as the weak, so that he could lead them to Christ. He could identify culturally with any group in order to minister to them.

Our identity in Christ must be shaped by Christ more than—way more than—ethnic and cultural heritage or anything else. Which is more important? That I am a white Southerner or that I am a Christian? That a person is Caucasian, African, Latino/a, Asian, or whatever? So many parts of our identity that we assume are determinative are not and do not deserve to be. Christ is not an accessory to our identity, as if we were making a small addition by letting him in; he takes over our identity so that *everything else becomes an accessory.* Christ is our primary and determining identity. I am not saying ethnicity is irrelevant and should not be recognized. Quite the contrary, ethnicity will be recognized and can be a significant foundation for life, but it must not trump Christ as the ultimate determiner of identity, and it must not be a source of division in the body of Christ.

Does the new identity from Christ obliterate our former identity? Some have said Christians do not have their own identity, but that is an obvious and gross exaggeration. We *do* have our own identity. We are still the same people with the same body in the same culture with the same history, but our identity is relativized, redefined, and placed under the controlling influence of Christ. Not all is changed, but all must be reevaluated in light of Christ's death and resurrection. Christians are people who belong to Christ, and that relation transforms their identity and opens them to a new future, even a radically redefined future.

As it does with all nine factors of identity, sin will invade and use our histories if allowed. Our histories may be viewed as so destructive that we cannot live positively, or viewed so positively that we do not feel we need God or think we are better than other people. Sin will attempt to deny the reality of negative aspects of our history, but not dealing honestly with our histories is itself a sin. The same is true of giving our histories defining force they do not deserve. Our histories shape us, but they do not get to manipulate us. We live out of our histories, but sometimes, like Paul, we live in opposition to them.

What will you do with your history? You need to own your own history, but do not let your history own you. You are not who the past says you are; you are who you, unavoidable history and all, choose to become in relation to God. You are not allowed to use your history as an excuse for your failures. People do. They were abused, and on that basis they excuse their abuse of others. There is neither justification nor integrity in that. Your history is not merely a predetermination; it must be assessed, filtered, and sometimes rejected.

Either your history will define you, or you, well aware of your history and its impact, will define your future. People often are trapped in their past or vainly attempt to put off life until the future. You cannot live your history or your future. Jesus called people to live in the present, aware of their past and pulled by their futures. What can and should you change? It may well be that the more history you have the harder it will be to choose something else, but even there the real issue is what you are *willing* to change, with God's help, to become the person God intends. Do not let stubbornness and arrogance, even if you are elderly, keep you from becoming who God intends you to be.

Sometimes our histories have worn us out and disabled us. Life often is hard and even burdensome. Still, even a burdensome history does not get to define us. Nor can our histories be used as an excuse, as damaging as they may be. We can be energized, reoriented, and called back to our true identity by the larger reality of Christ's history.

Our histories are important, but our histories too are given over to the grace of God. Each of us should say each day, "By the grace of God I am what I am, and this grace is not useless to me." Realize, though, that this freeing statement on identity will not leave you as you were, for grace is a power that puts you to work and that works in and on you.

An obvious point is worthy of reflection. To the degree that it is in your control, you need to take care of your history. That involves first analyzing and speaking truth about your history. It must not be merely forgotten. It also involves taking care of the history being made by present actions. You must not be naive about being manipulated or taken advantage of by someone else, and you need to be wise about your own actions. An ill-advised action can ruin a life, but why would you want to be ill-advised?

We Are Given a New Name

What does your name *stand for*? This is much broader than what a name may mean etymologically. The first item of our personal history is our name. The name we are given at birth is an important part of our individual history and shapes our identity. Often names connect us to individuals in our family or have religious or cultural significance. Even if we were assigned a name just because our parents liked it, it still shapes us. We seek to protect our names and reject attempts by others to disparage or change our names. Identity is directly tied to our names, as evidenced by Nazis and others attempting to reduce people to numbers.

Many people in the ancient world had two or more names because they lived in two or more cultures. Jews might have a Semitic name and a Greco-Roman name. In the New Testament, Saul was also Paul, a certain Jesus was called Justus (Col. 4:11), and Silas was called Silvanus. Names are important as well for Jewish or Christian identity. Names were often changed for religious reasons, such as Abram being changed to Abraham or Simon being renamed Peter.

A name in the Jewish world was not merely the handle by which someone was called. It stood for all the person was and represented. To do something in the name of the Lord meant to do it in accord with all he is and stands for. To call on the name of the Lord was to call on his character and actions, and to pray in the Lord's name was to pray in accord with all he is.

Believers were described as people who "bear the name" of God or Christ (Dan. 9:19; Mark 9:41; 1 Pet. 4:16), or have God's name written on them (Rev. 3:12; 14:1; 22:4). This is just a way to say God determines who they are. Christians are baptized into the name of Jesus (or the Father, Son, and Spirit), which is to say they are baptized into a new identity, into accord with who Jesus is and what he accomplished. Such expressions are really important. All these attachments of people to the name of Christ or God are descriptions of identity. Christians have a new name because they have been given a new identity. Christians have the responsibility of carrying the name of God—demonstrating the character of God in the way they live—to the society in which they live. The meaning of the name Christopher captures the idea: one who bears Christ. That is a history to live into.

By your conduct and relations your individual name stands for something in the eyes of those who know you. What have you made of your name by your history? Do people see someone with a trustworthy identity, someone "bearing the name of God" and reflecting the character of God, someone of true substance, trustworthiness, and value? That is what human identity is supposed to stand for. So, what does your name *stand for*?

FACTOR 3

You Are Your Relations

We live in dialogue.

— Daniel Migliore, *Faith Seeking Understanding*

"Reuven, listen to me. The Talmud says that a person should do two things for himself. One is to acquire a teacher. Do you remember the other?" "Choose a friend," I said.

— Chaim Potok, *The Chosen*[1]

When one welcomes his fellow man, it is considered as if he had welcomed the Divine Presence.

— Mekilta Amalek 3:245–246 (on Exod. 18:12)

"Through others we become ourselves."[2] Identity always involves a community, for our identities are always communicated to us through others.[3]

1. The instructions are found in Mishnah Avot 1:6.
2. *The Collected Works of Lev Vygotsky*, vol. 5, *Child Psychology*, ed. Robert W. Rieber, trans. Marie J. Hall (New York: Kluwer Academic/Plenum, 1998), 170.
3. See M. Heidegger, *Identity and Difference* (New York: Harper and Row, 1969), 41; note Philip F. Esler's comment: "Identity is defined in terms of groups to which we belong," in "Family Imagery and Christian Identity in Gal 5:13 to 6:10," in *Constructing Early Christian Families: Family as Social Reality and Metaphor*, ed. Halvor Moxnes (London: Routledge, 1997), 121–49, here 131. This has always been the case. Mark Reasoner, in describing

You cannot be a human by yourself. Your very existence depends on a community, and always has. You cannot conceive of yourself in isolation. Rugged individualism—or any other kind—is an illusion. A community gives the language by which rugged individualism is understood, and other people tell you how to be an individual. A community gives the language necessary for comprehending identity, and a community engages each of us in dialogue, telling us who we are and how we fit into a larger story.[4] We derive our identity from groups to which we belong. None of us is a mere individual, an isolated "I." Each "I" is part of a "we"; we are communal beings, and our brains are structured as social organs geared for relation. Other aspects of life make sense only when they enhance relations.

Our misguided, self-centered society, however, works against good relations. So many live destructively focused on themselves and the mistreatment of others, often from a sense of entitlement, as if the world owes them. Social media may be making things worse by heightening self-centeredness in an unreal world. "Life is posted and public. . . . You have to promote yourself all the time, it's a PR job."[5] People take selfies, enhance them, and celebrate their "self"-identity on social media, whether it is their real identity or not, but self-centeredness destroys life. You are not the identity created by social media any more than Matt Damon is Jason Bourne. The identity on social media is often a charade, a mask.

We may play in a virtual world, but we cannot live there. Relations are absolutely central to all we are and do, and after oxygen, relations are the most important part of life. Someone else gave you your first nourishment to keep you alive, and relations still provide access to the necessities of life and everything else. As with all identity factors, some relations are given and some are chosen. Some are handed to us (like family) and are avoided

---

the ancient Roman world and the cultures around the Mediterranean, says essentially the same thing: "All these cultures viewed a person's identity as constructed primarily of the groups to which they belonged." See his *Roman Imperial Texts: A Sourcebook* (Minneapolis: Fortress, 2013), 103.

4. Charles Taylor, *Sources of the Self: The Making of the Modern Identity* (Cambridge, MA: Harvard University Press, 1989), 34–39.

5. Emma Thelwell, "How Do You Help Young Girls Feel Happier?" BBC News, August 31, 2016, http://www.bbc.com/news/uk-37228930.

only with difficulty, but in many cases we choose those with whom we will construct our lives.

Life is relational, and any thinking person knows it. A commercial for football—of all things!—says, "Football is family." The promoters would like you to think this because they realize how important relations are. If you make football your family, you are hooked.

Why Are Relations So Important?

First, God created us for relation. To varying degrees, all of us have a need to belong, and this is a positive thing. We cannot exist alone. Solitary confinement is the ultimate punishment for the worst criminals. Enjoyment and satisfaction come through good relations, even if good relations are not easy to obtain. *Life finds meaning only in relations.* Everything else is merely an attendant factor. Second, whether with regard to the covenant in the Old Testament or discipleship and faith in the New, Scripture is about relations with God and with people. Third, other people tell us—for good or ill—where we fit in. Our identity is shaped in dialogue as other people tell us who we are and we negotiate the description. Fourth, and again for good or ill, we are shaped by the models around us and the circumstances of our relations. We draw strength and direction from relations. As one person put it, all things receive the characteristics of that in which they participate.[6] The old proverb is "Birds of a feather flock together." The people around us influence us and enable or disable us.

Our relations both affirm who we are and draw us out of ourselves. We are what others say of us and remember about us.[7] You cannot be who you are without the community around you, and they need you to become the people they should be. Charles-Augustin Sainte-Beuve said, "Tell me who loves, who admires you, and I will tell you who you are."[8]

6. Robert Letham, *Union with Christ in Scripture, History, and Theology* (Phillipsburg, NJ: Presbyterian and Reformed, 2011), 93. He derives the point from Athanasius. See Athanasius, *Against the Arians* 1.38–39 and 3.23, 33–34.

7. Miroslav Volf, *End of Memory: Remembering Rightly in a Violent World* (Grand Rapids: Eerdmans, 2006), 24.

8. Charles-Augustin Sainte-Beuve, "A Critic's Account of His Own Critical Method

That is clearly true among humans, but how are conclusions changed when we remember that the main one who loves us is God? Or, to quote my colleague Jim Bruckner again, with reference to both God and the Christian community: "Christian identity, at its center, is grounded in whom you love and in who loves you."[9]

Philosophers emphasize our relatedness. Mikhail Bakhtin said, "To be means to communicate. . . . To be means to be for another, and through the other, for oneself. A person has no internal sovereign territory, he is wholly and always on the boundary; looking inside himself, he looks *into the eyes of another* or *with the eyes of another*."[10] Seeing the face of another person summons us to responsibility. Each face is a voice that says, "You shall not kill"; each face is "a Sinai that prohibits murder" and calls the other person to responsibility.[11]

Being Individual and Relational

But how do we do justice to our individuality *and* to our relatedness? There is a sense in which you are *not* your relations, and in fact relations can be dangerous, destructive, and idolatrous. All good things can be subverted. Too frequently boundaries are violated so that people are not free to be the individuals God called them to be. People oppress others, hem them in, limit them, and demean them, often doing so to seek their own advantage. Far too many people attempt to live through someone else. Parents attempt to live through their children, which is almost always

('*Nouveaux Lundis*')," in *Library of the World's Best Literature, Ancient and Modern*, ed. Charles Dudley Warner (New York: R. S. Peale and J. A. Hill, 1897), 22:12666.

9. James K. Bruckner, "The Lord's Claim on Our Identity," in *Doing Theology for the Church: Essays in Honor of Klyne Snodgrass*, ed. Rebekah A. Eklund and John E. Phelan Jr. (Eugene, OR: Wipf and Stock, 2014), 184.

10. Mikhail Bakhtin, *Problems of Dostoevsky's Poetics*, ed. and trans. Caryl Emerson, Theory and History of Literature, vol. 8 (Minneapolis: University of Minnesota Press, 1984), 287; quoted from John Shotter, "Life Inside Dialogically Structured Mentalities: Bakhtin's and Voloshinov's Account of Our Mental Activities as Out in the World between Us," in *The Plural Self: Multiplicity in Everyday Life*, ed. John Rowan and Mick Cooper (London: Sage, 1999), 71–92, here 71.

11. Paul Ricoeur, *Oneself as Another*, trans. Kathleen Blamey (Chicago: University of Chicago Press, 1992), 336. The focus on the face is from Emmanuel Levinas.

destructive. Some attempt to live through a spouse, which is crippling and unhealthy. Understandably, the victims in these attempts react against such diminishing and manipulation in ways that often destroy relations.

The other problem with relations is that many people fail to become themselves, for they merely mirror people around them. They conform to the expectations and wishes of others. They do not analyze life for themselves and *in community*, and they do not seek God's intent for their uniqueness. They merely assimilate to the groups around them, even when trumpeting their difference. As Oscar Wilde put it, "Most people are other people. Their thoughts are someone else's opinions, their lives a mimicry, their passions a quotation."[12]

So how do we navigate living and learning in relation but remain the strong, independent person God wants each of us to be? Søren Kierkegaard is a helpful guide. He focused on the *importance* of being an individual and worked to persuade each person to become the unique being God called him or her to be. He dedicated his books to that "solitary individual," someone who is not just one of the crowd. He forced the question, How may *I* become a Christian? He would not allow people to hide in the crowd and insisted that people see themselves standing alone before God. He would not allow the "sideward glance," the sin of comparison, and said, "Now, by the help of God, I shall become myself."[13]

The process of "becoming myself" takes place in community. Each of us must be an individual alone before God, but we cannot just be individuals. Individuals exist to relate, and we find our identity and individuality by relating, which will include analyzing both one's community and one's self. There is a process of being receptive to shaping and resistant at the same time. Sometimes how the community, which includes our families,

12. Oscar Wilde, *De Profundis*, in *Collected Works of Oscar Wilde* (Ware, Hertfordshire, UK: Wordsworth Library Collection, 2007), 1084.

13. *Søren Kierkegaard's Journals and Papers*, ed. and trans. Howard V. Hong and Edna H. Hong, 7 vols. (Bloomington: Indiana University Press, 1967–1978), 5:443 (no. 6132). For the summary statements here on Kierkegaard, see his *The Point of View Etc. Including the Point of View for My Work as an Author, Two Notes about 'The Individual,' on My Work as an Author*, trans. Walter Lowrie (London: Oxford University Press, 1939); and Søren Kierkegaard, *Purity of Heart Is to Will One Thing*, trans. Douglas V. Steere (New York: Harper and Row, 1938).

shapes us is legitimate, and sometimes it is illegitimate. Identity always involves a discerning activity.

Even though Scripture emphasizes that we are responsible as individuals, Scripture knows nothing of the *individualism* of our society and in our churches. Contrary to popular belief, Christian faith is *not* primarily a mental activity, as important as the mind is. Faith inherently is a *relational* understanding of identity. Faith is the expression for the relation between two beings,[14] not mere thinking about ideas. How could it be otherwise if love and unity are the dominant characteristics of being Christian? If indeed we are created in the image of God, we will never understand what it is to be a person apart from our relation to God, a very personal God. We become ourselves most of all in relation with God, but relation with God is impossible apart from relation with other people. Life is caught up in the twin love commands, love of God and love of neighbor as oneself. As Jesus said, all God's instruction, the whole of the law and the prophets, depends on these two commands (Matt. 22:36–40 and parallels). The horizontal and vertical relations of human existence are never separated.

But why are we so relationally inept? With this identity factor we have to focus on sin's impact, most obvious with relations, given our fractured relations with God, with each other, and with ourselves. Sin is by nature about fracture. Sin is betrayal of the responsibility of relation and a destroyer of relations because of its self-centered character. Family is a key arena for the relational aspect of identity, but it is also a key arena of bad and destructive relations, which is the reason many flee family ties. Families are often dysfunctional for several reasons: envy, competition, violation of boundaries, and perhaps because family members know the truth of the distance between what we say we are and what we really are. Our attempts to validate our own existence often come at someone else's expense, especially in our families. Relations outside the family often are conflictual as well. All too often people who have been damaged by poor relations become violators of others as they repeat the offenses.

14. See Dag Hammarskjöld, *Markings*, trans. Leif Sjöberg and W. H. Auden (New York: Knopf, 1965), 97: "Faith is the marriage of God and the Soul," quoting Saint John of the Cross.

Somewhere the cycle of destruction must stop, and Christ's reordering of identity makes that possible.

Because of the difficulty and pain of relations, people retreat to relations they can control, to dealing as much as possible with people like themselves or with people who can be controlled, or they attempt to go it alone and keep relations to a minimum. That may insulate one from further hurt, but it is counterproductive and unenjoyable. Despite what we may claim, no one is a lone individual, nor can anyone make it alone. We were created as relational beings, first for relation with God but also with others, as difficult as relations sometimes are. You will never make it on your own, nor will you be healthy trying to do so.

John Calvin addressed the question "Who am I?" and argued that we cannot know ourselves without knowing who God is. God is the one who created us and unites us to himself. Consequently, the question "Who am I?" can only be answered by the question "*Whose* am I?"[15] This is what Paul asserted and every Christian ought to know: "You are not your own, for you were bought with a price" (1 Cor. 6:19–20). Christians belong to Christ, and their identity is determined by their Lord. We will never be whole without knowing to whom we belong.

Identity Is Participation in Christ

If relations are a major factor of our identities, Christian faith transforms identity because it transforms relations. In other words, Christ wants to raise your relational IQ and ability. It is no accident that the New Testament lists of sins to avoid are lists of community-destroying acts and the lists of virtues to embrace are lists of community-enhancing acts. (For example, see Eph. 4:25–32.) It is no accident that family terms, especially sibling metaphors like "brother and sister," are the most frequent New Testament descriptions of Christians, a frequency unprecedented in the ancient world.

15. Nico Koopman, "Christian Baptism and an Identity of Inclusivity, Dignity, and Holiness," in *Christian Identity*, ed. Eduardus Van der Borght, Studies in Reformed Theology 16 (Leiden: Brill, 2008), 67–81, here 72.

Life is relational and is *constructed in dialogue* with others. A human is a communicator and therefore relational. We know ourselves only in relation, and we are known only in relation. We do not have an identity by ourselves. Interestingly, when Moses asked God's name, God replied, "I am who I am." Only God can say "I am who I am." God alone has being within himself and is not dependent on external relations. Even God is relational, though, and the very existence of God is found in the "dance" of the relations of Father, Son, and Spirit.

While we were created for relation, something within us yearns for *individual* authenticity, for independence from everyone and everything, for the freedom to chart our own course. The attempt to author our story without God is the character of sin. Still, that yearning for individual authenticity is not itself sin. Individual authenticity and relation to God belong together. No one will ever be whole or attain ongoing value apart from God. Without God you are just a blip on an eternal radar screen, but with God you have ongoing value and freedom to be unique and who you were called to be. God neither desires nor expects you to be like someone else. Your relation to Christ determines you but also sets you free *and* in relation to all others in him and to all of humanity. Christianity is not an individual affair. We have a common identity in Christ, but that common identity is lived out individually in unique ways by each of us. We have already seen that people exaggerate when they say, "All is changed with Christ." No, much still remains the same. What is changed is that all else is reinterpreted and reframed through Christ, especially relations, and all is determined by him.

Unexpectedly, the language the New Testament uses to describe relation with Christ is more profound and intimate than many know. Our failure to do justice to the Christian good news is just at this point. People commonly describe conversion or faith as "asking Jesus into your heart." I am not *completely* opposed to such language, especially if people understand it, but it is hardly satisfactory. The language distorts the idea of faith, has a poor record of producing disciples, and is marginally biblical at best, especially in Paul. Where the language of asking Christ into the heart came from is unclear. *Neither Jesus nor any of the New Testament writers gives such instruction.* The one text that sounds like this, Revelation 3:20, is addressed to people who are already Christians. Further, if faith means a person asks Christ into his or her heart, that person is the dominant personality, and Christ is about one inch tall, a diminutive player in life and one who can be hidden away when convenient.

Paul's writings contain only five occurrences of the idea of Christ *in* a person: Romans 8:10, 2 Corinthians 13:5, Galatians 2:20, 4:19, and Ephesians 3:17.[16] (Some would add Col. 1:27, but the Greek word *en* in that verse probably should be translated "among," that is, "among the gentiles.") Much more significant is that the Greek expression *en Christō* ("in Christ") or some equivalent expression (such as "in the Lord," "in him," or "in whom") occurs 164 times in Paul's writings. He views faith as *being taken into Christ*. He also uses "in the Spirit" nineteen times and "in God" three times. Not all the uses of *en Christō* and equivalents should be translated literally as "in," since other nuances are present,[17] but clearly the fundamental way Paul spoke of Christian faith was of being *in Christ*. This is something much deeper than the relation of a disciple to a teacher, and something much more profound than usual conceptions of faith. *In Paul's understanding, Christian identity derives from being in Christ, from participation in Christ. This is the primary relation and what has ultimate defining force. Relations have been taken to a radical new level.*

The focus on participation with Christ is *the* dominant idea in Paul's writings. Salvation takes place in Christ, people are described as "in Christ" or "in the Lord," and actions are done "in the Lord."[18] Romans 6:1–14 is a compelling text on participation. Here believers are said to have been baptized—plunged—into Christ and into his death, buried with him, grafted onto a death like his to enjoy resurrection with him (vv. 5–6), with their old self crucified with Christ and their being raised with Christ to live with him in newness of life. They are to consider themselves dead to the tyrant sin but living *in Christ Jesus* in relation to God (v. 11—note the blend of indicative and imperative again). Dying and rising with Christ is what faith is about.

Even the few texts that speak of Christ in us are still about participation. In Galatians 2:19 the focus is on being crucified with Christ and on

16. Additional texts allude to the idea of Christ and especially the Spirit in us. For example, see 1 Cor. 3:16; 6:19.

17. The Greek word *en* often has the connotation of "by" or "with."

18. See as examples Rom. 8:1; 16:3, 8, and 12.

such a oneness with Christ that Paul's words are hard to grasp: "*I am no longer living*, but Christ lives in me." He clearly *was* living, as is acknowledged when he added, "What I now live in the flesh . . ." Christians are people who have been displaced from their own being, crowded away from themselves, and if a person is not willing for this to happen, he or she cannot be a Christian. This is not merely some mystical union with Christ, and it is not too weird for "normal" people. Humanity needs this disorientation from self and reorientation to God. Remember Miroslav Volf's statement from earlier in the book: "Paul presumes a centered self, more precisely a *wrongly* centered self that needs to be de-centered by being nailed to the cross."[19] In dying with Christ and calling him Lord we obtain a new center for the self.

Participation is *the* essential ingredient in Christianity. Christ died for us, but we died with him, or his death is of no effect. I know of no other way for the atonement to make any sense. The cross is not some remote event of the past, but the means of our own death and our own resurrection to new life.

We have difficulty grasping what Paul means, for we do not speak of being *in* any other person. Some argue that we have no way of embracing Paul's thought since our understanding of personality and individuality precludes any idea of being in Christ, no matter how nice the latter may sound. Are we that impoverished? The idea of a mere individual is an illusion. We were created for such relation with God. Also, did we not notice that it is no easier to think of Christ in us than it is of our being in Christ? Paul has a "spheres of influence" theology.[20] Life is either lived in Christ or lived in sin and the flesh, and existence is always housed somewhere. Paul just assumed that faith made Christ the context in which we live. "Paul evidently felt himself to be caught up 'in Christ' and borne along by Christ. In some sense he experienced Christ as the context of all his being and doing."[21] That is what New Testament faith is about.

19. Miroslav Volf, *Exclusion and Embrace: An Exploration of Identity, Otherness, and Reconciliation* (Nashville: Abingdon, 1996), 69.

20. See my "Spheres of Influence: A Possible Solution to the Problem of Paul and the Law," *Journal for the Study of the New Testament* 32 (1988): 93–113.

21. James D. G. Dunn, *The Theology of Paul the Apostle* (Grand Rapids: Eerdmans, 1998), 400.

To speak of being in Christ or of losing self to find Christ is not about loss of identity, absorption in the divine, or negation of self, as in Buddhism. It is to say that one's true self is only known in relation to God and in being determined by God. Justice is still done to particularity and individuality. In fact, being in Christ requires a more robust idea *of the individual*, for it underscores the responsibility, decision making, and action of each person, not in isolation but through the Spirit and in relation to others.

Being in Christ is a recognition that our relation with Christ defines and determines every other relation and action. Being a Christian means *being one with Christ* to such a degree that we are aware that we live in him and are bound to him. He is the environment or force field, the sphere of influence, within which we live and which determines our thought and conduct. This is what the early church understood when it said, "Jesus is Lord." *Participation* in Christ reconstructs identity. This is not about perfectionism; it is about a relation and involvement that supersedes every other relation but also determines every other relation.

As strange as the language of being in Christ or God may be, some people in the ancient world—both Jews and Greeks—got it. The psalmist prayed, "Lord, you have been our *dwelling place* from generation to generation" (Ps. 90:1), and God was often viewed as a fortress or refuge (for example, Pss. 18:2; 46:7). Paul told the Athenians, "For in him we live and move and exist" (Acts 17:28).[22] John Calvin thought this idea was already present in the concept of the image of God in Genesis 1.[23] With Christians such intimacy with God is enhanced and moved to the center of thought. Now it is not just existence in God; it is life taken up in and with Christ and hidden in God, as Colossians 3:3 says: "Your life has been hidden with Christ in God." Whatever else we may say, Christian faith is about

22. On participation see my "The Gospel of Participation," in *Earliest Christianity within the Boundaries of Judaism: Essays in Honor of Bruce Chilton*, ed. Alan J. Avery-Peck, Craig A. Evans, and Jacob Neusner (Leiden: Brill, 2016), 413–30.

23. See his *Institutes of the Christian Religion*, ed. John T. McNeill and trans. Ford Lewis Battles, Library of Christian Classics, vols. 20 and 21 (Philadelphia: Westminster, 1960), 2.1.5; 2.2.1; and 1.2.1; J. Todd Billings, *Union with Christ: Reframing Theology and Ministry for the Church* (Grand Rapids: Baker, 2011), 33; and J. Todd Billings, *Calvin, Participation, and the Gift: The Activity of Believers in Union with Christ* (Oxford: Oxford University Press, 2007), 79 and 167.

Ancient baptistery at Mamshit in the Negev of Israel

Photo courtesy of Bruce Einspahr

participation with the God revealed in Jesus Christ, not merely thinking thoughts about God, and participation is the ultimate form of relation.

The most poignant examples of people who "got it" are those who constructed cross-shaped baptisteries. From the fourth to the sixth century, various countries around the Mediterranean had cross-shaped baptisteries. The person being baptized went down four or five steps into the center of the cross and was baptized there. People took their new Christian identity standing in the middle of the cross. They knew what it meant to enact Paul's language of dying and rising with Christ. They were not merely thinking thoughts; they were participating with Christ.

Why we have not emphasized faith as participation more is a mystery, for all great Christian thinkers throughout church history focused on participation, especially John Calvin, who spoke of being engrafted into Christ,[24] and Martin Luther, who said, "But faith must be taught correctly, namely, that by it you are so cemented to Christ that He and you are as one person, which cannot be separated but remains attached to Him

---

24. Calvin, *Institutes of the Christian Religion* 3.1.1; see also 3.11.10.

forever and declares: 'I am as Christ.'"[25] More poignant is the statement of Luther's wife, Katharina von Bora, who reportedly said on her deathbed, "I will stick to Christ as a burr to cloth."[26] She understood.

To speak of participation raises theological issues, but it also has *huge* advantages. Suddenly the dense and often convoluted discussions of atonement find clarity and fresh prospect. In the person and work of Christ, *God was participating with us* to bring us to himself (2 Cor. 5:19), and by the Spirit's work of joining us to Christ in faith *we participate* in the death and life of Christ. Oneness with Christ is assumed when we speak of his death being our death, his death being for us, and his life being our life. Dying and rising with Christ expresses the ongoing participation we have with Christ. Baptism and the Lord's Supper are both about participation with Christ. Among many texts, note Galatians 3:27, "You who were baptized into Christ have put on Christ," and 1 Corinthians 10:16, "The cup of blessing which we bless, is it not a participation [Greek: *koinōnia*] with the blood of Christ? The bread which we break, is it not a participation [Greek: *koinōnia*] with the body of Christ?" Participation is the very nature of faith; it is knowing God experientially, participating with God, not merely knowing things about God. Ethics are totally reorganized by participation. Note how incredulous Paul is in 1 Corinthians 6:15–17 that one who is joined to Christ could commit sexual sin. With a focus on participation, the weary and wasted discussion of faith versus works goes away. You will work; the only question is from what identity.

"Participation" is the language the church should be—*must be*—using to describe the gospel and conversion. The gospel is a gospel of participation. Faith in Christ is participation with Christ, and participation with Christ will change your identity. Such language would energize both the church and the lives of individuals. It would help prevent the "failure to launch" of many people who claim to believe in Christ but never become disciples of Christ. It would negate the thought that one can believe in Christ and not work with and for Christ.

What role do humans have in union with Christ? The Spirit is the one

25. Martin Luther, *Lectures on Galatians 1535*, in *Luther's Works*, vols. 26 and 27, ed. Jaroslav Pelikan (Saint Louis: Concordia, 1963), 26:168.

26. "Katharina von Bora," *Wikipedia*, last modified March 29, 2017, https://en.wikipe dia.org/wiki/Katharina_von_Bora.

who creates union with Christ and places us in Christ, but do we accept it and engage it? If we do not, nothing happens. But what does "accept and engage" mean; how does the Spirit accomplish creating this new union; and what is the interaction of God's Spirit with the human spirit? I know of no easy answers to these questions, but perhaps the last question already makes a wrong assumption. It assumes that we start out with God and humans isolated from each other and that we need to figure what part is God's and what part is ours. Rather, a more biblical view is the awareness that we do not exist apart from God and that in all we do we have to do with God. Any action we take—right or wrong—is a response to God and involves God, and any action of God toward us also involves us.

I have argued that *geography is identity*, and nowhere is that more true than here. That phrase and its importance first occurred to me when I was trying to explain what Paul meant by the words "in Christ." There is a real sense that Christians live in Christ, that he is their new geography, the "place" that determines who they are and how they will live. This thought is the basis of both salvation and Christian living. Christ's death and life are effective for us because we are in him and one with him. A pattern in Paul's use of this language seems clear. When Paul speaks of salvation, he usually speaks of being *in* Christ (e.g., Eph. 2:13: "But now *in* Christ Jesus . . . you have been brought near"). When he speaks of Christian action, he usually uses "*in* the Lord" (e.g., Phil. 4:1: "Stand firm *in* the Lord"). Although the pattern varies, he often describes other people and their work as *in* the Lord (e.g., Rom. 16:12: "Greet Tryphaena and Tryphosa, who labored *in* the Lord").

In John's Gospel and letters the thought is more reciprocal. We remain in Christ, and he remains in us, just as the vine and branches are united and remain together. In John's writings as well we are never instructed "to ask Jesus into our hearts." In the Synoptic Gospels, participation with Jesus is expressed as following him, but it is no less attachment to Jesus.

Identity Found in the Family of God

The reality of being in Christ reconstructs all thought concerning relations with other people. Conversion itself is sociological both in its origin and in its result. Nearly all of us experience conversion because of relations with specific people or communities, what they represent, and their drawing us into Christ. Conversion into Christ also includes conversion into a community. The church is not some afterthought but is inherent in being joined to Christ. Paul assumes that by being in Christ you are *both part of Christ and part of the other people in Christ* (see 1 Cor. 6:15; Eph. 5:30; and Rom. 12:5 and Eph. 4:25). These texts and many others point to a depth of relation, a solidarity and union, with Christ that exceeds what we think possible. Unity with Christ *and his people* is established. Our relation to Christ determines us but also sets us in relation to all others in him and to all of humanity. The obvious and most fundamental metaphor Paul uses to describe these new relations is the *body of Christ*. We are taken into Christ and made part of him and one with him but also part of other people in that body. In Christ we belong to other people, and they belong to us. Obviously other people have only derivative defining force; Christ is the ultimate definer. Clearly Christianity is not an individual affair, and the idea of a merely individual Christian is an impossibility.

People in the ancient world were driven to achieve honor and avoid shame, and the primary means for both involved family and the groups to which one belonged. This was a major factor in determining one's identity—and still is. One had honor and a valuable identity if one's family had status and acted in reputable ways, and one had honor by belonging to a particular group, whether it be a trade guild, an association, or a status group like the equestrians. Our society is not driven so *overtly* by quests for honor, but our identity and value are still determined partly by our relations and the groups to which we belong or do not belong. Everyone wants to belong to a reputable group, even if it is only as a fan of a reputable sports team. The New Testament confronts all misplaced human quests for honor, which nearly always are at someone else's expense, and offers a different understanding of honor and shame. Honor is given by the grace of God and in relation to God. Christians are honored by being in Christ. Honor and shame for Christians are conditioned on whether one acts in accord with the character of Christ and the honor and identity given by God. Language such as "the elect" or "children of God" is an attempt to express the honor *given* by God and by being in relation to God. A new identity-shaping group is formed that trumps all other groups.

The relational aspect of faith is emphasized also with language drawn from the family. For us family is usually the most important set of relations we have. Relations with family and tribe have always been stronger than relations with country or some other entity. The importance of family relations was even stronger in the ancient world. Jesus and the New Testament writers emphasize that faith creates a new family. Our true family, as much as we may love our historical families, is the family of God, those doing the will of God (Mark 3:31–35 and Eph. 2:19–22). God is our ultimate Father; the Spirit is the one who enables us to say "Abba, Father" (Rom. 8:15; Gal. 4:6); and we are adopted into the family of God. Family metaphors such as "children," "brother," and "sister" are the most frequent way of describing those in Christ. Honor is now not something one seeks for oneself; rather one seeks to honor God and promote the well-being of brothers and sisters.

This is not merely about me and my kind, and the issue of racism must be faced. Participation with Christ obliterates the divisions and illegitimate boundaries we think are normal, as Galatians 3:28, Ephesians 2:11–22, and Colossians 3:11 make clear. If being in Christ creates the unity of the body of Christ, we cannot tolerate the divisions and attitudes that separate people. Being part of Christ and part of each other—including people of other races—requires that we practice the unity God has created. To do less is sin.

Early church confessions are also instructive about relations, for confessions did (and do) more than assert ideas people held. They also showed to what groups people belonged and what relations were most significant to them. In 1 Corinthians 15:3–4 Paul quotes a confession of the early church: "For I delivered to you first of all what I received: that Christ died for our sins according to the Scriptures, that he was buried, that he was raised on the third day according to the Scriptures." With this confession Paul marks out the relation of Christ *for* and to believers, his own relation to ones who handed the tradition down to him, his relation to those to whom he now hands it, and the relation of believers to Christ and to each other. To confess someone means, at least in part, to declare publicly to whom one belongs. To say "Jesus is Lord" means, first of all, that one's primary and determinative relation is with Jesus. Other relations are not negated—this is not individualism; they are reoriented and redefined by Christ.

Nor should we think of the relational aspect of our identity only in terms of relation to Christ and other Christians. If we take seriously the fact that humans are created in God's image and that we are to mirror God's own character, then we stand in potential and positive relation with all other humans. Myrto Theocharous, a Greek friend and Old Testament scholar, put it this way: "Your identity is revealed in your encounter with the stranger; that is the moment that you know where you come from: whether you come from a Father who brings near the ones who are far off or not."[27] How we relate has its origin in our God. Being from such a Father, we embody a hospitality and graciousness that mirrors God's grace. Any narrow and self-centered identity or any identity that disparages other people is excluded by the nature of the facts.

This, however, raises the issue of accountability. Sometimes people speak of the "accountable self," the part of our self that holds the rest of our self accountable. Being in relation involves accountability to each other. What do we owe each other? We do not owe the same to every person, but we do owe every person. Cain's question—"Am I my brother's keeper?"—is still a foundational question. What do other people owe us? How we treat people is predicated on the nature of the relation, on how we have read their identities, and on how we understand ourselves in relation to them. We and they are accountable to each other and to God. Unfortunately, people in our society have little sense of accountability. I will address the issue of accountability again in discussing identity and the future, but Jesus's parable of the sheep and the goats (Matt. 25:31–46) says judgment will be based on how we related to other people and ministered to them. How we treat others is an encounter with Christ—"Whatever you did to one of these least brothers of mine, you did to me" (Matt. 25:40). Since Christ is the one who energizes our relations with others as well, he is the origin and recipient of everything we do.[28] This is a level of participation we did not expect.

At the same time, we need to be attentive to the *quality* of our relations. While we should be open to relations with all kinds of people, not all relations will have the same significance or influence on us. Conver-

27. Myrto Theocharous, "Loving the Least: Human Trafficking in Greece," Langham Partnership, July 27, 2007, http://us.langham.org/loving-the-least-human-trafficking-in-greece/.

28. See my treatment of this parable in *Stories with Intent: A Comprehensive Guide to the Parables of Jesus* (Grand Rapids: Eerdmans, 2008), 543–63.

sion restructures identity, and it does so partly by giving us new sets of relations in a new and positive community, that is, with the community of Christ followers.

Relation with Christ not only sets us in relation to other people, but it redefines how relations are to be lived. A good deal of the instruction in Scripture focuses on proper relations, not only with directions concerning such things as love, anger, or sexual relations. Basic life questions such as "Am I my brother's keeper?" or "Who is my neighbor?" force us to think through what we are supposed to be and how relations are lived out. People are more important than things. Truth is required in dealing with relations. Legitimate boundaries must be preserved and honored. (Conflict is always a result of perceived violation of boundaries and devaluing of relations.)

Often our operative question is, "What is in it for me?" We use people and see relations as transactions conducted for our own profit. Relations can and should be beneficial, but the goal of our relations must not be lodged in our own self-centeredness. Other people are not furniture in our lives nor opportunities for us to take advantage of—to make a transaction for our profit. Rather, they are opportunities for us to be truly human and live relationally. Recognition of another person is a recognition of our responsibility to nurture and care for the image of God in us and the other person. The Roman philosopher Seneca said, "Wherever there is a human being there is the opportunity for a kindness."[29] Surely Christians have better reasons to say the same. If the character of God is to be reflected in us, God's care must be evident as well in seeking the good of the other person. If we are aware of our responsibility and accountability for other people, we will not view them as opportunities for transaction to enhance our own being. We will treat people as a goal in themselves and not as a means to our own pursuits.[30]

We cannot deal in detail with the character of Christian relations, but the following should be obvious:

1. Relations must be built on both truth and love, two realities that are *not* in conflict. Love rejoices with the truth (1 Cor. 13:6). Love refuses

29. Seneca, *On the Happy Life* 24.3.
30. Alasdair MacIntyre, *After Virtue: A Study in Moral Theory*, 3rd ed. (Notre Dame: University of Notre Dame Press, 2007), 46, following Kant.

to let go, and truth is willing to confront. Good relations cannot exist without authenticity.

2. Good relations will honor people because they are made in God's image. Therefore the importance of each person will be affirmed by the way he or she is received and treated. The Christian faith requires hospitality to others. Immanuel Kant asserted that the only unqualified good is a good will.[31] His point was that any good we imagine could lead to negative results, but a good will is positive in itself. Good will toward others is an unqualified good. Christians call this commitment to good will for the other person *agapē*, the love reflecting God's own love for us.

3. Priority on relations will require investment in learning about relational skills and in developing sensitivity and ability to read people. You can *learn* to relate well. Self-centeredness will be excluded, and willingness to forgive will be ready at hand.

4. Good relations will both enable people and hold them accountable, which will require the willingness to invest in people. Good relations take time.

5. Good relations will exclude anger, bitterness, belittling, hostility, lying, slander, and any other attempt to establish the priority of one's own existence at the cost of someone else. Dietrich Bonhoeffer spoke of the ministry of holding your tongue.[32] Words can be highly destructive and divisive, and once spoken they cannot be retrieved. We should be very careful in what we say to others, especially children whose brains will be structured partly by the way we relate to and care for them.

Crucial to healthy relations, of course, is a proper sense of self, neither disparaging nor overestimating oneself, which indeed is the first step to obeying God. It is no surprise that humility is the first item mentioned in Romans 12:3–5 and Ephesians 4:2–5, key passages explaining how Christians are to live. Although we are responsible for our lives, our lives are not really about us and our desires. Our lives are supposed to be about what is

31. Cited by Ricoeur, *Oneself as Another*, 205. See Immanuel Kant, *Groundwork of the Metaphysics of Morals*, trans. and ed. Mary Gregor and Jens Timmermann (Cambridge: Cambridge University Press, 2012), 9.

32. Dietrich Bonhoeffer, *Life Together*, trans. John W. Doberstein (New York: Harper and Row, 1954), 91.

good, pleasing, and complete in obedience to the will of God, as Romans 12:1–2 says. All of us seek to attach ourselves to that which is good, and the good this passage seeks is relational, living as individuals bound together and mutually supportive of others in the body of Christ. This text and others do *not* assume equality. In fact, any focus on equality is a distortion, unless we are specific about the arena being assessed. In truth, we are not equal. We are all different with different abilities and gifts. The biblical material assumes difference, but different does not mean less valued. The body imagery insists on the care of all in the body and assumes that each person will contribute to the good of the whole community.

Trying to keep life for yourself destroys life. Giving it away creates it. This is the foundation of discipleship and expresses Jesus's intent in saying, "The one who wishes to save life will lose it" (Matt. 16:25 and parallels). This is especially true of our relation to him. Life is not about you even when it is about you. You are not the goal of life even when you are the subject of life.

If life is relational, who are you when a key relation, especially a spouse or some other close determiner, is no longer there? The death of a close relation leaves a gaping emptiness and can be destructive. Still, no relation is given ultimate defining force except our relation with Christ. Anything else is a form of idolatry. We know who we are by knowing whose we are. All other relations must be held with an open hand because they are not permanent and cannot be the source of ultimate definition. Further, except for relation with Christ, no *particular* relation is determinative. All relations exist in a network of relations, and indeed, even our relation with Christ does.

On Sin and Relations

Reflection on sin and relations is essential. Sin is so destructive because it is rooted in self-centeredness, which violates boundaries and destroys relations. Martin Luther defined sin as *homo incurvatus in se*—a human turned in upon himself or herself.[33] Like shavings planed from a piece of

---

33. Martin Luther, *Lectures on Romans, Glosses and Scholia*, in *Luther's Works*, ed. Hilton C. Oswald (Saint Louis: Concordia, 1972), 25:291 (on Rom. 5:4). See also 25:159. Some point to Augustine in his *City of God* 12.6 and 14.28 for the roots of this thought.

wood curl in on themselves, we too, when separated from God, curl in on ourselves. This leads to fracture in all relations, to fracture in one's own being, to bad transactions (i.e., trading the truly valuable for counterfeits), and often to abuse of power. The results are so negative that philosophers and theologians regularly speak of sin being its own punishment. Self-centeredness, the essence of sin, is the death of wisdom, and it ruins life. The opposite of self-centeredness is not self-negation; it is love.

Sin involves relations another way. Sin nearly always requires other people to be complicit; it requires other people to be involved or to be silent, to look the other way or to avoid truth telling. David's sin with Bath-sheba (2 Sam. 11) could not have occurred without other people being complicit: Joab, the messengers of David, other soldiers, and Bathsheba were all complicit. They knew and could have stopped the sequence of events, costly though it may have been.

The biblical teaching on relations is especially important for men, for people often assume that men are by nature insensitive and not particularly good at either communication or relations. This is not necessarily true, and must not be true for Christian men. No one can say about relational ineptness, "That is just the way I am." Again, that may work as a confession of sin but not as an excuse. You can change, and relation with Christ demands that you change in your relations with other people. Show me how you relate to people, and I will know who you are and I will know if you understand the message of Jesus and the New Testament.

Relations will be dealt with in a different way in the next chapter, but at this point, what will you do with your relations? Is your external community one to be trusted, one to be chosen, or should you change it if possible? Can you change it without being disloyal to yourself and disloyal to your relations? Should past relations be valued and nurtured, corrected, or avoided? What new relations will help you become the person God intends? Granted the need to be hospitable to all, with whom should you join yourself to have your Christian identity enhanced? If your primary relations are not rooted in your Christ identity, your identity will not flourish. The people you are with will shape you, and you will shape them. Your identity is at stake. Make wise choices.

FACTOR 4

You Are Your Mind

<hr>

Without learning you cannot be a person who loves God; accept learning as necessary.

—*Sentences of Sextus* 251

Do not go outside, come back into yourself. It is in the inner self that Truth dwells.

—Augustine, *True Religion*

In America today the main heresy is not atheism, it's superficiality.

—Tom Long, "Christ's Uncomfortable Words of Comfort (Mark 4:10–12)"

You are indeed your mind. You are the result of how you think about yourself. Logically this chapter should come last, but it is too important for that. By focusing on our physical and psychological makeup, on history, and on relations, we have built a foundation for understanding identity, but the clear determiner of identity is *what we do with all the factors* related to us. We need to focus on this process now.

The internal self-interpreting, self-directing memory is the most complex, fascinating, enjoyable, and determinative part of identity, and it is the reason Scripture speaks so frequently of the mind. To be human is to be aware of—to think about—oneself *as a self.* To be human is to think, to remember, to evaluate and value, to choose, and to assign meaning. Identity results from such actions. Your mind—the internal self-interpreting, self-directing memory—collects, interprets, and prioritizes everything else and in effect says, "This is who I am because of what matters to me, and therefore I will live accordingly," even if you are unaware of the process. Without such thinking there is no identity. Given that, why would anyone cloud the mind with alcohol or drugs—or the inane drivel we are handed each day by our society?

If thinking is the source of identity, why are we often so unconscious and uncaring about how and what we think? Should we not be highly attentive, concentrated, and caring about how self-interpretation takes place? This self-interpretation, this process of making sense of ourselves, *is* the process of identity formation. It makes us who we are.

For all the significance of our bodies, of being born into a history, and of our relations, identity is still about the uniqueness of each person, even if that can never be perceived apart from other people. Identity is personal; it is about each of us individually and how we understand ourselves as *separate* from other people, no matter how much we are joined to them. It is about *self*-consciousness. We are ultimately responsible for and to ourselves, even though others shape us. An Old Testament scholar said, "The basic phenomenon peculiar to man [and woman] is the consciousness of responsibility."[1] To be human is have moral responsibility—responsibility for what we have been given, for what we do and why we did it, and for how we relate to others. *Oughtness,* then, is at the center of identity. Oughtness results from an evaluation of the good to which we should attach ourselves, an investment to some degree in the good we discerned, and an evaluation of ourselves as to whether we did indeed attach ourselves to the good or why we did not. We have been given this life; what will we make of ourselves so as not to waste life? Our mind sorts, organizes, explains, values, and chooses—at least to some degree—what we will be and do. A main point in Scripture is that we will be held responsible for what happens with this process.

1. Walther Eichrodt, *Man in the Old Testament,* trans. K. Smith and R. Gregor Smith, Studies in Biblical Theology (London: SCM, 1951), 9.

How many selves are there? People speak of multiple selves: the minimal self (the purely immediate and rather base self responding to needs and desires), the agentic self (the self that acts), the responsible self, the accountable self, the summoning self, and the executive self, just to name some of the most obvious. With self-interpretation we are both the one interpreting and the one being interpreted. We have a variety of drives and desires that are part of us but are, hopefully, controlled by us, but who controls us when there is self-control? Who is talking when I talk to myself? The self is always at some distance from itself, at least when it is aware of itself.

We do not need to explain the complexity of the self—nor can we—but several facts seem foundational:

> We all know fragmentation within ourselves because of the conflicts between our desires and goals and our sense of what we should be. We are divided within ourselves.
>
> We all need purpose, a sense of value, some sense of coherence (if not unity), and redirection away from self-centeredness. We need to be decentered and then recentered on something worthwhile.
>
> We all are aware that we are not what we should be, which means— even if we cannot name it—that we are aware of the summoning self, both communicated by others and discerned on our own, that calls us to be what we should be.
>
> At some level an executive self is formed to decide how we will navigate the conflicts, tensions, and difficulties of life. Even if we say we have no coherence in our being, there is an executive self making the judgment.

We must ask, "From which self do I live?" Clearly many people live most of life out of the minimal self, the rather low-level self that responds to desires. The minimal self does not care about consequences of its actions, either for itself or for others. If you live from the minimal self, you will encounter maximal pain, or even maximal destruction, for yourself and for others. You need a strong, well-informed executive self. Is the executive self well founded, well instructed, and actually "in control," or is your executive self unable to lead because it is submerged somewhere in the morass of a complex and conflicted life? Is your executive self unable to make executive decisions?

Though Scripture does not use the language I have used, much of Scripture is directly concerned with these very issues: dealing with desires and goals, our purpose and value, our failures to be who we are, and the ordering of our lives to be who we really are. Patrick McNamara, a neuroscientist, argues that every religion addresses the problem of the divided self and that the purpose of every religion is to create an executive self. Religious experience for him involves a "decentering," which periodically takes the self "off-line," out of working memory temporarily for repair and construction, and then links it back with an ideal possible self for a more effective and mature executive self.[2] This precisely describes Christian faith and what worship seeks to do. Faith unites us to God and orders our lives, and worship allows the self to take itself off-line, to examine itself honestly in communion with God, realize the self it is summoned to be, and go back online with a newly ordered perspective, an executive self.

But where do we get a legitimate summoning self, that self in front of us calling us to be what we should be? The one society offers us is often twisted. Part of the summoning self may be inherent in being human, but if so, it can certainly be muted or ignored. Clearly Scripture offers us a summoning self with its assertion that humans are created in the image of God, with directions for how we should live, with examples of right living, and especially with the example of Jesus Christ. Surely one purpose of the church is to help us form a legitimate summoning self. Will we stifle the summoning self, acting like it is not there or finding some reason to not apply it to ourselves? The summoning self is not some general model, though, and it is not static. *Your* summoning self is not the same as everyone else's. While the summoning self is modeled on scriptural directives and Jesus Christ, it is highly personal, unique to the individual, and calls each of us to be the individual we were intended to be. Also, the summoning self is in transition as one gains or loses abilities and opportunities, as one ages, etc. Clearly too, people around us com-

2. Patrick McNamara, *The Neuroscience of Religious Experience* (Cambridge: Cambridge University Press, 2009), 5, 30–32, 40–42, and 147–51.

municate what a summoning self should be like; this is part of the task of a family, the church, and education when rightly perceived.

What is the relation of Jesus Christ to the summoning self and the executive self? It would be easy to think Jesus was the summoning self and that naming him as Lord makes him the executive self, but that would be naive. The summoning self may be modeled after Jesus's character, but it is much more specific to each person. My summoning self will not be the same as that of my son or daughter or someone who lives in another culture. Jesus shapes—or seeks to shape—the summoning self but is not the summoning self. The same is true for the executive self. Naming Jesus as Lord does not make him the executive self. There is still an executive self in each person that chooses naming Jesus as Lord, repeatedly chooses to follow him, and repeatedly decides what it means to follow him. Who denies when we deny ourselves, take up our crosses, and follow Jesus? The very self we deny is the self that must act. The executive self remains as the arbiter of one's own being, even when it is given over to Christ. The executive self must find a goal and purpose outside of itself, something worth striving for. Jesus and his kingdom give a vision worth being the purpose of life. Part of what Scripture does, which we need so desperately, is give us right desires and a vision of what life from God should be.

But this is to get ahead of ourselves. The process of self-interpretation is complex, but it centers around three interrelated actions: *memory*, *valuing*, and the *dialogues that take place in and with the mind*. The internal self-interpreting, self-directing memory has to do with memory and vision, what we think is good and our relation to it, what we say about ourselves and what others say about us, and our sifting and editing all of it to decide and assert who we are. After describing memory, valuing, and the dialogues, we will see how Scripture addresses these very issues.

Memory

When I turned fifty-eight, my daughter gave me a box in which she had placed fifty-eight notes, each one a memory of some event or time of enjoyment in our lives. Each memory structures our relationship. For all of us, all our memories define us and cement relations that enable or disable life, productivity, and enjoyment. They provide a framework within which we live, and they enable or disable belongingness and meaning. Meaning is the value we give a set of relations, whether relations with people around us or the relation of words we seek to understand. If meaning is a valuation placed on relations, memory tells us which relations are important and invests significance into the relations we have. There is no more important relation than our relation to God, our Creator, even though we often forget it. Memory helps us understand reality, but memory is not reality. You cannot live in a memory in healthy fashion, but memory can enable you to live healthily. By memory we construct reality and know who we are.

Without memory identity does not exist, at least in terms of self-consciousness. We literally remember who we are. Our memory is our life. The continuity of memory creates a narrative of self-understanding, although it is not done in isolation from others. Augustine said that in his memory he met himself, but he also asserted that in our memory we find God.[3] Identity derives from a sense of sameness—a continuity of remembering—even while life is in constant change. Memory is the basis for forming character and for trust in relations. Memory allows us to know and be ourselves and to know how to relate to others. The failure of memory, such as when people experience Alzheimer's disease, amnesia, or other attacks on memory, makes identity a difficult and excruciating subject.

Memory, however, is not as simple as one might think. It is not just the collection of remembered events, and it is not merely an automatic function. We do not remember everything, and we only partially control what is remembered. Memory is sometimes chosen, is sometimes forced on us, and sometimes just happens. Some things we can never forget, some we repress in an attempt to avoid remembering, and memories fade over time. Some memories are *embodied* rather than conscious (not just "muscle memory" but other embodied traits, experiences, practices, etc.) and so may survive severe memory loss. An example of this is a man with

---

3. See Augustine, *Confessions* 10.8.13–14 and 10.24–25.35–36. See also 3.6 and the discussion in Charles Taylor, *Sources of the Self: The Making of the Modern Identity* (Cambridge, MA: Harvard University Press, 1989), 135–36.

Alzheimer's whose wife faithfully brought him to church. He gave little indication of awareness of what was happening unless it was the singing of a hymn he knew well or the recitation of the Lord's Prayer. Then he suddenly became aware and involved.

From memories of people, experiences, and thoughts we construct our identity, but memory is not merely about the past. *How* we remember shapes the future. Memory is already an ordering. It arranges people and experiences for recall and priority, and indeed, as one person put it, memory is like a battleground for everything.[4] What will we choose to remember, and how will we arrange the memory? The arrangement occurs because items are important, enjoyable, or negative, and one needs the information for the future, but one needs it also for self-understanding. How do I stand in relation to what has happened and to the people I have met, and how will that memory contribute positively to my future?

Memory is rarely merely an individual act. It involves others and discussions—even if never verbalized. Other people help us remember, sometimes filling in the blanks we missed or lost and sometimes challenging what and how we remember.

Memories shape us, both our own memories and memories others instill in us, but they are always partial and always only partially reliable. Memories are only partially reliable—and sometimes not reliable at all—because even as our memories shape us, *we shape them.* We often remember in the way most beneficial to ourselves, which is not only unfair to others but may be a lie. If we rewrite memory to avoid the truth of what we or others did, we falsify our own being. *Even remembering is an ethical activity.*

The psalmist said God desires truth—*integrity*—in the inward being (Ps. 51:6).[5] My Old Testament colleague Bob Hubbard says the inward being refers to "any place inside humans that is so hidden, secretive, and inaccessible that it can get away with anything (or cause anything) with-

---

4. Binsar Pakpahan, "Identity and Remembrance," in *Christian Identity*, ed. Eduardus Van der Borght, Studies in Reformed Theology 16 (Leiden: Brill, 2008), 105–17, 108.

5. The NIV has "Yet you desired faithfulness even in the womb." While the Hebrew word 'emet includes ideas of both "truth" and "faithfulness," this translation is odd. The parallelism with the second part of the verse shows the focus is on understanding in the inner being.

out detection."[6] We prefer lies. Lies are more inspirational than the truth, but you cannot live well there. Lies are more inspirational than the truth because they deceive, offer the unattainable, and ignore the harsh—or even not so harsh—realities of life. Witness Genesis 3 and the lie "You will be like God," to say nothing of the lies people tell themselves to avoid reality. (This should give pause to those who think preaching is only to inspire.) Real truth, God's truth, is the only inspiration that does justice to truth and gives real hope. The complete truth, God's truth and its promises, is indeed more inspirational than any and all lies.

Once again the biblical focus on the heart and truth in the inward parts points to something crucial. Without truth your identity has no adequate foundation. In Scripture the heart refers to the controlling center of one's being, which sounds very much like the executive self. Even the executive self can be deluded—or self-deluded. If the heart/executive self is key for the internal self-interpreting memory, how do we get it to be honest, just, not defensive, and willing to obey? Surely here the grace of God and the Spirit of God must be the foundations on which we stand.

Valuing

A quite wealthy woman gave gifts to her employees each Christmas. She gave her farrier, the man who put shoes on her horses, a signed blank check. When he pointed out to her that no amount was specified, she told him to fill in the amount he thought appropriate. Should he put $15 or $15,000 or even more? If he puts $15, what does he think of his identity? If he takes advantage of her and writes an enormous number, what does that reveal about his identity? I confess, in his shoes, I would have begged her to fill in the amount.

The point is often made that a person's identity is determined by what *matters* to him or her, by what the person finds *valuable* enough to make *commitments* to. What you value gives a vision of what you should be and do, and in the process values or devalues you. This is something beyond dignity; it is about achieved honor. Every person has equal dignity be-

---

6. Private communication.

cause he or she is created in the image of God. Honor, however, rests on a foundation of inequality.[7] Dignity may be true of all, but honor does not come to all. Dignity is a gift of the Creator. Honor is achieved as a result of attachment to something good and living accordingly. Honor is about what a person is and accomplishes. But there are two kinds of honor: the honor that comes from humans and the honor that comes from God (see John 5:44). Honor from humans often involves self-centeredness and often is a distortion of life. Honor from God assumes rejection of self-centeredness and then living as God intends.

Everyone wants to be respected, to be valued, but whose respect do we seek and why? Respect gained by attaching ourselves to the good and by living faithfully presupposes that the individual and the society know what is good, but often people do not. Attaching oneself to the good is accomplished either by *doing* something that is good, *possessing* something thought to be good, or *associating* with others or something thought to be good or valuable.

The internal self-interpreting, self-directing memory is very much about valuing and the *honor* that comes from assigning value. Valuing is what makes us human and is at the heart of any treatment of identity. Humans choose what they care about, and in the process they demonstrate who they are and set the course for their actions. All of us want to attach ourselves to what is valuable and good so we can see *ourselves* as valuable and good,[8] even if it is not true. A violent Jamaican drug lord reportedly said, "I am no saint, but I am a good person." All of us want to label ourselves as good, even if we are not, and therefore, because it is about the good, valuing is a *moral* issue.

Valuing is part of the foundation for living. The good both attracts and motivates us to be good. An early Christian advised, "Think about good things so that you may also do good things."[9] This is Paul's point in Philippians 4:8 when he urges people to think on what is true, honorable, right, etc. The less we are attached to the good, the less sense of worth we have,

7. Carl Elliott, *Better Than Well: American Medicine Meets the American Dream* (New York: Norton, 2003), 41.

8. Taylor, *Sources of the Self*, 47: "to make minimal sense of our lives, in order to have an identity, we need an orientation to the good."

9. *Sentences of Sextus* 56.

but who determines what is good? We learn what and how to value. While some knowledge of "the good" may be innate, mostly we are taught what is good by parents and society, even though every human orientation to the good is already skewed. Should we not be much more conscious in naming what is good and in thinking about values and teaching them?

Who teaches values in our culture? The indoctrination of Germans in the 1930s, lined up in neat rows by the hundreds of thousands, is astonishing to us. They listened to a demagogue and bought into an ideology seemingly without question, giving allegiance and absolute obedience almost beyond belief. One can understand their vulnerability after the shame of World War One; here was someone giving them honor and value, and they bought it. We would not line up by the thousands except for a rock concert or a sports event, but we line up by the hundreds of thousands in front of our TVs. We are not so vulnerable and do not *usually* listen to a demagogue, but we are indoctrinated just as much and seek honor and value from places and people who cannot rightly give it.

Morality is learned, but little *substantive* teaching of morality occurs in our society. Individually we need language and models of the good to enable our internal conversation about the good. Of course, much of the language about what is good is provided by Scripture, which seeks to orient us to the good, a good that comes from and is found in God.

If valuing is about the good, it is about finding worth or honor for ourselves. "I am worth something because of my attachment to the good." The good may be universal "goods" about which all (or most) agree, or the good may be more limited—say a hobby—which individuals choose as part of their personal identity. People in effect say, "I value these realities as good and attach myself to them, and therefore I am valuable." Does your choice for attachment merit the attention you give?

The self-interpreting memory then is largely, even if unconsciously, about value and honor and how we see ourselves because we think we do, or do not, have value. Where do we find value and honor for ourselves? Family is a huge source for attaining or not attaining value and honor. "I have value and honor because I belong to a valuable and honorable family"—or not. Groups and associations convey honor as well, as do personal and worthwhile accomplishments. Some think wealth conveys value, but it does not, at least not true value. It conveys privilege and responsibility but not value and honor. A quest for value and honor stands behind envy, pride, shame, and much negative activity as we seek to pull others down or push ourselves up at their expense. The problem with our honoring systems is that we gauge honor by comparing ourselves with other humans, which, although understandable, is not sufficient.

All of us know at some level what we should be, but for various reasons we do not achieve the good we acknowledge. There is "a load of compromisin' on the road to my horizon," as a country song puts it.[10] We are not willing to put forth the effort or to deny our baser self. We settle for something far less than we should be, often rebelling against what we know we should be. Knowing we are choosing something less, we trade off pieces of our own soul so as not to notice. In effect, we move the boundary stones of our existence to reshape our own standards,[11] but we cannot easily hide from ourselves. Knowing ourselves involves judging ourselves. Our internal memory knows that we cheated, and when we realize that we are not good, that we are sinners, we have to do something to live with ourselves and avoid depression, insanity, or destruction. This can lead to honesty and reorganization of ourselves, to avoidance of reality, or to egotistical self-justification to others and to ourselves.

Not many paths are open to us. We can try to ignore the reality, but we know we are kidding ourselves. We can try to convince ourselves we are good enough by lowering the standards. We can redefine what is good; we can argue that we are no worse than everyone else; or we can attempt to align ourselves with something or someone who seems good or is at least better than we are. Such thinking is behind the adulation and identification with "beautiful and famous" people. Actually the attempt to align ourselves with some good outside us is not a bad idea, except for the choice of what is good. Scripture seeks to align us with the good, but it holds out that the only good sufficiently worthy is the God revealed in Jesus Christ. The vision of the good becomes clear in the face of Christ, and with that the summoning self is not an unattainable goal but the specific and individual call of Christ aided by the Spirit.

10. "Rhinestone Cowboy."
11. See Søren Kierkegaard, *Purity of Heart Is to Will One Thing*, trans. Douglas V. Steere (New York: Harper and Row, 1938), 141.

But if identity is about attachment to the good, why do so many choose to identify with what is not good, with what we know is wrong, insane, and destructive—such as music and videos that demean women or movies that focus on gore and violence? Is it rebellion against the good, rebellion against hypocrisy, embracing our failure, a desire to prove we are tough and not naive, or what? The media often—sometimes even literally—tell us it is good to be bad, which is inane, but it is their way to persuade us to accept an approach to life or to buy a certain product. One thing is clear. Sin is not merely wrong acts; sin is to a large degree the act of transvaluing, assigning value to items not worthy of the designation and ignoring what is truly valuable. Obviously if we choose to satisfy our minimal self at the expense of the summoning self and God's intent, we have been deceived into a bad trade. That is precisely the description of sin in Romans 1:22–32, the exchange of the truth of God for a lie.

Similarly, guilt and shame are not merely the awareness of having done wrong; they are in part the awareness of not living up to our own standards. As any number of people have pointed out, guilt is a result of the tension between what one is and what one should be, an awareness of the difference between the perceived self and the summoning self. Guilt is actually an awareness of one's own dignity and the failure to live accordingly.[12]

What happens when someone lies to himself or herself? We know the truth but seek to live elsewhere, and the lie is a sword piercing our own internal unity. The summoning self knows we did not speak truth, so we seek to hide our conscious and acting self from our summoning self. In effect, we are like deceptive attorneys twisting truth for our own interests. The more we fail to meet our own standards, the more guilt we feel, the more we seek to evade our summoning self, the more we compensate for our wrongdoing, the more we develop feelings of inferiority, the more we attempt to cover feelings of inferiority or are taken down by them, the less human we really are, the less healthy identity we have—all while often holding other people to the standards we do not meet but know are right.

Also, what happens when values conflict, as they certainly will? That is

12. On guilt, see Patrick McNamara, *Spirit Possession and Exorcism: History, Psychology, and Neurobiology*, 2 vols. (Santa Barbara, CA: Praeger, 2011), 1:34–43.

why we have an executive self, and we need a strong, well-informed one. The executive self has the task of prioritizing competing values, *inhibiting* pursuit of lesser values, and making sure that the goals of higher values are attained. There will be conflict within ourselves. The temptation to settle for less than we really are or to seek an easy way out can be strong. Such struggles are at the heart of our identity and continually shape us in positive or negative directions. Christians believe they do not struggle alone, but that God is present and a help in dealing with the conflict. This is not escapism or some easy answer; it is an awareness that life is intended to be lived with God. Christians do not find their identity by themselves but are continually being shaped by the character of Christ. Christ becomes the *salient*, the determinative, part of identity. Christ's character and commands prioritize values, inhibit pursuit of lesser values, and give a vision of good goals to pursue.

Dialogue

We have already seen that identity always involves dialogue, both with oneself and with others who tell us who we are. Language is the fundamental human characteristic, the one that distinguishes us most from all other animals. With the *internal* dialogue we converse with ourselves, often unconsciously, about how to interpret what has happened, about what has value, about the divisions within our being, about how to justify ourselves for not attaining the summoning self, and about how we will view and present ourselves. The dialogue with oneself is not merely a third factor, for the dialogue is about values and memory. The three items are intertwined. The internal dialogue is extremely important for identity, especially with regard to creating a strong, well-informed executive self.[13] It is the way we live with ourselves. An earlier generation called

13. Note Paul Ricoeur, "The Summoned Subject in the School of the Narratives of the Prophetic Vocation," in *Figuring the Sacred: Religion, Narrative, and Imagination*, trans. David Pellauer, ed. Mark I. Wallace (Minneapolis: Fortress, 1995), 262–75, esp. 271 and 274: "Conscience is fundamentally a principle of individuation rather than an instance of accusation and judgment . . . the call of conscience is a call of the self to itself. . . . The Christian is someone who discerns 'conformity to the image of Christ' in the call of conscience."

this internal dialogue "conscience." People now do not frequently speak of their conscience, for what reason I do not know. In the end, though, conscience is not broad enough. It tends to be thought of only as a voice reminding of wrongs committed, and obviously one's conscience can be callused and easily ignored. The internal conversation is much broader, is always active, and relates to all parts of our being. Even if dishonest and twisted, the internal conversation still goes on.

Sometimes people give themselves an unrealistic positive evaluation that everyone, including God, knows is wrong. This is a defense mechanism that allows them to live with themselves despite the truth. Actually facing the truth can be devastating, especially if one has no sense of the grace of God.

The more frequent and more destructive problem with the internal dialogue is the artificial negative evaluation and accusing voice within. Whether because of fear or awareness of failure, most of us know at some level the internal accusing self that says, "You are inferior, not good enough, not loved, and never going anywhere." If we allow this negativity to define us, we will never be who God says we are, but what can we do when the internal conversation is a negative one? Who are students who have successfully navigated graduate school but cannot find employment? They doubt their self-worth even though they are the same successful people with the same abilities but have no option to demonstrate it. Are they suddenly less valuable because no one else has occasion or time to recognize their value? How can they deal with the negative internal voices? Joni Eareckson Tada, a quadriplegic who developed a significant ministry, said in dealing with loneliness and suffering, "Part of my Christian growth is grabbing my thoughts by the scruffs of their necks and jerking them into line. I will not allow thoughts to take me down these dark roads."[14] Indeed, we must rebel against such thoughts, and "As long as the self can say 'I,' it is not impossible to rebel."[15] The negativity cannot stand where there is a focus on image of God, faithfulness, forgiveness, participation with Christ and the Spirit, and the destiny God's promises

14. Tim Stafford, "A Heaven-Made Activist," *Christianity Today*, January 2004, 46–50, here 50.

15. W. H. Auden, "A Christmas Oratorio," in *For the Time Being* (London: Faber and Faber, 1945), 61–124, here 66.

entail. We can still say, "By the grace of God, I am what I am" (1 Cor. 15:10). Even the internal dialogue must be instructed and brought into conformity with who God says you are.

The dialogue between the individual and the external community is equally important for identity, for identity is always communicated to us, even if the communication is often confusing. We find identity in community and in conversation with others. Amanda Knox, who was convicted of murder in Italy, then declared not guilty, then convicted again, and then acquitted again, reportedly said, "After everyone has branded me, who am I?" For all of us, though, the dialogue between the individual and the external community takes place much more generally and all the time.

People make immediate judgments about us on first sight regarding age, sex, attractiveness, threat level, possibility, level of importance, and level of needing to engage. Those judgments are communicated either explicitly or implicitly, and we are trained to discern such signals easily. Within seconds of seeing a person we make judgments about how safe, interesting, or desirable that person is. Other people tell us what a "good" person looks like, who we are, how to be an individual, and where we fit in. *By attention or inattention they communicate to us an interpretation of our value, and they either help us arrive at a healthy self-understanding or create obstacles that prevent it.* It is here that racism often rears its sinful head. A community also gives the language necessary for comprehending identity and engages us in our self-understanding. Other people are constantly communicating to us who they think we are. We may be able to control most of our internal dialogue, but we do not easily control what others say about us. The identity they seek to give us may be right or wrong, and the quality of the external assessment of us depends to a large degree on the quality of the people addressing us. Especially when people are young, the external community can enable or disable people quickly. While we cannot control what people say, we can control how we assess the communication. Is their assessment a foundation on which we can build, a critique that is incorporated for positive change, or an error or belittling that we must reject and prove wrong?

We dialogue internally concerning what others are saying about us, our values, and our identity. We either agree or disagree, develop feelings of pride or inferiority, rebellion or frustration, and then we decide how we will act. With language, including language to ourselves, we construct the world in which we will live. While this is true generally of all language, it is specifically true with what we tell ourselves about ourselves.

The dialogue with the external community is not merely about others telling us who we are, for they also tell us who we *should* be, how far short we fall of the standard, and what value results. The very existence of others is part of the summoning self, for their existence before us calls us to responsibility, the responsibility to be a human in relation to others.[16] The standard placed before us may be—often is—skewed, and itself must be evaluated. The way we respond to what others say indicates who we are. At the same time the community is describing us, we are describing them, and in our telling others who they are, we are shaping ourselves and determining how we fit with them. Self-respect is directly tied to respect for other people.

The assessment of us by other people is an enormous factor in shaping our identity. We are who other people say we are—unless we disprove what they say by performance. The only way to reject a community's assessment of us, as we have noted already, is by performance.

For Christians a powerful feature of the dialogues with ourselves and with the external community is *the Holy Spirit*. The Holy Spirit is part of that external community addressing us, whether we are Christian or not. We do not perform these conversations by ourselves, for the Spirit engages us, speaks to us, and guides the process, if we are willing to listen. The Spirit provides the most important voice shaping our identity and communicating what a person is supposed to be. If one takes seriously a message from *God*, conflicting assessments by humans tend to fade. The purpose of Scripture and the work of the Spirit is to transform our thinking. Suddenly our value, importance, and sense of belonging are not

16. Emmanuel Levinas, with his emphasis on the significance of the face of the other person, wrote, "Access to the face is straightaway ethical" (*Ethics and Infinity: Conversations with Philippe Nemo* [Pittsburgh: Duquesne University Press, 1982], 85). Paul Ricoeur extended Levinas's point by saying, "Each face is a Sinai that prohibits murder" (*Oneself as Another*, trans. Kathleen Blamey [Chicago: University of Chicago Press, 1992], 336). See p. 90 above.

established primarily by the human community but by the grace and love of God. The purpose of our lives is removed from our self-centeredness and found in our relation to God. Messages sent by people and society do not enter our being unfiltered but are discerned as to whether they fit with God's intent.

Obviously the dialogue with the external community is directly related to the subject of "separation from the world." "World" in such an expression is used of society gone off its rails and, if not hostile to God, at least indifferent to God. The truth is that part of our external community is often a society off its rails. We are not born resistant to shaping by this world. We have to be taught to analyze and resist the shaping of a way of life contrary to what humanity is supposed to be. This is a continual process and is the reason Romans 12:1–2 instructs us not to be conformed to this age but to be continually transformed by the renewing of the mind so that we can discern the will of God, that is, what is good, pleasing, and complete. The problem, of course, is that "the world" is not merely something external to us. Often, even when we choose otherwise, "the world" is in us, for we internalize the messages from the world about our own identity.

The important point is that being continually transformed, as Romans 12:1–2 instructs, is a mind thing. To be a Christian is to commit oneself to thinking and learning and to a life of the mind, at least to some degree. I am not referring to formal education, as important as that can be, but regardless of the means, your mind must be under constant revision, under construction all the time, to be what God wants you to be. Why must there be a constant renewing of the mind? Because you are changing each day, your circumstances are changing, the world is changing, and your mind was deficient anyway. We need a continual God-directed renewal process in our heads, but God will not hit you on the head and make it happen. God seeks to engage you, to participate with you. You will have to give attention to construction of your mind in relation to God. The purpose of this is so you will be smart enough to make good decisions in forming your own identity. You will have to be serious about learning.

Scripture's Treatment of Memory, Valuing, and Dialogue

Almost anywhere we look in Scripture the issues of memory, valuing, and dialogue are the concerns of the text. Christians (and Jews) are thinkers—or are supposed to be—which explains why Chaim Potok could say, "A shallow mind is a sin against God."[17] Too often we have been an embarrassment because of the shallowness of our thinking. For Christians (and Jews) memory is enormously significant. Identity is about remembering the history of God's acts in Israel, in Christ, and in the church, a history that is part of our own history. Life and worship are structured especially around the exodus and the death and resurrection of Jesus, which is obvious with the acts of memory ritualized in Passover and the Lord's Supper. We know who we are because of some sense of how we fit with what God has done and is doing. In the history of God's actions we find our true selves.

Much of the Bible is about memory enhancement. It provides aids to remember who we are, what our relations are, and who we are to be. God's instructions did the same for ancient Israel. People were told to build a memorial of twelve stones so their children would ask, "What do these stones mean?" and they would have an opportunity to tell the story of entering Israel (Josh. 4:3–9) and thereby enhance identity. People were to go up to Jerusalem three times each year to remember Passover, Tabernacles, and Pentecost, the first two to remember the wilderness wanderings of Israel and the third to remember the giving of the law. (The feasts were also connected to thanksgiving for harvests.) Jesus directed regarding the Supper, "Do this in remembrance of me." Christians worship on the first day of the week to remember the death and resurrection of Jesus.

The role of prayer, worship, and meditation belongs with the self-interpreting memory; these acts are avenues for our minds to remember, to interpret, and to be reformed with the identity God calls for. Memory in acts like Passover, the Lord's Supper, and baptism is not mere thinking about the past; it is an act of *participation* in which an event is made

---

17. Chaim Potok, *In the Beginning* (New York: Fawcett, 1975), 381.

real in our own being.[18] These are not and must never be dead rituals. The Lord's Supper and baptism are identity-shaping acts based in identification with a crucified and risen Lord. They are reminders of, and an engagement with, who we really are. These acts and other acts of worship address issues of self-esteem, accountability, and responsibility. The interaction of self-description and community description is reframed in worship because individual and community are both part of the body of Christ. Of most importance is God's description of who we are as communicated in Scripture reading, worship, and prayer. For Christians, identity is founded in who God says we are, affirmed and tested by the interaction of self and community.

Perhaps one of the easiest places to see the self-interpreting mind's work with memory, valuing, and dialogue is in Paul's letter to the Philippians, especially 3:3–11.

> For we are the circumcision, the ones who serve by the Spirit of God and boast in Christ Jesus and place no confidence in the flesh, although I could have confidence in the flesh. If anyone else thinks they have reason for confidence in the flesh, I do more. I was circumcised on the eighth day, from the people of Israel, from the tribe of Benjamin, a Hebrew of the Hebrews, with respect to the law, a Pharisee, with respect to zeal, persecuting the church, with respect to the righteousness that is based on the law, blameless. But these things which were gain to me I considered loss for the sake of Christ. More than that, I consider all things loss because of the superior greatness of knowing Christ Jesus my Lord, on account of whom I have suffered the loss of all things and consider them crud that I may gain Christ and may be found in him, not having my righteousness, the kind that comes from the law, but the righteousness that comes through the faithfulness of Christ [or "faith in Christ"], the righteousness of God based on faith, so that I might know him and the power of his resurrection and participation in his sufferings, being conformed to his death, if somehow I may attain the resurrection from the dead.

18. See Nils Dahl, "Anamnesis," in Dahl, *Jesus in the Memory of the Early Church: Essays* (Minneapolis: Augsburg, 1976), 11–29. Cf. Deut. 5:3 and Mishnah Pesahim 10:5.

In verse 3 and throughout this section, an identity is being asserted over against another group with a different value system. One can almost hear the conversation with the external community. Taking over a valued Jewish self-description, Paul asserts, "We are the circumcision," which is odd to our ears, but it was a way of saying, "We are the people in covenant with God." Labels are shorthand identity enhancers—or destroyers—and the early church borrowed stacks of Old Testament descriptors of Israel to frame their identity positively, terms such as "the elect," "a holy nation," "children of God," and even "children of Abraham." In going on to say that Christians do not have confidence in the flesh, Paul is saying, "We have found something more valuable and trustworthy than a mere human perspective."

Especially in verses 4–10 Paul focuses on the memory of his own life and the change in values Christ brought. He does not disparage his Jewishness. In fact, elsewhere he is proud of it (Rom. 3:1–2; 9:1–5; 2 Cor. 11:22–23), but it is not what ultimately defines him. His value system has been reoriented by his knowledge of and attachment to Christ. Realities and accomplishments previously valued have been so discounted that they are rejected in favor of knowing, participating with, and being shaped by Christ. New values and thinking have brought a new identity.

In the verses that follow this section, the focus is still on the self-interpreting mind. Paul is happy to forget the things behind (Phil. 3:13), things he clearly does not *literally* forget, for he has just spoken of them. What he means is that those former realities no longer are the real determiners of his identity.[19] The prize—hear "value"—of the high call of God in Christ Jesus (v. 14) is the ultimate determiner of who he is.

The dialogue with the external community is clear in 3:15–18: "Let us think this way. . . . God will reveal to you. . . . Be imitators of me . . . watch those living this way . . . many live as enemies of Christ." The descriptions involve three participants: those in the community, especially those who embody the group ideals and merit serving as models; those who oppose the identity of the believers; and *God.* There is also an appeal for dialogue

---

19. The tension between this text and Eph. 2:11, where Paul urges his readers to remember their past, is only superficial. Both texts urge Christ as the ultimate determiner of identity.

in 4:2–5, with instructions to help those in the community in conflict and to demonstrate gentleness to all, including those not in the community.

Valuing reenters the picture in a big way in 4:8–9, where believers are asked to focus their minds on a list of what is good—the true, the honorable, the just, and other virtues acknowledged by all. Focusing on the good shapes into the good. It is almost as if Paul said, "Think on those things that are part of your summoning self, things we taught you and you have seen in us—and do them."

Much of the rest of Philippians also relates to memory, value, and dialogue, but two more texts must be mentioned. In 1:9–10 Paul prays that the love of the Philippians may increase *in knowledge and understanding so that they can discern* what really counts—hear "value." That they may have smart love to make judicious decisions points to a love-directed and wise executive self, the very purpose of religion. This focus on discerning is a frequent focus in Paul's writings and is central to Christian living.[20] In 2:5–11, the so-called hymn, we find "Let this mind be in you which was also in Christ," which says in effect, "Have the same kind of executive self that Christ had."

The Beatitudes of the Sermon on the Mount relate especially to the internal self-interpreting memory. "Blessed are the poor in spirit," "those who mourn," and "the meek" all have to do with the rejection of arrogance and the realization of the need for God. "Hungering and thirsting after righteousness" and "the pure in heart" have to do with values, and being called children of God and dealing with persecution have to do with the external dialogue. Of course, statements like "You are the salt of the earth" and "You are the light of the world" are direct identity statements.

Another obvious text about valuing and the internal dialogue is Romans 7, where Paul says the very thing he wants to do—the good—he does not do, and the thing he hates, evil, he does. Whether Paul refers to his pre- or post-conversion experience and whether he refers to himself autobiographically or speaks of humanity more generically are heavily debated but should not divert us from what is important here. All of us know the conflict of desires—or selves—within us, a conflict between a baser self directed by sin and a summoning self to which we do not attain. The text points out that sin uses

20. See Rom. 12:2; 14:22; 1 Cor. 11:28; Gal. 6:4; Eph. 5:10; and 1 Thess. 5:21.

the good, even something as good as God's command (7:7–13), and turns it to a baser, self-serving but deadening purpose. Verse 24 ends with a lament, a cry of anguish: "Wretched human that I am, who will deliver me from this body subject to death?" Here is the cry of one who knows the guilt of failing to reach the summoning self. Also obvious is the already deceived nature of the self-interpreting memory. The valuing activity is already skewed.[21] The dialogue is not over, though, for 7:25 points to deliverance already in force through God's grace in Christ, a deliverance explained in chapter 8.

In fact, any text dealing with sin relates to the self-interpreting memory. With regard to the internal conversation, Romans 1:20–23 is obviously relevant with its focus on sin being a fracture within one's own being. Sin is at some level the acceptance of a lesser self than the ideal self, the failure to be who you are supposed to be, one bearing the image of God. Sin is not merely wrong acts. Sin is first of all ignoring, silencing, and forgetting the real self, which is supposed to be in relation to God. The ideal self knows its value; when that is silenced, we are given over to an unproven mind that leads us in the wrong direction. The value of being human is lost or at least hidden. We end up hiding from ourselves.

Clearly the very tool we use for memory, valuing, and our dialogues is already skewed because of our self-interest.[22] Again, Pascal's line nails it: "Our own interest is again a marvelous instrument for nicely putting out our eyes."[23] Still, our mind with its self-interest *is* the instrument by which we must move toward God. It only needs a better understanding of its *real and valid* self-interest. Life is not found in ourselves but in relation with God and other people. We gain life by losing it (Matt. 16:25). We need a conversion of our values, of the way we dialogue with ourselves and others, and even of our memory, a conversion bound to life with God both now and in the future.

Two points are crucial. First, there is no way forward unless we are willing to be displeasing to ourselves, a point that various Christian thinkers have made.[24] In other words, we will not change unless we are dis-

21. Cf. the double-minded person in James 1:7.
22. See Ps. 36:2; Jer. 17:9–10; Eccles. 9:3; Mark 7:21–23 and parallels; Rom. 7:14–25; 2 Cor. 4:4.
23. Blaise Pascal, *Pensées* (New York: Modern Library, 1941), no. 82.
24. See, e.g., Augustine, *Confessions* 10.2, and John Calvin, *Institutes of the Christian*

satisfied with who we are. If we are not willing to examine ourselves, be honest, and admit our shortcomings even when it hurts, we will never be who God calls us to be. Self-defense has to go out the window. Now we understand more easily God's desire for truth in the inward parts. The willingness to be displeasing to oneself, honesty, confession, and repentance are foundational for identity and life. This is part of the reason humility is essential to Christian faith and the reason a mirror is a powerful spiritual formation tool. The person in the mirror knows the truth—and knows he or she knows. Hiding does not work. But this humility before God does not degrade us; on the contrary it establishes us.

Second, we do not do these identity tasks alone. The very texts that speak of the deceitfulness of the human heart also speak of God engaging us and enabling transformation. The psalmist, in anguish over his sin, still says God taught him wisdom in his inner being and asks God for further cleansing (Ps. 51:6–7).[25] We will never know ourselves and our motives completely or eradicate the sneakiness of our own egos. Perhaps this is why Paul focuses more on *being known by God* than on knowing ourselves or even knowing God.[26] My former colleague Richard Carlson had a sign on his door that merits thought: "Jesus knows me; this I love." God knows us in ways we cannot know ourselves, and being known by God creates a dynamic of change to bring us more in line with God.

God does indeed know us and comes alongside us filling in the blanks. God's Spirit enables us and gives us courage to face ourselves and to be honest about life. God brings about right remembering, transformation of values, and honest dialogue with ourselves, with each other, and with God. None of this is easy. It is work, but it is good work and continual work, the very substance of life. This continual interpreting and choosing ourselves makes sense of Jesus's focus on faithfulness. The one who is faithful in the least things, who shows a continuity of identity found in relation to God, is also faithful with much.

Everyone wants to be valuable. What makes for an honorable and

---

Religion, ed. John T. McNeill, trans. Ford Lewis Battles, Library of Christian Classics, vol. 20 (Philadelphia: Westminster, 1960), 1.1.1: "We cannot seriously aspire to him [God] before we begin to become displeased with ourselves."

25. Note texts like Ps. 25:7–9; Eph. 4:17–24; and James 4:8–10.

26. 1 Cor. 8:3; 13:12; Gal. 4:9.

valuable life? It is not the number of hits on our social media. The quest for honor in the ancient Mediterranean world is well known,[27] a quest that Jesus's disciples assumed was legitimate. Repeatedly their concern was who among them was the greatest (e.g., Matt. 18:1–5 and parallels and 20:20–28/Mark 10:35–45).[28] This quest for honor is an attempt to get the external community to assign value, which may be appropriated by the internal self-interpreting memory and translated into self-esteem. We want that external community to affirm our existence, to shower glory on us so we have confidence about living.

Even if the external community affirmed us, that affirmation would be fleeting and in the end ineffective. The identity we should be pursuing is the exact opposite of self-glorification, for true identity is not found merely in the self. We do indeed need to be decentered from ourselves and recentered in Christ. Your identity is not merely about you; it is about you in relation with and for people around you and with and for your God. In fact, this reorientation is precisely what conversion is about. Treatments of conversion are discussions of identity, and if identity is a narrative construct, conversion is about rewritten autobiographies.

It is easier just to go through the motions of life and not face ourselves and not make the hard decisions, especially if we are not conscious of our need for God. If we choose this route, we will never be who we really are, and the result will in the end be disaster. The issue of "dying and rising"—or losing life to find it—is crucial here. We cannot become who we are supposed to be without the willingness to lose who we are. We become ourselves by not being self-centered. Self-centeredness obliterates a broader awareness of life, for it sees only itself, whereas giving up self-centeredness opens us to God's larger world and the people in it.

Remember, though, that God is part of the external community, if we are willing to listen. Who God says we are may be a confrontation forcing us to face our failures, but it will also be an affirmation of God's love for us and of our value. It will be an indication of who we are supposed to be and the beginning of change. The psalmist asked God to test him and examine

27. See Bruce Malina, *The New Testament World: Insights from Cultural Anthropology* (Atlanta: John Knox, 1981), 27–50.

28. See also the discussion of honor in John 5:41–44, and 12:43 on seeking glory/honor from God.

him (Ps. 26:2), and Paul urged the Corinthians to test themselves to see whether they were in the faith (2 Cor. 13:5). Surely we too need to examine ourselves, stripped of pretense, and made vulnerable before God. With such a stance the Spirit of God can transform us. If we thought about our own identity more, about our remembering, our values, and our internal and external dialogues, we would find first a sensitivity to God, then a sense of direction, energy to engage life, freedom to be who we are supposed to be, rebellion against culture's manipulation of us, appreciation of community and its importance for life, and the realization that life is not merely about one's self. We would be on the way to being who God says we are, and we would have a healthy internal self-interpreting, self-directing memory.

By being aware of such a transformed internal self-interpreting memory, we can appreciate Paul's description of Christians as those who have the mind of Christ and who make Spirit-assisted judgments (1 Cor. 2:15–16). Our dialogues—especially with our self and God, our memory, and our valuing—all take on a more robust character. It is clear as well that we have a responsibility to guard our minds and both our internal and our external conversations. Our very being is at stake in how we think, remember, value, judge, and converse with ourselves, with each other, and with God. With our memories we partly construct the universe in which we will live. Construct honestly and well.

How will you remember, how will you value, and how will you handle the conversations of your life, including the conversation within you? Having good goals is necessary but insufficient. Most would affirm good goals, but goals are not attained without the commitment and discipline to work toward them. Can you, will you, evaluate the messages bombarding you every day, even when you do not realize how pervasive they are in life? To what will you give your mind? You will give it to something. Give it to learning about the good, the true, and the valuable. Give it to *honest* self-assessment. Give it to God for continual renewing.

One further point must be made explicit. The discussion of memory, valuing, and dialogues presupposes that you will *decide* with God's help how your identity is shaped and lived. Do not be passive in making good decisions.

FACTOR 5

You Are Your Commitments

My identity is determined by what matters to me, by what I find valuable, by my commitments.

—Svend Brinkman, "Identity as Self-Interpretation"

We find our identity and meaning when we discover our vocation.

—Anthony Thiselton, *Interpreting God and the Postmodern Self*

"You make yourself real by telling the truth";[1] yes, and you make yourself real by the commitments you make. We exist only by committing ourselves.[2] We are what we choose, actually choose, not just claim to choose, for our commitments are lived, or they are not commitments. Things to which we give our life shape our life. Our choices reveal who we really are. Life consists of making—and rejecting—commitments. Should we not be more conscious of our commitments, of what we do to life, of what life does to us, of who is influencing our commitments, and should

1. Thomas Merton, *No Man Is an Island* (New York: Harcourt, Brace, 1955), 188.
2. Charles Larmore, *The Practices of the Self*, trans. Sharon Bowman (Chicago: University of Chicago Press, 2010), 97. See also 65, 104, 107, and 143.

we not evaluate the commitments we make? *Sentences of Sextus* again provides sound advice: "If you love what you should not, you will not love what you should."[3] In other words, wrong commitments prevent good commitments. Saint Clare of Assisi is reported to have said, "We become what we love, and whom we love shapes what we become. If we love things, we become a thing. If we love nothing, we become nothing. Imitation is not a literal mimicking of Christ, rather it means becoming the image of the beloved."[4]

An athlete does not succeed without commitment; nor does anyone else. Schools—good public ones like charter schools—often have uniforms, songs, pledges, and strict discipline. They seek students who will make a commitment to be what the school embodies, and if they do, the students succeed. Why do so few churches have expectations of high commitment?

We are urged to "sell out" or to be "all in," for success requires commitment. Søren Kierkegaard said, "All religion has to do with passion, with having passion."[5] Nothing great happens without passion. If that is true, then nothing great happens without commitment, for passion engages. All people who are respected—athletes, musicians, leaders, people successful in careers, people who have stayed faithful in difficult situations—have made great commitments. No one wins a marathon without commitment. Much success is based on a single commitment, one extreme commitment, but life requires multiple commitments. All of us know people who succeeded in one aspect of life and failed at the rest, such as professional athletes great at their sport but unable to handle money and relations. So, how do we manage our commitments? You will commit to something. If you do not commit heavily, you will never be successful. If you do commit heavily, you may be narrow, myopic, and stressed out.

3. *Sentences of Sextus* 141.

4. This saying is attributed to Clare, but I have not been able to verify that in her published works. It appears to be a summation of thought expressed in her letters. Thomas Merton, drawing on Thomas Aquinas, said something similar: "Hence, the things that we love tell us what we are." See his *Thoughts in Solitude* (New York: Farrar, Straus, and Cudahy, 1956), 22.

5. Søren Kierkegaard, *Attack upon "Christendom," 1854–1855*, trans. Walter Lowrie (Princeton: Princeton University Press, 1946), 185.

Commitments of No Significance

Commitments are crucial, but many in our society make commitments to fantasy—fantasy football, movies about zombies and imaginary heroes and never-never land. So many are occupied with sitcoms, movies, and sports, as if that is all there is, and others give themselves to alcohol, drugs, and sex without responsibility. Maybe we have not dealt with reality rightly if we think we need to escape it. Balance in life, relaxation, and enjoyment is one thing, but escape is something else. A news channel reported that 7,300 people in Iowa gathered to break the Guinness record for the number of people doing the hokey pokey.[6] Don't people have anything better to do, no better commitments? Is life not more important than that?

The teacher in the book of Ecclesiastes looked at life, even with all its goodness and enjoyment, and found it meaningless, or at least frustrating. If "meaningless" is the label for such a temporary life, even with its goodness, what label should we use for a life of fantasy and entertainment?

What label should we use for life that is debilitating, filled with evil or suffering? Much of the world knows only suffering, deprivation, and victimization of one form or another. In such a world, what commitments should we have in the midst of suffering, and what commitments might make the world, or at least the part within our reach, a saner place, and what commitments would lead to an identity worth having?

Many people in our society have nothing *important* to which to give themselves, and it is evident in the trivia that occupy their lives. Little of it matters at all, from sports to entertainment media. It is banal and of little use. By the end of the day it is gone. Clint Black sings a song with the words "Killing time till there's no more time to kill."[7] For many that is an apt commentary on their lives; they are hanging around, waiting for death, with no real investment in anything important. They commit to the banal with little thought. They merely commit to what others commit to, which means they are not really living. Commitments reveal values, and identity is very much about values, as we have seen. Surely the waste of

6. CNN on September 4, 2010.
7. "No Time to Kill."

135

a life is sin. What is worth your commitment? You are largely the result of the commitments in which you invest, and you have only so much capital. Where will you invest it? Jesus asked in Matthew 16:26, "What will a person give in exchange for life?" Apparently some will trade life for just about anything.

Important Commitments— Conscious Choices Carefully Made

We have commitments, even if we did not mean to make them. Some commitments are handed to us, such as family involvements, certain necessary tasks, and locations, but we still have to choose how to handle them. Society clamors for our commitment. Our commitment will make other people rich and reinforce *their* identity. Lack of commitment to the commitments of the society is a threat to the society, for it is an indictment of the society's values. There are often repercussions for not committing to society's commitments, but if Christians are not actually going to be different, why bother?

We are what we love, but it is not that simple. Our commitments include things we love, but out of necessity or choice we often commit to things we do not love. Such commitments still shape us, even if we do not want them to. Sometimes people have no choice in their choices—from child soldiers to sex slaves to victims of illegitimate, systemic pressures and dehumanizing situations, concerning which one can only weep and concerning which God is surely cognizant. How does this relate to identity? Sometimes identity is something done to us. Sometimes we end up as broken people in a broken world. How much responsibility do we have for what we do not control, and how much capacity do we have for choices? Are we merely trapped? How does the gospel address such situations and bring freedom? Freedom *is* the focus of the gospel. (See Gal. 5:1 and a host of other texts.)

While some commitments happen by default and some are attached to us without our even noticing, the most important commitments need to be conscious choices carefully made. We must not allow our lives to be shaped by default. We need to be aware of what is happening to us, who we are becoming, and what choices we must make to be who God says we are.

Some have said the most important commitment we can make is the commitment to be ourselves. We will get to that, but there is a prior commitment, and it is the commitment to the truth. We do indeed make ourselves real by telling the truth. We can never be our true selves without a commitment to the truth, even the painful truth, and it is the only adequate foundation for life. Truth requires the willingness to face the facts of human existence with its joy and potential but also its sin and fragility, its temporality, and its uncertainty. Given its uncertainty, life is necessarily contingent. We do not know what will happen in life; we do not know the secrets of the universe; and we do not have ultimate answers. Truth also requires us to be honest about our own sin, our own biases and blind spots, and our own failures. We seek to ignore and evade such uncomfortable truths, to insulate ourselves against them, but they will not go away. That is one reason church is so important. If it is a good church, church is the place where people will not let you believe your own lies. We need to be confronted with the uncertainty and fragility of life and with our own limitation and defensiveness, and because of this, life is always a life of faith—in *something*. In what will you place your trust? Christianity says only God merits such trust—and commitment.

After commitment to the truth, commitment to be ourselves follows and is absolutely crucial. Commitment to *be* ourselves is a universe away from commitment *to* ourselves, which, wrongly understood, only leads to self-centeredness. The person who lives for himself or herself lives for a fool.[8] Commitment only—or even mainly—to ourselves is a dead end and destructive of life. Commitment to *be* ourselves is far different and is the only foundation for health, legitimacy, and peace. We can be no one else: "Be yourself; everyone else is already taken."[9] That presumes, of course, not being your sinful self but at least a person on the way to one's summoning self.

8. Walter Beran Wolfe adds, "If you live only for yourself you are always in immediate danger of being bored to death with the repetition of your own views and interests" (*How to Be Happy though Human* [New York: Farrar and Rinehart, 1931], 360).

9. This quotation has been attributed to Oscar Wilde, but I have not been able to verify that.

We need a commitment to our own identity—not as it is but as it is supposed to be. Søren Kierkegaard pointed out that people content to be like others fail to become themselves, and he stressed that selfhood is an achievement, something one must become.[10] Commitment to be ourselves does not mean just commitment to what is, nor does it tolerate the hypocrisy of being different people with different groups. *It is a commitment to be who God calls us to be.* We need a commitment that enhances identity within us and prevents self-centeredness. If I do not have something that puts me in myself, I am nothing. If I do not have something that takes me out of myself, I am self-centered and myopic.

My son-in-law soccer player tells me soccer is a constant struggle between who you are and who you want to be. I suppose any sport is, but so is life—or it should be. The problem with many people is that they are not engaged in the struggle for identity.[11] They merely desire to be entertained and settle for who they are told to be, which means they fail to become who they really are and should be. At least make the choice to be something worthwhile! All of us follow a script, as if in a drama. From where did you get the script you follow? No doubt, much of it is from family, some is from society, some from friends, and some from within your own being. Much of the script may be good, but it must be evaluated. Do you trust the author(s) of your script? Do you merely plagiarize from the script of others? Christians, of course, have, or should have, a commitment to the centrality and authority of Scripture, which, *rightly understood*, is *the* trustworthy script for human life.

Kierkegaard's urging people to become the solitary individual they are supposed to be deserves further attention, for it leads to commitment. He wanted people to avoid merely being one of the crowd and actually become who God intended them to be. He knew they would stand before God in eternity as an individual, not as one of the crowd.[12] He was not

10. See Søren Kierkegaard, *The Point of View Etc. Including the Point of View for My Work as an Author, Two Notes about 'The Individual,' on My Work as an Author*, trans. Walter Lowrie (London: Oxford University Press, 1939), 115–36. See the treatment of C. Stephen Evans, *Kierkegaard on Faith and the Self: Collected Essays* (Waco: Baylor University Press, 2006), especially 265–71.
11. This is not to ignore or diminish other struggles that many have merely to live.
12. This was a frequent theme for Kierkegaard. One of the easiest places to find it is in

talking about *individualism* but about the authenticity of one's own being. That takes work, discernment, and commitment, and it is quite clear that being our true selves presupposes that we *know* who we are, a person created in the image of God. Being oneself stems from being committed to the God revealed in Christ and reflecting his character.

Our commitments involve our body, our relations, our place, our investments, our tasks, our values, our ideas, our ideals, and our oppositions. For many of these we are not even aware of making a commitment; it is just the way things are. Remember, with all aspects of identity some things are given and some are chosen. Some commitments are handed to us, but we still have to evaluate their legitimacy and negotiate how they will affect us and how we will deal with them. Will they be an occasion for complaint or an opportunity for life?

We all have a hierarchy of commitments regulated by our executive self.[13] Some commitments are more important than others, and the less important will be arranged under them and, if necessary, sacrificed to them. Our higher commitments can easily turn into idolatry, which is why Scripture is so concerned with idolatry, and why the earliest Christian confession, "Jesus is Lord," is so important. For the rich young ruler in the Gospel story, money had become the idol to which he sacrificed the idea of following Jesus (Matt. 19:16–22 and parallels). Any commitment other than to the God revealed in Jesus Christ is potentially idolatrous, and commitment to Christ deserves to be our strongest and determining commitment. Commitment to Christ engages us with Christ and creates a proper hierarchy of commitments, one that places all other commitments in relation to God and regulates them by the character of God. It gives the executive self the directions for doing its job.

The other really crucial fact is that our commitments are an expression of our values—or a failure to meet them. This is only a variation of the material about values in the discussion of the self-interpreting memory. Identity results from our attaching ourselves to what we think is good. Integrity depends upon commitments that are an approximation to our values.

---

his *Purity of Heart Is to Will One Thing*, trans. Douglas V. Steere (New York: Harper and Row, 1938), 11–21, 184–97, and 208–16.

13. See pp. 110–12, 115, above.

Recognizing and valuing the good should lead to committing to the good, but it does not necessarily do that. We need to be conscious of committing to the good and holding ourselves accountable for that. From the sense of the good we develop a sense of "oughtness," which shapes the executive self and leads to a sense of responsibility—and guilt when we do not measure up to our own sense of what ought to be. Oughtness is more fundamental than character. Character is the result of successful development of oughtness. Oughtness is the process of recognizing the good and committing to it over time. It is taught by others, learned from experience, *and* is a development from one's *own* recognition of the good worthy of attachment.[14] That involves two steps: recognition of the good and the willingness to make an ongoing commitment to it. Some people recognize the good but, for whatever reason, do not commit to it—on their own admission. Is it because they fear they cannot meet their own standard of what is good and settle for less? Do we alter the good or find excuses why the good does not apply in our case?

In settling for less, not even being willing to embark on the road to the good, we fail to be our true selves. Especially for Christians, commitments need to be conscious, thoughtful, and determined. In the Southern Baptist tradition in which I grew up, people often joined the church on a "profession of faith," which often was no more than a nod to ideas. Profession is not enough; what is needed instead is a commitment to be who God has called us to be in relation to himself.

Scripture's Call for Commitment

Much of Scripture seeks to get readers to make good commitments, most obviously in imperatives seeking to direct life or texts advocating right choices. The list of such texts is long, but think on these few. "Commit your way to the Lord" (Ps. 37:5). "You cannot serve God and money" (Matt. 6:24/Luke 16:13). "Consider yourself dead to sin" (Rom. 6:11). "Present your bodies as a living sacrifice" (Rom. 12:1). "Commit yourself to a faithful Creator" (1 Pet. 4:19). "Live worthy of the calling with which

---

14. Apparently oughtness is also to some degree a result of our own hardwiring.

you were called" (Eph. 4:1). "Imitate God" (Eph. 5:1). "Do nothing from selfish ambition . . . think this way" (Phil. 2:3 and 5). "Live in him" (Col. 2:6). "Think on things above" (Col. 3:2). "Love each other" (1 Pet. 1:22).

The virtue lists, those passages saying "Put off bad qualities and put on good ones" (like Col. 3:5–15), are an attempt to say that negative qualities do not fit a Christian identity and positive ones are required in a Christian identity. Obviously such a discussion requires of us a commitment to Scripture as the place where our true identity as people created in God's image and for relation to God can be found. This is why Christians emphasize Scripture's centrality and authority. Scripture seeks to tell us who we are.

Such commitments are really a commitment to a way of life, to the sacredness of life, and to having a certain kind of identity. We give our lives an orientation by the commitments we make, and orientation is at the heart of identity. Where is your identity pointed? The call of Scripture is for a commitment beyond oneself, a refusal to think that life is just about "me." Still, commitments involve rather complex ideas.

Think again of your body. To what does your body, including your gender, *commit you*? If you are female, for example, you have a possible commitment to motherhood that never crosses a man's mind. Size, physical attractiveness and ability, and mental capacity or the lack thereof enable or limit commitments. Our culture at least implies what you should do with your body. How will your commitments steward your body? The body may commit a person to a wheelchair, or to athletics, or to thought and creative possibilities, or merely to a struggle for survival. Some will have multiple options, and some will have multiple challenges.

Also, to what do *you commit* your body? In light of these questions, 1 Corinthians 6:12–20, a text treated briefly before, takes on surprising significance. Paul asserts that all things are possible for him, but not all things are profitable, and that he will not be dominated by (brought under the authority of) anything. The body is not merely for food and definitely not for sexual sin. *It is for the Lord, and the Lord is for the body* (v. 13). Suddenly the *body* takes on new significance. The body first and foremost is placed in relation to the risen Christ, destined for resurrection, and viewed as a recipient of the benefits of being in relation to Christ. The assumption is that in relation to Christ humans control their bodies—not the reverse, especially in relation to sexual practice—and that the body and its sexuality are good, positive, and to be used positively. The body too is joined to Christ and is a temple of the indwelling Spirit, for it belongs to God. Given this thinking, our commitments with our body are rearranged and placed first in service to Christ. Obviously too, care of our bodies is assumed.

Think too of your relations. Every relation—whether family, friends, work, or chance encounters—involves commitments and responsibilities. Relations too are placed in a hierarchy of values, and integrity depends on how we carry out the different values of our relations. Love and friendship are commitments that must be lived out. Failure to live out relational commitments—to do justice to the nature of the relation with specific people—is a betrayal that damages the other person, for we know intuitively that relations are about valuing people, and we have some sense of what the relation should mean. Christian identity will not allow relations to be devalued and discarded.

The character of God provides the foundation for our relational commitments. The primary revelation of God in Exodus 34:6 is that God is a God full of covenant loyalty and faithfulness, sometimes expressed as "full of grace and truth" or "full of steadfast love and faithfulness." The Hebrew words in this verse, *chesed* (lovingkindness) and *'emet* (truth), both have to do with covenant loyalty. "Covenant" in Scripture is a way of speaking of promises and relations. Because of his love, *God makes commitments* to us. God establishes a covenant relation and makes promises to his people, and God keeps his commitments. God is a faithful God. Similarly, our relations bind us with commitments and expectations, and our identity is shaped by the way we keep faith with our commitments. All of us decide about a person's identity from how he or she keeps faith with relations. Is this person to be trusted? We too are known by how we handle relational commitments, even with the recognition that not all relations are the same or merit the same commitment.

Our commitments regarding investments of interest, time, and money also shape us. For each of us these are limited resources, but they determine who we are. Tell me where you spend your time and money, and I will tell you who you are and how self-centered you are. A car commercial asserts, "The things we make make us," which is a recognition that we are largely the result of our commitments and investments. What makes you?

Dangerous Commitments

Commitments are the things to which we give focus, and surely sin has as much to do with misplaced focus as anything. Sin is not merely the acts we should not have done, but also is the whole orientation of life in the wrong direction, which is why Scripture focuses on idolatry so much. When we honor the wrong things, we give away the value and dignity God gave us, and we mar our identity. To repeat a statement from the *Sentences of Sextus*, "Whatever you honor most will rule you. Honor what is best that you may be governed by what is best."[15] To put it another way, people who worship worthless things render themselves worthless, a point made in 2 Kings 17:15, which says the Israelites followed after worthless idols and themselves became worthless (also Jer. 2:5). We become like what we worship and that to which we commit ourselves, which is scary.

For most people desires, pleasure, and self-satisfaction are at the top of the list of commitments. We commit to what we think will make us happy: money, resources, possessions, and enjoyment, all of which are important, but they do not make a life. Even wealthy people, who think they have no needs, still need God. The parable of the rich fool in Luke 12:16–21 tells of a man who had many resources to enjoy life but had forgotten God and the brevity of life. Just when he was ready to enjoy his good fortune, life was over. After his death, to whom did his things belong? Possessions do not make a life, and you are not your stuff. A salesman in a high-end audio store commented to me, "People do not have peace, so they buy pieces." Worse still, possessions, fragile as they are, often become possessors and dictators; they have to be stored, cared for, and guarded. We do not so much own them as they own us and manipulate our lives.

Pleasure and entertainment are perhaps the controlling commitment for most in our society. We desire to be amused—to death. Georg

15. *Sentences of Sextus* 41–42.

Carstensen, the founder of the amusement park Tivoli Gardens in Copenhagen, obtained a five-year charter to create Tivoli by telling the king, "When the people are amusing themselves, they do not think about politics." The words stand on a plaque near an entrance to the park.[16]

Actually, when people are amusing themselves, they think about nothing, which means our society is in serious trouble. We give our attention to useless, meaningless items. We watch staged "reality" shows, endless sports, and comedies that require laugh tracks so we know when to laugh. We even watch people lose weight! Are we bored to death or what? Entertainment wants to live your life.[17] We appear to have little purpose other than to exist for entertainment and our own enjoyment. We are so scattered we are diffuse. We are indeed a mile wide and an inch deep. If we are to a large degree what we do, what paltry identity have we constructed?

Entertainment and leisure are not worthy goals for life. We need diversion, yes, but we need purpose and focus more. Psychologists point out that people are happiest when they have some sense of involvement in *important* issues, even if life otherwise is precarious. We need commitments worthy of life, or life itself is devalued and without meaning. What are you if your highest commitment is to your own pleasure?

Interestingly, much of the ancient world viewed pleasure and desires themselves as *bad*. The Roman philosopher Cicero (first century BC) said, "Intellect . . . has no deadlier foe than pleasure," and "In pleasure's realm there is not a single spot where virtue may put her foot." Pleasure for him was the bait of sin.[18] A second-century Christian added, "God does not listen to one who loves pleasure."[19] Why did some in the ancient world discount pleasure and Stoics and others reject desire? Obviously, other people in their time were pursuing pleasure. Presumably those suspicious of pleasure saw that pleasure frequently disoriented life and

16. Something similar was said by Oliver Wendell Holmes Sr.: "Give us the luxuries of life and we will dispense with the necessities" (*The Autocrat of the Breakfast-Table* [Boston: Phillips, Sampson, 1859], 143).

17. Robert Short, *The Parables of Peanuts* (San Francisco: HarperSanFrancisco, 2002), 9.

18. Cicero, *De senectute* 12.40–41; at 13.44 he quotes Plato, *Timaeus* 69D. See also Seneca, who says pleasure "has in it nothing of nobility, nothing worthy of the nature of man" (*De beneficiis* 7.2.2).

19. *Sentences of Sextus* 72.

enticed people in the wrong direction. The Bible does not view all desire as wrong or all pleasure as wrong, even though it knows that desire easily is distorted into greed, that pleasure can be idolatrous, and that life is in relations, not things.

The rejection of pleasure by some ancients, though, should give us pause. Pleasure is not the highest good, should not be given so much focus, and can never satisfy. The fourth-century church father Jerome said, "Pleasure always creates a hunger for itself and when indulged does not satisfy,"[20] which means it disorients and distracts from proper goals. The question of what we are to pursue is crucial, and our own happiness is not the goal, depending of course on how one defines happiness.

Committed to Two Geographies

Your commitments also involve commitment to a location—or several locations. Commitment *to a location* is a major identity-shaping factor, for geography is identity. As we have seen in discussing relations, the true location of a Christian is *in Christ*. He is the sphere of influence within which we live. Christians actually have two geographies, and therefore two commitments to location. We live *in Christ* and in a particular community, city, state, and country—or multiples thereof.

Where you live determines your identity because location determines languages, customs, expectations, and celebrations. I have visited Ecuador, but I am not an Ecuadorian. Visiting a geography does not make you a resident; only living there will give you that geographical identity. People are happy to visit Jesus every now and then. Visiting Jesus can make you feel good, especially if you do not listen, but it does not change your life. Faith is not about visiting Jesus; it is being incorporated into him and participating with him. If you have true faith, your life has been hidden with Christ in God. He is your primary location and, therefore, your primary commitment. You have been inserted into Christ. How does that affect your language, customs, expectations, and celebrations?

20. *The Letters of St. Jerome*, trans. Charles Christopher Mierow, Ancient Christian Writers 33 (Westminster, MD: Newman, 1963), 21.13.2 (p. 117).

Perhaps the most obvious evidence of this dual geography is in Paul's opening words in the letter to the Colossians: "To the holy and faithful brothers and sisters in Colossae in Christ" (1:2). Rarely do I remember sermons very long, but years ago a sermon on this text asked two simple questions I cannot forget—what does it mean to Christ that you are "in Colossae," and what does it mean "to Colossae" that you are in Christ? Obviously being in Christ carries a commitment of the highest order and reframes all other commitments. Our commitment to being in Christ brings with it a commitment to faithfulness, to critical thinking about what fits with Christ, to being conformed to Christ, and to working on behalf of Christ. Again we see the importance of the Christian focus on the mind.

Suddenly the second geography, the place we live, is not merely a physical locale but a place for living a Christlike identity and serving on behalf of Christ. It is a place for investment. Geography is itself a vocation. What is the significance to Christ that you live where you do, and what is the significance to your locale that you live in Christ?

Many people do not consciously choose the physical location where they live. They are there by default. Others make a choice for any number of reasons. In either case, the physical location determines us, and we should be conscious about how our identity is being affected by our geography. Does our physical location help or hinder life with Christ? What should it mean for us to commit to a place? How critical must our thinking be so that we do not merely assume what is assumed in our locale. What is wrong elsewhere is still wrong in "Vegas." Clearly, too, we should not think of location merely as communities or regions of the country. The location may be the building in which we live or work. Such a location still determines us, and of course, at least to some degree, a location is determined by us, or should be.

Moving geographically will affect identity, but it does not convey the identity we should have. Gregory of Nyssa, writing about pilgrimages to the Holy Land, made the point that we do not come closer to God by changing our place.[21] We come closer to God and to being truly human

21. Gregory of Nyssa, *On Pilgrimages*, in *Nicene and Post-Nicene Fathers*, series 2, 5:383. Seneca had made the same point. See his *Moral Letters* 104, "Why travel cannot set you

only by changing the way we think and live as the Spirit of God engages us.

Commitment to life in Christ also changes how we view "other geographies." While we can live only in one geography at a time, we do not confine our care to our own geography. Christ opens up our limited geography to a perspective on God's whole world. We will return to this topic when we treat boundaries.

Commitment as Imitation

Commitment to something good means that we will imitate people we think achieve the good. Imitation—for all of being yourself—enters into the very heart of our being and is unavoidably part of identity.[22] Imitation can be a good thing. We all have mentors and models for life. You will imitate someone, even when attempting to be yourself. Who will you choose? Never in the history of humanity has so much adulation been given to so undeserving few. Why do we adulate attractive people, movie stars, and the like? Is it some twisted sense of attaching ourselves to the good? There is no real benefit in it for the person adulating, and adulation rarely leads to identity formation. Any association with the person is an illusion, for we have no real connection to the person. Most do not deserve to be role models, and they do not really shape our identity or make us better. At most they may influence the way people dress or express themselves, but even there the influence is short-lived. Today's "star" is a vague memory a short time later, and we move on to the next illusion.

Scripture offers several role models for imitation, all pointing in the same direction. If humanity is created in God's image and likeness, then God's character is the primary role model deserving commitment from us. Paul's instruction in Ephesians 5:1 for believers to *imitate God* at first glance may seem a bit outrageous, but if humans are created in God's im-

---

free" (Loeb 3, pp. 191–211, uses the title "On Care and Health and Peace of Mind"): traveling will not improve one's condition; one has to change oneself. See also his "On Travel as a Cure for Discontent": "The person you are matters more than the place to which you go" (*Moral Letters* 28.4; Loeb 1, p. 201).

22. Larmore, *Practices of the Self*, 33.

147

age, then what makes better sense? Much about God we cannot imitate—his power, his knowledge, or eternal being—but imitating God's character is the most important part of our identity formation. First and foremost we need a commitment to God both as the source of our identity, the ultimate and determinative good, the one to whom we are accountable, and the one we are to please. Humans are to take their character from their God, which presupposes that they know God's character, the revelation of which is part of Scripture's purpose.

The call to follow Jesus (e.g., Matt. 16:24) presupposes that he should be imitated, that he embodies the character humans should have and that he is the visible image of God's character. Paul asks his readers to imitate him as he imitates Christ (1 Cor. 11:1), and the writer of Hebrews assumes that Christians of character should be imitated (6:12). Identifying with models that help us mirror the character of God is precisely what Christian identity is about.

Such commitment to God rearranges attitudes and beliefs, at least if we are willing to reflect critically on our mental assumptions. You cannot take your character from your God and have disdain and disregard for the people God created and cares about. This is not to suggest that a commitment to God on our part suddenly fixes all errors of our thinking. It is the realization that every thought is indeed "taken captive" and made obedient to Christ (2 Cor. 10:5). This is a process whereby life is continually placed in relation to God, evaluated by the revelation of God in Christ, and adjusted to bring thinking into line with the will of God. In that process our desires, assumptions, and ideals are rearranged. Christian ideals are not utopian or too hard, not even those of the Sermon on the Mount that so many seek to avoid. The ideals are a call to be what God created us to be and to reflect God's own character. Peace and satisfaction lie nowhere else.

Some people, however, do not choose what is good and true for their own advantage but choose instead *against* other people whom they do not want to be like. In the process they fail to become what they should be. On the other hand, of course, sometimes we learn from negative examples and choose to go the opposite way. But in any case, what we oppose, hate, and fight shapes our identity. Alasdair MacIntyre says, "It is often and perhaps always through conflict that the self receives its social definition."[23] In other words, people take their identity by opposition. We gain a sense of who we are by not being like the others. This is one reason our society has become so antagonistic. No matter what the other side is doing, people oppose it because it is the other side.

We might prefer to say we do not fight, but if we are not opposing some things, we cannot be doing the will of God. Some realities we must oppose, and we are not allowed to turn a blind eye toward them. If we do not fight evil, what are we? But how will we fight? Here is one of the largest failures of Christians. In fighting we too often forget who we are and become like what we fight. Even in fighting we are still to be defined by Christ. *To fight evil without becoming evil is the task of all Christians,* and maybe one of the biggest obstacles for humans, as war after war attests. Can we care for and love the opponents, despite the evil we fight? Love of enemies is not some impossible ideal but precisely a reflection of the character of the God we serve.

Final Thoughts on Commitment

Commitments are crucial, but they need to be realistic. Knowing what is realistic requires wisdom and sensitivity to the will of God. Sometimes people make commitments to what cannot and will not be. A friend reported on his commitment—following the will of God, he thought—to pursue an academic career. For various reasons the plan for teaching never worked out, even with a PhD in hand. He had to come to peace with the realization that his commitment was not enough; there were other factors shaping his identity that precluded his desire. He was frustrated until he decided "to stop living in the zip code of daily thinking about and wondering what happened in my own academic experience."[24] But how does one determine what is realistic? How does one remain faithful when a legitimate commitment is the source of frustration? No easy answers exist, but surely here as elsewhere one lives by an honest and continual

23. Alasdair MacIntyre, *After Virtue: A Study in Moral Theory*, 3rd ed. (Notre Dame: University of Notre Dame Press, 2007), 31.

24. Private correspondence.

reassessment of the will of God. That presumes, of course, an honest and foundational commitment to seek the will of God and engagement with other Christians in finding it.

A number of biblical texts view commitments as attachments. Commitments and relations are intertwined. Romans 12:9 urges, not surprisingly, that we attach ourselves to the good. First Corinthians 6:17 describes believers as attached to the Lord.[25] Other texts speak of being attached to—clinging to—God and his commandments.[26] Deuteronomy asks for a commitment to the teaching of God. The Israelites were told to teach their children the Torah in their homes, when traveling, and both day and night—in effect, always and everywhere. They were told to bind the Torah on their arms and on their foreheads and to write it on their doors and gates, commands orthodox Jews still literally obey. In effect, they were told to focus their lives on—to make a primary commitment to—God's instructions for life. They were to tie the Torah on their heads and arms so that it shaped all thinking and all doing (Deut. 6:6–9). Can—should—Christians do less?

The identity factors are intertwined. We saw that commitments involve relations, but they lead to actions, and they create boundaries, as the following chapters show. But you must ask yourself two questions: Are my commitments worth my life, and what have they made me?

25. The NIV and NRSV translations both use "united," which is understandable, but the word in question, *kollaomai*, conveys the idea of being bound closely to or clinging to. It is used of sexual relations in 1 Cor. 6:16, and a compound of this word is used of the marriage relation in the Greek translation of Gen. 2:24 and in Eph. 5:31.

26. Deut. 4:4; 10:20; 11:22; 13:4; 30:20; Josh. 22:5; 23:8; Pss. 63:8; 119:31; and Jer. 13:11.

FACTOR 6

You Are Your Actions

It's always easier to learn something than to use what you've learned.

—Chaim Potok, *The Promise*

God is worshiped not by moods but by action. But this, too, has the problem that it can so easily turn into pettiness and temptation in the form of meritoriousness.

—Søren Kierkegaard, *Søren Kierkegaard's Journals and Papers*

Let's get something straight right from the beginning. If you do not act like a Christian, you are not a Christian. Yes, I am willing to die on that hill. There is no such thing as an identity that does not act. If you do not treat people, especially spouses and other family members, from and with Christian virtues, there is serious doubt that you are Christian. And no, I do not believe in salvation by works, but I do know that faith involves attachment to and participation with Christ, and if that is the case, you cannot be attached to Christ without acting in accord with his character to some *large* extent. Identity informs behavior. All things do indeed receive the characteristics of that in which they participate.[1] We cannot participate in the life of Christ without taking on the characteristics of Christ and his teaching so that his life shapes what we do. I am not talking about perfection but about a serious living out of faith. Agreeing with Christian ideas and goals does not make one a Christian; it makes one merely an admirer of Christianity.

The Absolute Necessity of Action

Do Christians have to do anything? The question is silly. I want to emphasize as strongly as I know how the importance and necessity of action for identity, especially Christian identity. The self is a self because it is an agent; it decides and acts to achieve a goal, and in doing so reveals who it really is. Being a competent human is about being a person who establishes values and moves toward them. A second-century Christian said, "When you know for what reason you exist, you will know yourself,"[2] alluding of course to the Greek philosophical quest to know yourself.

A reining horse is highly trained to perform a series of maneuvers such as figure eights and galloping and then immediately doing an abrupt sliding stop. What is impressive is that some reining horses are so well trained that they do the whole routine without a bridle. They do what they are. Similarly, cutting horses—horses trained to separate a cow from the herd and prevent her returning to it—have been known to do this on their own when turned out to pasture with cows. They know who they are, and they just do it.

Knowing for what reason you exist presupposes that you will, or at least should, act to accomplish the reason you exist, that the reason for which you exist will provide an organizing center of your life and give you goals, and that you will seek to meet the goals of your own being. That requires decision making, which is already an action, and implementation of the decisions. With actions we are not speaking merely of physical acts. Focusing your life is an act; conscious thought and speaking are acts.

1. Robert Letham, *Union with Christ in Scripture, History, and Theology* (Phillipsburg, NJ: Presbyterian and Reformed, 2011), 93.
2. *Sentences of Sextus* 398.

Study and learning are acts, and commitments and actions are closely related. Commitment without action is no commitment.

Identity cannot be shaped without doing. Humans are notoriously adept at tearing being from doing, which will be treated below, but doing expresses who we really are. Affirming ideas without practicing them is hypocrisy, a failure of courage, and a hiding from oneself. Life is not merely about thinking; in fact, thinking by itself can be a defense against being and doing. Life is about being and *doing.* Judgment in Scripture is always according to works, *not* according to what one knows or thinks.

I am *not* diminishing the importance of thought or of theology—quite the contrary, given the earlier chapter on the self-interpreting, self-directing memory. Thinking is absolutely crucial, and as I have tried to emphasize, Christianity has a huge focus on the mind, on learning, and on continually renewing the mind. But Christianity is not merely about thinking the faith. Thinking—theology—is useless unless it is backed up by life, and in fact, thinking often is an excuse for not acting. Identity is about ethics, for it is about values and actions. Reason does not necessarily produce action; passion and investment do when one actually cares about life and acts.

No one emphasized this more than Søren Kierkegaard, who said deliberation is only brought to a close when we care enough about something to stop thinking and act. He emphasized that he needed to be clear about what he must do, not what he must know. He asserted that God is worshiped not by moods but by actions, that Christianity is Christianity in action, that Christianity is not doctrine but an existence-communication, and that most dangerous of all is intellectualizing, which is a defense against genuine understanding.[3] Kierkegaard derided people guilty of such intellectualizing with the label "professor," one who knows about but does not do. He complained of pastors who were like swimming instructors who cannot swim and never get in the water but instruct others in swimming. Like many, he emphasized that Christianity is entirely a gift, but with the gift comes obligation. Real knowing includes doing.

---

3. *Søren Kierkegaard's Journals and Papers*, ed. and trans. Howard V. Hong and Edna H. Hong (Bloomington: Indiana University Press, 1967–1978), 1:14. See also Søren Kierkegaard, *Attack upon "Christendom," 1854–1855*, trans. Walter Lowrie (Princeton: Princeton University Press, 1946).

Kierkegaard's words sting, but Western Christianity is pervasively guilty of intellectualizing Christian faith and not living it. What we do shows what we *really* think. If we proclaim a gospel that does not lead to doing, we proclaim an alien gospel, one that fits neither with Jesus nor with any part of the New Testament. One does not really know if one does not do. Or, as my colleague John Weborg put it, "Some things are never known until they are put into practice."[4]

The message people hear from some Christian pulpits, however, is, "Just believe; you do not need to do anything," which has resulted in a superficial and useless religion. This is a gross distortion. How did anyone get from *any* part of the Bible that you do not need to do anything? What are all those commands, imperatives, exhortations, virtue and vice lists, and examples for, if not to call us to action? Both Old and New Testaments are about covenant with God, about living in relation with God and reflecting his character, and obedience is stressed throughout. The idea that Christianity is about what you believe and that it does not matter what you do is a huge lie, a perversion of the faith, and perhaps the most self-deluding thought ever perpetrated on anyone.

What is the end goal? That you agree with certain ideas or that you actually *become* a person who lives with God and reflects the character of God, a person who is alive and productive, who chooses important tasks and lives life with integrity, the very thing for which you were created? There can be no question. If faith is participation with the God revealed in Christ, acting in keeping with God and God's desires is necessary. You cannot participate and be inactive.

Actions, of course, can be wrongly performed and wrongly motivated. Actions can be legalistic, uncaring, unwise, insincere, and unrelated to the reality of relation with God and neighbor. Actions can be distorted as easily as any other part of life and used for self-serving ends, especially to try to prove oneself or to make oneself look good. Nothing in a focus on action suggests earning merit. Martin Luther rightly said, as far as humans are concerned, "There is no such thing as merit."[5] He empha-

---

4. John Weborg, "Scripture Demands More," *Covenant Companion*, September–October, 2016, 46–49, here 49.

5. The comment is in *Dr. Martin Luthers Werke*, 69 vols. (Weimar: Böhlau, 1883–

sized, as every Christian should, 1 Corinthians 4:7: "What do you have that you did not receive, and if you received it, why are you boasting as if you did not?" All we are and have and anything we do worthwhile are a gift of and engagement with God. We act not to gain merit but because we are God's, not to gain standing with God or others but because God has given us standing and engaged us.

The focus on action has nothing to do with legalism or with faking. It has to do with an honest identity lived with integrity. Mature identity results when thinking and acting are unified. Only here will one find freedom and peace. The integrity of thinking and acting being unified removes many of our problems and especially any separation of evangelism and social concern. A division of the two can result only from hypocrisy or a misunderstanding of the breadth of the gospel.

For years I have advocated a hermeneutics of obedience, that is, a process of interpreting Scripture that insists first on openness to hear and willingness to obey. In fact, often the Hebrew verb for hearing *means* obeying and is so translated (e.g., see Exod. 19:5; 24:7). This approach to reading Scripture is both a stance and a performance, a stance ready to hear and obey and performance of the action. *Right interpretation results in performance.* What counts is not knowing *about* texts but knowing texts well enough to do them—that is, knowing texts experientially and with your whole being, not knowing about God, but living with God in such a way as to reflect God's character.

"We are what we repeatedly do. Excellence, then, is not an act, but a habit."[6] You are what you do habitually, not what you do once. Jesus's exchange with a legal expert in Luke 10:25–28 is revealing. The lawyer asks, "What thing [singular] having done [aorist] will I inherit eternal life?" In effect, he asks if there is some single act he can perform to gain life. After the commands to love God and neighbor are brought into the discussion, Jesus says, "Be doing this [present tense, an ongoing action] and you will live." In effect, Jesus says, "Be this kind of person with your

---

1993), 18:769.33. See the treatment of John M. G. Barclay, *Paul and the Gift* (Grand Rapids: Eerdmans, 2015), 101n45.

6. Will Durant, *The Story of Philosophy: The Lives and Opinions of the World's Greatest Philosophers* (New York: Simon and Schuster/Pocket Books, 1991 [originally published 1926]), 76, summarizing an argument from Aristotle. See *Nicomachean Ethics* 2.4 and 1.7.

actions." In what follows in the parable of the good Samaritan the lawyer again thinks in the singular. Who is my neighbor? Jesus again points to character. Who proved to be neighbor?

To be a mature person presupposes the ability to assess what has value and to act accordingly *and* to take responsibility for one's actions. All such thinking and acting assume the capacity for wisdom and self-control, two of the four cardinal virtues of the ancient Greco-Roman world.[7] These virtues are affirmed repeatedly in Scripture, as are the presuppositions of competence and the possibility of living ethically. Self-control is one of the most important lessons anyone can learn and is badly needed in a time when self-gratification, unkindness, addiction, and violence are so prevalent. Self-control is the root of all action and all success. No musician, no businessperson, no athlete, nor anyone else is even moderately successful without self-control. Self-control is itself an action, and it is the assumption of every New Testament imperative.

Self-control is the most important achievement of any human, for here is the basis of rejecting the urges and desires of the minimal self, the basis of choosing higher value possibilities for successful living, and even the ability to listen to and give oneself to God. Such internal action to close off wrong desires is foundational to all other actions. We will never choose good things unless we control the attraction to lesser and bad things. We spend a great deal of time teaching children self-control, for without self-control they can never succeed or even be bearable. We expect people to control their anger and their urges, or we do not want to be around them. Jesus, Paul, and James assume people *can* control their anger (Matt. 5:21–22; Eph. 4:26 and 31; James 1:19–20). Desires and temptations are always present. Everyone has inclinations to varying de-

7. The four being temperance (self-control), fortitude (courage), justice (righteousness), and prudence (wisdom). Saint Augustine, discussing the morals of the church, said: "Therefore, these four virtues—would that their efficacy were present in all souls as their names are on all lips—I would not hesitate to define as follows: temperance is love giving itself wholeheartedly to that which is loved, fortitude is love enduring all things willingly for the sake of that which is loved, justice is love serving alone that which is loved and thus ruling rightly, and prudence is love choosing wisely between that which helps it and that which hinders it." *The Catholic and Manichean Ways of Life*, trans. Donald A. Gallagher and Idella J. Gallagher, Fathers of the Church 56 (Washington, DC: Catholic University of America Press, 1966), ch. 15 (p. 22).

grees both for good and for bad, but inclinations do not make an identity; actions do. Inclinations are mere proclivities. Temptations themselves are not sins until they are embraced, nurtured, and enacted.

We assume a fairly high level of self-control, even apart from Christianity or another religion, and expect people to control themselves. Still, there is a long religious tradition that has worried about and debated whether and to what degree humans can control themselves. Is the human will so bound by sin that it is incapable of good? Is free will really free? Is any good accomplished really only God's work? Many are convinced only of human inability, but the stress on human sinfulness does not preclude human obedience to God *in communion with God.* Sin is not Lord; Christ is. Any thought of Christian self-control and obedience presupposes the activity of God's Spirit in us enabling what we do. The relation of God's action and human action is extremely complex and too frequently not even thought about, let alone discussed. We will revisit these issues later in this chapter, but too often the question is framed wrongly. It assumes an isolation of the human from God, but that is already a distortion. To anticipate, especially for Christians, any talk of self-control does not mean control by one's self. It means self-control through the help of God's Spirit, and God's Spirit is indeed active in the world.

Actions define life, and you will not be happy without some sense of being useful. The psychologist Erik H. Erikson said, "All, sooner or later, become dissatisfied and disgruntled without a sense of being useful."[8] Humans were created, not merely for enjoyment, but to be productive, to "tend the garden" (Gen. 1:28), mirroring God's own creativity. Without a sense of purpose, of actually doing something useful, people become bored and dissatisfied, which is obvious in our society with so many people seeking amusement or self-"medicating" with alcohol and drugs.

But what does it mean to "tend the garden" in a modern world, especially when technological advances seemingly render humans redundant? Already in 1985 Wendell Berry wrote an article entitled "What Are People For?" as a protest against technology taking over life.[9] That fear has become a reality.

8. Erik H. Erikson, *Identity and the Life Cycle* (New York: Norton, 1980), 91.

9. Wendell Berry, *What Are People For? Essays by Wendell Berry* (San Francisco: North Point, 1990), 123–25.

What *are* people for anyway? Are millions of people "unnecessary" now, and is wealth only to be accumulated for the enjoyment of the few at the top? *All* people still have the task of mirroring their Creator and caring for each other. Love of neighbor includes some level of care and responsibility for neighbor. The idea of "caring for the garden" in Genesis 1 was about working with the land to be productive and caring for and stewarding the land. Unfortunately, relatively few today work with the land, but the instruction is not so narrowly limited. "Useful work"—good work—is any work that furthers life and productivity and enables and promotes human existence, for that honors God. We can devote our efforts to trivial activities, but our societies cry out for people to work to meet enormous needs and help all of us to flourish and live meaningfully. This is not just for religious professions; it involves all kinds of employment that promote life. The requirement is not just that some people or some professions address the needs but that all do. Each of us has his or her responsibility, and some can do much more than others. You cannot fix all the problems in the world, but you can choose good work that honors God and God's world. To what good will you give yourself?

What greater good is there than doing the will of God? Commitment to do the will of God defines Christians. The more we do the will of God, the more our identity is shaped by orientation toward God. Life with Christ gives us purpose and good work to do. God's work in Christ is to be our interest and our investment. *Such work is not "church" work; it is life work.* Only a minority will have "religious" employment or even be in the "helping" professions, but no matter what the job, our work matters to God. Nor is the work merely our employment. The work will be within our own families and relations, will address needs in our communities, will confront evil and suffering in the world, will create order and beauty, and will be engaged with living and speaking the teaching of and about Christ. It will be relational, and it will focus on gaining wisdom and living wisely throughout our existence. It will also show that in naming Christ as Lord we honor ourselves.

We are what we do. Our commitments are lived or they are not commitments. Doing is an essential—absolutely essential—part of Christianity. You are not a Christian if you do not live as a Christian.[10]

---

10. Note the comment of Justin Martyr, the second-century apologist (*1 Apology* 16): "And whoever are not found living as he taught are not to be recognized as Christians, even

This is the imperative of the faith. Knowing him is not merely knowing about him.

How did we end up with an understanding of the faith in which people do not need to act? Conversion to Judaism involved accepting practices, not merely ideas, and conversion to Christ does as well. All of the Bible, including Paul's letters, has a heavy emphasis on action, on living the faith, on obeying the will of God. I will mention only a sampling of the focus on actions.

The teaching of Jesus heavily emphasizes actions. He castigated the Pharisees for saying and not doing (Matt. 23:3–36). The Sermon on the Mount repeatedly calls for radical obedience that disciples are to perform. The sermon has a heavy focus on doing; the Greek verb for doing occurs twenty-two times in Matthew 5–7. Jesus asserted that he did not come to destroy the Old Testament law and prophets but to bring them to fulfillment, that is, to show how deeply they direct life and are accomplished through the love commands. Jesus's teaching in the sermon gives the characteristics of disciples of the kingdom. Good trees produce good fruits (Matt. 7:16–20); people with an identity shaped by the kingdom produce works fitting with the kingdom. The Sermon on the Mount is not unreasonable and does not lead to legalism or salvation by works.[11] Legalism and salvation by works are not the issues Jesus was addressing in the sermon, nor was he worried about them.[12] The sermon is the bright light of the gospel and is eminently reasonable and shows what life should be. All of us would love to live in a community where the Sermon on the Mount was lived, and that is precisely what the church should be.

As is well known, Dietrich Bonhoeffer, writing about discipleship and the Sermon on the Mount, lamented the cheap grace that so many buy into—grace without cost or effect—and asserted that only those who obey

---

if they speak the teachings of Christ with their tongues. For he said that not those who only speak but also those who do the works will be saved. For he said this, 'Not everyone who says to me, "Lord, Lord," will enter into the Kingdom of Heaven, but the one who does the will of my Father who is in Heaven.' . . . And we request that those who do not live according to his teachings, and are only called Christians, be punished by you as well" (see *Justin, Philosopher and Martyr: Apologies*, ed. Denis Minns and Paul Parvis [Oxford: Oxford University Press, 2009], 16.8–9 and 14).

11. See pp. 42–45, above.

12. Legalism is an issue in material dealing with the Pharisees.

can believe, and only those who believe can obey.[13] He was absolutely correct.

Paul emphasized actions as much as anyone, and his rejection of works, which will be treated below, has nothing to do with devaluing *obedience*. In fact, Paul described his whole ministry as bringing about the "obedience of faith" among the gentiles (Rom. 1:5; 16:26). He used "obeyed" and "believed" in synonymous parallelism, two ways of saying the same thing (Rom. 10:16). Three times he used a formula to say that neither circumcision, which his opponents were insisting upon, nor uncircumcision really mattered. What does matter is expressed differently each time. In Galatians 5:6 what really matters is faith *working* through love. In Galatians 6:15 what counts is a new creation, and in 1 Corinthians 7:19 what counts is *keeping the commandments of God*! In Romans 8:4 he expects people to fulfill the righteous commands of the law by living in keeping with the Spirit of God. Everywhere Paul expects believers to act in ways fitting with faith. Sins must be put off and not practiced, and actions in keeping with the God revealed in Christ must be put on and lived. The vice lists exclude actions that do not fit identity in Christ, and the virtue lists demand actions that fit the identity (see Gal. 5:17–26; Eph. 4:17–5:21; Col. 3:5–17).

First John is very emphatic that if you do not keep Christ's commands, if you do not mirror his character, you do not know him. Note especially 2:6 ("The one claiming to be in him [Christ] should live just as he lived") and the assertion in 3:6–9 and elsewhere that the one in Christ by default cannot live a life of sin. All of Scripture mirrors the same theology. The issue is not perfectionism; it is living a Christ identity, one that does justice to the fact that humans are created in God's own image and have been transformed by encounter with God's Spirit. There is forgiveness for sin, but there is rejection of any thought that it does not matter what you do. All of Scripture has this focus on proper actions.

Deep down all of us know the necessity of worthwhile action if we are to be worthwhile. Yet, our society focuses more on enjoying leisure and on being provided for and entertained, even if it leads to the abuse of others. The goal seems to be avoiding work, particularly the way re-

---

13. Dietrich Bonhoeffer, *The Cost of Discipleship* (New York: Simon and Schuster, 1995), 70.

tirement is advertised, but retirement is quite difficult for many, for they lose all sense of purpose, meaning, and worth. Granted, work is no fun if it is mere drudgery, so how do we establish sound practices of work? Entertainment has its important place, but it should not be the idol it is, and it can never satisfy the need to be productive and worthwhile. Our jobs may be drudgery at times, but even when that is the necessity, they support the possibility of life and meaningful action elsewhere. While our jobs do partly define us, we are not our jobs. Some jobs we do because we have to, not because of who we are. In the end it is not our jobs that say who we are; it is the God in whose image we are made.

One of my friends took a job reading gas meters—at one level not much of a job, but she considered it a gift to help her make it through a tough time. During that job she wrote the lyrics for her first album. What does life do to us when we do seemingly meaningless jobs? How do we maintain and grow our identities in difficult times? Actions, good habits, and following good examples in these circumstances are especially important, for practices shape us, and faithfulness in practices solidifies who we are.

That Christian actions are necessary cannot be denied, but the point is not merely that we should do such acts. The point is that our actions—and specifically Christian actions—both express our identity and, even more importantly, *shape* our identity. Actions are a means to our identity, not merely a consequence of our identity. We act because of who we are but also in order to become who we should be. Jesus told people to love their enemies *in order that* they may be children of their heavenly Father (Matt. 5:44–45). Good actions develop good character, and good character produces good actions. The same dynamic works for bad actions.[14] We are what we do. Some things change your identity if you do not do them, from not cutting your hair to not committing sinful acts. Some things change your identity if you do them, from coloring your hair blue to practicing acts of love. Who we are is shown by what we do, and what we do solidifies and shapes—or distorts—who we are.

Each act is a learning process. Actions, like all learning, structure our

14. See Max Lee, "Ancient Mentors and Moral Progress according to Galen and Paul," in *Doing Theology for the Church: Essays in Honor of Klyne Snodgrass*, ed. Rebekah A. Eklund and John E. Phelan Jr. (Eugene, OR: Wipf and Stock, 2014), 56.

brain. Morality and immorality are both learned. Self-centeredness appears to be innate, but morality and immorality are both learned, with the latter being more easily self-taught than the former. Right actions are part of the process of unlearning wrong actions. How does one discern from one's identity what acts to do? Most do not discern; they merely fall into habits without thought. Habits are crucial in forming identity, but one needs to discern which habits to adopt. Bad habits lead to a bad identity; good habits help shape a good identity, or at least the possibility of a good identity. Habits alone cannot do the job, but a proper identity will not be formed without good habits. Also important are examples—leaders and others who best embody the traits of the desired identity—and the confession of Jesus as Lord is meaningless if he is not indeed the example we follow.

People look at the directions to slaves and masters in Ephesians 6:5–9 as irrelevant, if not embarrassing, but when I was writing a commentary on Ephesians, this passage had more impact on me than any other.[15] This text subverts slavery, even if many did not notice. Slaves are told that they belong to Christ, not their masters; that they serve Christ, not their masters; that they are to please Christ, not their masters; that they will be rewarded by Christ, not by their masters; and that they are no different from their masters. The masters are told to treat slaves the same way slaves are to treat the owners—How was that heard?!—for they too have a Master in heaven. In effect, Paul asks for mutual submission of slaves and masters, which surely raised eyebrows! Clearly Paul knew slaves did not take their identity from their jobs but from their Lord, even if their jobs could not be changed.

Obviously among our most important actions, especially in tough times, are acts of worship, and often worship is an act of protest against the valuations society places on us and suggests for us. I said earlier that church is the place people go to take their identity and declare their allegiances. Worship is crucial to all aspects of identity because in worship we remind ourselves who God is and who we are. We participate in rituals that trigger our memory, we renew our commitments, and we make

15. See *Ephesians*, NIV Application Commentary (Grand Rapids: Zondervan, 1996), 323–24, 326–29, and 331–33.

our values clearer. All of us have rituals, even when we say we do not, but some rituals are better than others. Rituals can be perfunctory, or they can be life giving and life preserving. Rituals in worship are habits we practice that maintain and shape our identity. Such habits must not be perfunctory or poorly thought out. Our lives are literally at stake, so worship carefully.

Actions, though, are not isolated from other factors of identity. Rarely are actions merely individual acts; they are relational and engage us with other people. Actions reveal our commitments, and they partly determine our future, either opening or closing off new possibilities. Our actions will be the basis on which people evaluate us, trust us, and give opportunities to us. We are responsible for our actions, especially before God, and will give account for them.

Before we leave this focus on the necessity of actions shaping our identity, we should ask what pieces of our identity we must defend at all costs, and what may be given up. We will act to defend identity, and this causes issues at numerous levels. Most wars are fought to defend an identity. Racism has its roots in defending identity. Knowing we are not like others becomes a threat to our identity. But why should this be? Why are we so willing to belittle or mistreat others just because they are different? Does our stance betray egotism gone awry, a fragility of identity that is threatened by the least interference, or both? Why do we not tolerate difference better? But what about our identity should we defend, and how will we defend it? What will you do to defend your Christian identity, for that must be defended, and will your actions doing so remain Christian? It is an easy thing to try to defend Christianity with non-Christian actions.

The Relation of Faith and Works

Does Paul's discussion of faith and works undermine the necessity of actions? Did he not repeatedly write about salvation apart from works? Indeed he did, but *nothing* he said supports the suggestion that actions and obedience are unnecessary or irrelevant, even though people have wrongly concluded such things. Paul himself in Romans 3:8 acknowledges distortion of his words: "Why should we not say, as some slander us to say,

'Let's do evil that good things may happen,' of which the condemnation is just." James, of course, argues against the error of thinking faith can be unproductive, and surely he is reacting to a perversion of Paul's thought.

Three points need to be made about Paul's discussion of faith and works, which treats subjects far different from what people think. First, his understanding of faith is way more comprehensive and of a different character than is typically assumed. Second, his rejection of works is rejection of a specific kind of works and not a lessening of right actions. Third, Paul, like the rest of the New Testament, everywhere insists on a productive and active faith, one that demonstrates the character of Jesus Christ by its actions. Each of these points deserves attention.

Faith is not merely about thought and mental convictions; it is about *participation* with Christ, being grafted into him, and made one with him, part of his body. Faith is not mere thought but life, not mere thinking but being and *practices*. Yes, faith involves believing the facts about Jesus's life, death, and resurrection, but even more it is such a deep trust that it leads to a *living involvement* in those facts. For Paul faith is primarily understood as being *in Christ*. It is relational and participatory, for it is about living in covenant with the God revealed in Christ. Such a relation is not static or passive; it is life lived and determined by that relation, and this understanding of faith is what the whole of Scripture is about. This argument about the character of faith was laid out in our chapter on relations and does not need to be repeated here. Right thoughts are not faith, for a faith that is not lived is not faith. Paul was not attacking works in any way that would separate believing and doing. Obedience is an essential part of faith.

The Protestant Reformers, the very people many think were opposed to works, emphasized that faith must be performed. They were opposed to penance and the idea that one can purchase or earn salvation. They and theologians before them insisted that faith never comes alone; justifying faith is inherently active.[16] Luther is quite clear about this, saying things like "But he does not truly believe if works of love do not follow his faith,"[17]

---

16. See Stephen Chester, "Faith Working through Love (Galatians 5:6): The Role of Human Deeds in Salvation in Luther and Calvin's Exegesis," in Eklund and Phelan, *Doing Theology for the Church*, 41–54.

17. Martin Luther, "Lectures on Galatians 1535, Chapters 5–6; Lectures on Galatians

and "It is impossible to be a believer and not a doer."[18] John Calvin argued that faith is always joined to good works and that works are a condition of salvation.[19] The church needs to start emphasizing what the Reformers knew, that faith is participation with Christ, not thought about him, and no one can participate without acting. Such participation means having the attitudes Jesus teaches, doing the acts Jesus did, showing the compassion, grace, and moral integrity he did. It means being involved in the mission of Jesus regarding the kingdom of God, being a servant of and witness to the kingdom and the newness that the risen Christ brings.

With regard to the second point, the *works* Paul argues against, we are in the middle of the discussion of the "new perspective" on Paul, which stresses among other things that Paul was not arguing against salvation by works and Jews were not trying to be saved by works. The new perspective did not get everything right, but it forced a clearer explanation of what Paul argued against. First, one should realize that when Paul uses the plural "works," nearly always the word has a negative connotation.[20] For example, Romans 3:28 says, "We consider a person to be acquitted by faith apart from *works* of the law." However, when he uses the singular "work," nearly always the word has a positive connotation,[21] as in "Be steadfast, immovable, excelling always in the *work* of the Lord" (1 Cor. 15:58) or "that in everything, always, having enough of everything, you may have ample resources for every good *work*" (2 Cor. 9:8). The plural "works," either explicitly or implicitly, refers to "works of the law," not actions in general, while the singular "work" usually refers to the obedience God expects.

1519, Chapters 1–6," in *Luther's Works*, ed. Jaroslav Pelikan (St. Louis: Concordia, 1964), 27:30.

18. See "Cordatus' Controversy with Melanchthon," *Theological Quarterly* 11, no. 4 (1907): 193–207, here 199. He adds (200): "because faith is always operative, or it is not faith."

19. *Calvin's Commentaries: The Epistles of Paul the Apostle to the Galatians, Ephesians, Philippians, and Colossians*, trans. T. H. L. Parker (Grand Rapids: Eerdmans, 1965), 96 (on 5:6). See Chester, "Faith Working through Love," 48–49.

20. The exceptions are Rom. 2:6 (an Old Testament quotation) and, with the explicit addition that the works are good, Eph. 2:10; and a few times in the Pastoral Letters.

21. The only exceptions being 1 Cor. 5:2, which the context makes clear concerning the man committing incest, and 2 Tim. 4:18, which mentions "evil work."

The expression "works of the law" is used in refuting the arguments of the "Judaizers," people who were trying to force Jewish marks of separation on gentile Christians, especially circumcision, food laws, and Sabbath keeping. They argued that these "boundary markers"—works characterized by law—would give gentile believers the identity they needed. These boundary markers are Paul's primary concern with "works," but they are not his only concern. In Romans 4 Paul points to Abraham's salvation by faith, not works, but this happened for Abraham even before any command for circumcision or food laws was given. With "works of the law," therefore, we must think of any attempt to obtain standing before God or present oneself to God and others based on human action. It is the attempt to establish identity over against others by oneself, one's own heritage, status, or effort. It is an attempt to stand on one's own by striving after the law, as if doing certain acts gave you the identity you needed. No work, no matter how significant, is sufficient grounds to gain access to God, nor can any work be the *foundation* of your identity. The source and foundation of identity are in God, God's grace, and God's having created humans in his own image. You are a human because God says you are, not because you kept the rules, and this has enormous consequences for all kinds of issues. Still, if the grace of God gives an identity, largely by creating relation with God, does one have the identity if it is not expressed? Can one have an identity and not act in accord with that identity? Everything in Scripture or logic says otherwise. You do not become who God says you are merely because God said it. The reality must be accepted and lived.

Access to God is granted as a gift of grace, but neither Paul nor any other writer would think access to God was not itself transformative. Remember, for Paul grace is an enlivening power that enlists people in work with and for God (1 Cor. 15:10). Actions do shape identity, but they are not the foundation for the identity we need. That comes only by the grace of God who created us in his image, participated with us in the incarnation of Christ, and called us to live in relation with him, but we cannot live in relation with God without acting accordingly. Faith must be lived.

The problem Paul opposed, of course, is not the primary problem of the church today. People may sometimes still think they can do something to gain standing with God, but our problem is more that people do not think they need God at all or anything in relation to God, and that they can go on doing what they wish. But relation with God is crucial for life; yet an encounter with God that does not produce transformation of life is not truly an encounter with God. We should remind ourselves as well that judgment is always on the basis of works, the way one has lived.

A number of years ago there was a debate that was totally misguided— the Lordship debate.[22] People argued, as some had before, that you could take Jesus as Savior but not as Lord. Having Jesus as Lord was desirable and commendable but not necessary. Texts linking "Lord" and salvation like Romans 10:9 were understood as invoking Jesus's deity, not his role as Master. The argument has no basis and cannot derive from any honest reading of the New Testament. Jesus as "Savior" is not even the primary subject for most of the New Testament. The two most important christological confessions of the early church were "Jesus is Lord" and "Jesus is the Christ." "Savior" really was not *that* important a term, which is evidenced by the fact that the Greek word for Savior, *sōtēr*, occurs only twenty-four times in the New Testament, sixteen of which are in the Pastoral Letters, 2 Peter, and Jude. The verb form *sōzō* (save) occurs 106 times, and the noun *sōtēria* (salvation) forty-six, so salvation language is important. I am *not* saying salvation language is unimportant, but it is merely one way to talk about the significance of Christ's work. The real point is that to be drawn into the saving power of Jesus is to be drawn into his transforming power. You cannot have Jesus as Savior but not Lord. For those claiming to have faith, there is no escape from the importance and necessity of living according to the Lord in whom they have faith. The short of this is that the faith-works discussion is largely a waste of time. Faith works or it is not faith. You will work, but from what identity?

As for how sin affects the conversation about faith and works, sin is still a reality for Christians, but Christians are people who do not take sin for granted, are alert to its presence both in themselves and in the community, and deal with it both to avoid its fragmenting power and to undo its effect.

22. For a summary of the debate, see Millard J. Erickson, "Lordship Theology: The Current Controversy," *Southwestern Journal of Theology* 33 (1991): 5–15, or Randall C. Gleason, "The Lordship Salvation Debate," *Evangelical Review of Theology* 27 (2003): 55–72.

For the third point, as already indicated, Paul, like the rest of the New Testament, everywhere insists on a *productive and active faith*. Paul's emphasis on action, obedience to the will of God, is no occasional topic, touched on by a few verses. It is the assumption and emphasis of every letter he writes.

Any thought of passivity is excluded. Paul's letters provide for his communities the theological basis and motivation that kick people out of inactivity and direct action in positive ways toward the good. For example, he urges people to present themselves as a living sacrifice to God, which is their logical/spiritual service, and that they stop being conformed to this world but continually be renewed so they can discern what is God's good, pleasing, and complete will (Rom. 12:2; see Eph. 4:17). One can deny the ethical necessity of Paul's letters only by ignoring huge chunks of every letter, not merely the recognized "ethical" sections of the letters but also the prayers and doxologies with which they start and much of the "theological" sections as well.

If we use Philippians as a test case, of the 104 verses in the letter, at least 56 have to do with ethical action expected of believers. In short, Christians are asked to live in a way worthy of the gospel of Christ (1:27); the same point is made explicitly at Ephesians 4:1, Colossians 1:10, and 1 Thessalonians 2:12. All of Paul's letters evidence such a focus on action.

We do not begin by grace and then, having been given salvation, live from our own efforts. In Galatians 3:1–6 Paul flatly rejects such an idea when he asks, "Having begun by the Spirit, are you now completed by the flesh?" With "by the flesh" he means "by that which is merely human." The way we enter into life with God—by grace and the working of God's Spirit—is the way we continue. Christian faith is always about participating with God in whatever we do. We never go it alone.

Nor does a focus on action have anything to do with legalism. You can keep rules, but doing so will never make you ethical and certainly will not grant freedom, which for Paul is the summation of what life in Christ is about. Nor did Paul have a negative view of the law. The law could be twisted and made a servant of sin, but the law itself is good and holy and is summed up in the love commands (Rom. 7:12–13; 13:8–10). But the obligation to moral action was not in some external law (which the Torah was never intended to be since it was about covenant with God—participating in life with God). Moral obligation comes from one's identity in Christ,[23] from one's new geography in Christ, and not from any action you do on your own. Living in accord with identity in Christ leads to morality, if identity is properly understood, and it grants maximal freedom.

The focus on a productive and active faith is evident as well in the blend between the indicative and the imperative (between statements and commands; "you are, now do"), which is frequent in New Testament writings, especially Paul's. The purpose of the indicative statements is to give understanding, to shape our minds to grasp what is true about God and ourselves, and the purpose of the commands is to move that understanding into life and action. Our identity is determined by such lived thought, and authenticity depends on thought and action matching well. Our attitudes about sexuality, possessions, the poor, etc., are not mere ideas; they are part of a coherent whole displaying our true identity. Authenticity results when indicative and imperative are put together. The grace statement of identity comes first, but then you are called to live out that identity. Faith is the act of living out the identity God says you have by grace, but what God says is not reality unless it is appropriated. You can still reject what God says about you and be diminished, but faith takes hold of Christ and life is transformed by God's Spirit. The imperative is a necessary and essential component. Unless the identity is lived out, it is not real. Relation with Jesus produces action; how could it be otherwise?

People want to ask how much is God's part and how much is our part. Wrong question! The idea of life apart from God is already an error, and there is no thought of action apart from our relation to God. This is not about establishing a relation with God but about living because of and in response to that relation. It is about participation with God. Even giving yourself to God is not an independent act. All such acts are done in relation with God through the agency of the Holy Spirit; they are not independent human acts. The error of much human thought is in thinking we do our acts alone. Instead, in all we do we have to do with God. Even responding to God is a God-assisted act.

---

23. See Halvor Moxnes, "Asceticism and Christian Identity in Antiquity: A Dialogue with Foucault and Paul," *Journal for the Study of the New Testament* 26 (2003): 3–29, especially 25–28.

The Relation of Being, Thinking, and Doing

Why do we tear being, thinking, and doing apart? Is it because actually keeping them together is hard work? Do we tear them apart because keeping them together requires self-analysis and forces us to deal with the various selves clamoring for attention and license? Is our own self-defense at stake because doing what we know we should do will not allow laziness and mere self-gratification, and the failure to do what we should do is self-indicting? Are we more content with the illusion of being? Appearance is easier than being a person of substance. In the attempt to avoid doing what we know we should, we persuade ourselves little by little that what would be right for others does not really apply in our case. We are content with having fooled others that we are thoughtful and moral, not with actually being thoughtful and moral. But looking good is not good enough.

Being precedes thinking and doing, but being can hardly be described in the abstract, other than the affirmation that a person exists. To say more we must immediately speak of where this being fits and what it does—how it relates to persons, places, and things, and what acts it performs. Meaningful human existence includes consciousness, that a person is aware mentally, analyzing and responding. Thinking drives life, which is the reason for the huge focus in Scripture on the mind and for the importance of theology, not as some abstract discussion but as an understanding of what faith is about and how it is lived. But life and faith are about how thinking and actions cohere, how our understanding of truth leads to specific *actions*.

On the other hand, the process of being, thinking, and doing is not so simple. Rather than a straight line from being to thinking to doing, there are conflicting desires and thoughts, often undetected, vying for dominance, and often derailing good intent. A constant conversation buzzes in our brains, even if we are unaware of it, and the inclination is to affirm the thoughts that enhance our own pleasure and self-image. Perhaps we do not so much tear thinking and doing apart as affirm one line of thought as good but implement another that is thought to be to our advantage, even though it is the opposite of the good. Thoughts, temptations, and feelings may impact our identity, but what we do with them is what really counts. You are what you *do*. You are not your temptations or even what you feel. This is crucial for those with addiction or wrong kinds of sexual attraction. Such cravings and attraction do not have to be an identity.

There is tension here, for we are tempted to do what is not us, to not be ourselves, the selves God created. At some level we choose our identity because we choose our actions from the options available to us. We choose to enact what we value and not to enact what violates our values, at times rejecting even part of ourselves because we know those parts go against God's intent. Unfortunately, sometimes we reject the very part of ourselves in line with God's intent and choose to go our own way to our own loss. The key question is whether we actually *want* what God intends or whether we want our own agenda. Every rejection of sin involves such a choice. Action involves both choosing for and choosing against. Identity acts, but not all aspects of identity are to be acted out. Some parts of our identity we reject in order to affirm and enact other parts. We have all kinds of desires—pieces of our identity—that will destroy our true identity if acted out.

One focus of the Dallas Holocaust Museum is on three young men who, with only a lantern, one pistol, and four pairs of pliers, stopped the twentieth train transporting Jews from Belgium. They enabled 231 Jews to escape, and *all* survived the Holocaust. Youra Livchitz, one of the three, commented, "The finest of all human struggles is against what we are and for what we should become."

That is commentary on Jesus's instruction to deny self, take up a cross, and follow him. The desire to keep being, thinking, and doing together is not with regard to all thinking but with regard to correct thinking that affirms what is right, chooses it, and pursues it. This requires a brutal honesty with ourselves, the willingness to face what is wrong with ourselves, especially our self-centeredness and distorted ego. It also requires a strong executive self that is committed to the right, rejects wrong thinking and motives, and chooses what is right, even if it is at some cost. It requires a determined commitment to truth and fulfilling what it means to be in the image of God. If you are not willing to obey the truth, you will never understand the truth. Often we must choose not to be who we easily could be. Christians believe that the Spirit of God is heavily engaged in the whole process enabling us to be who God says we are. Our identity in Christ is in front of us calling us beyond what we presently are. If you are to become who God says you are—or should be—you must be willing to change, to stop being the false you in order to be the real you. You get your real identity by giving up the false one you have. That is what passages on discipleship, conversion, and dying and rising with Christ are really about.

Clearly knowing right and doing right are two different things, and if right thinking is not acted upon, it is not really believed. Action establishes the validity of thought and the depth of conviction. Action does not have to be chronologically later than thinking. Nor is there a necessary sequence from thinking to doing. There is a reciprocal action. Sometimes we act intuitively and come to understanding in the process. Actions do structure our brain. In fact, most of the time we act first and then learn; we form identity from doing. Certainly this is the way children learn.

Having a positive identity presupposes values around which life is organized. The tragedy, though, is that many abort the thinking process that determines and chooses values. They so quickly mute any thought that is not about self-enhancement and self-amusement that any option for positive identity construction is lost. Entertainment is the goal of our society, but it is addictive, numbing, and in the end devaluing. Entertainment as the goal is an anesthetic, dulling the pain of superficiality and meaninglessness. It will make life one big compromise that never achieves worthy goals.

Not Just Any Action

Of course, not all actions are good. Actions can be compromised or just plain sin. They can proceed from wrong motives; they can be an attempt to prove oneself illegitimately; they can be destructive or legalistic; they can be an attempt to deceive or impress others, to draw attention to oneself; or they can be self-centered, the essence of sin. I say again, the person who lives for himself or herself lives for a fool. Actions can be merely frenetic and neither motivated by nor productive of love. If we are Christian, for all the need to establish and take care of ourselves, our actions must be in communion with God and motivated for neighbor. Our actions are guided by the two great commands—love of God and love of neighbor.

Still, life is messy. We know that sometimes people have no choice in their choices; they are forced into actions by violence or circumstances beyond their control. How much capacity do we have for choices then, and how do we navigate truly tricky situations? There are no easy answers, but the issue always is how one lives out a Christ identity and expresses faith in action (Gal. 5:6) in a sinful world. Even where circumstances beyond our control force something on our identity, this does not change the reality that the only ultimate determiner of our identity is who God says we are.

Sin is about wrong action, action contrary to God and destructive of self and neighbor. Sin *is* the abuse of power, and you do have power, more than you know. What will you do with your power? Will it result in good action that develops identity or wrong action destructive of life itself?

Judgment

There is another reason to focus on actions. We will be held responsible for what we do. No one wants to think about God judging us, but without judgment life is meaningless. We want a God who loves but makes no demands. God is indeed love, but love itself demands because it cares, a point made by C. S. Lewis long ago.[24] We expect more from people we love, for we care about them. God is the same. The God of the Bible cares about us, and the God of the Bible has demands for the people he created in his own image.

Unlike previous generations, few churches now even mention judgment. Earlier generations sometimes had a distorted and exaggerated view of judgment, and no one should go back to that approach. Scripture is much more cautious about the character of judgment, even while emphasizing its seriousness. Still, judgment is the consistent focus of Scripture, nowhere more than with Jesus's own teaching. If there is no judgment, no one needs salvation. Wherever judgment is treated, it is always according to works; it is an evaluation of what one did, not the facts one believed.

24. C. S. Lewis, *The Problem of Pain* (New York: Macmillan, 1962), 45–48.

The judgment scene in Matthew 25:31–46 is a classic text on the subject. Some attempt to avoid what is obvious in this text—that judgment is about how identity was revealed in actions, not by what someone claimed—but the attempts will not work.[25] Matthew has a judgment focus at the end of each of his five discourses, and 25:31–46 at the end of the fifth discourse is the climax of Jesus's teaching. The concern of this passage is to stress the importance of mercy and love reflecting God's own character. We will be judged on how we reflected God's character, the very purpose for which we were created. You will not be judged compassionate because you gave to a compassion charity; you will be judged compassionate if you lived compassion, which will include your giving but is much more. You are not ethical because you studied ethics and like to talk about ethics. This only produces Kierkegaard's "professor." You are ethical only if you live ethically.

To think that one can claim Christian faith and still live from greed or envy, practice sexual sin and covetousness, or express oneself with anger and ill will is sheer delusion. Further, we are directed to do everything in word and work "in the name of the Lord Jesus" (Col. 3:17), which is to say in keeping with who he is and what he has accomplished, and in whatever we do to work from the depths of our being (literally "the soul") as to the Lord and not to humans (3:23). Life in Christ involves work, and passivity is not allowed. If you are not working for Christ in some sense, you are not a Christian. If you take the gift, you get the Giver, and he will not leave you alone. He will change you, and he will give you good work. What else could "Jesus is Lord" mean?

Actions, good actions, are crucial for your well-being. You will never be happy without something important to do, some sense of usefulness. You will never be happy without love of other people (and that does not mean without sexual love). Love is not merely a feeling. Love is an action—a choice to care, to commit, to enjoy, to help and support others in the face of problems, to seek solutions, and to remain faithful even if there are no solutions. Our lives are too often marked by indifference or a halfhearted concern that knows something should be done but does not

---

25. See my *Stories with Intent: A Comprehensive Guide to the Parables of Jesus* (Grand Rapids: Eerdmans, 2008), 551–63.

engage. Action is the only remedy for indifference and abortive concern.[26] Action kicks us out of our complacency.

In the end judgment will be an assessment of identity. In effect, God will ask, "Who are you and how did you show it?" Were you who God intended *you* to be? You will not be measured by someone else. The question is *you*. An ancient rabbi, Rabbi Zusya, realized this and said, "In the world to come I shall not be asked: 'Why were you not Moses?' I shall be asked: 'Why were you not Zusya?'"[27]

Søren Kierkegaard said the life of the rigorously religious person is essentially action,[28] but it is not just the *rigorously* religious. This is true of everyone, even if it is especially true of the religious. Life is about doing—rightly understood. Who you are is shown in your actions, and being who God says you are will mean that your actions demonstrate a God-determined character. There is no thought of either perfectionism, of proving yourself, or of actions required only of the "spiritual." There is no loss of a focus on grace; grace is the power driving the actions of a Christian's life. For Christians passivity is not an option. Act and show who you really are.

26. Note Elie Wiesel's comment in his Nobel Prize acceptance speech: "And action is the only remedy for indifference: the most insidious danger of all" (*Night with Connections* [Austin: Holt, Rinehart, and Winston, 1988], 190).

27. See Martin Buber, *The Way of Man according to the Teachings of the Hasidim* (London: Routledge and Kegan Paul, 1950), 18.

28. Søren Kierkegaard, *For Self-Examination; Judge for Yourself!*, ed. and trans. Howard V. Hong and Edna H. Hong (Princeton: Princeton University Press, 1990), 11.

FACTOR 7

You Are Your Boundaries

Without boundaries we can know what we fight against, but not what we fight for. The absence of boundaries creates nonorder, which is the end of life.

—Miroslav Volf, *Exclusion and Embrace*

Your identity travels more than you do. Protect it.

—Ad for an identity-protection firm

"Good fences make good neighbors." "Something there is that doesn't love a wall."[1] Both statements occur in Robert Frost's poem "Mending Wall," which describes Frost (or an "I") repairing a wall with his neighbor. Frost seems not so sure about walls and wonders what he is walling in and walling out. The contrast between the two statements points to both the positive and negative aspects of boundaries. We need boundaries, but wrongly understood, they diminish life. Life is about boundaries, but it is also about seeking intimacy and relations despite our boundaries.

Identity is established by difference, by recognizing what we are and what we are not, and that is based on boundaries, whether geographical,

1. Robert Frost, "Mending Wall," in *Modern American Poetry: An Introduction*, ed. Louis Untermeyer (New York: Harcourt, Brace and Howe, 1919), 81.

social, religious, occupational, or other. I am me, not you. I am human, not God. Identifying others or oneself is a means of differentiation, and at the boundary between what we are and what we are not we know who we are.[2]

The first thing God did was create boundaries separating the land from the sea and the light from the dark, between species after their kind, and between male and female. God's choosing Israel was about boundaries. The law at Sinai was about boundaries, marking off the distinction between God and humanity and marking off boundaries dealing with spirituality and worship, time, property, life, and relations. The tabernacle and the temple were symbols of God's presence, but they also marked boundaries. God was in the midst of his people, but boundaries still limited access. Pantheism attempts to remove the boundaries between God and his creation. Mysticism attempts to remove the boundaries between God and the individual. God may be one with us, but God is neither contained by nor identified with creation or an individual. God is a distinct being who existed before creation and can exist without creation. God certainly exists apart from any particular person. God is not what we are, even though we are created in God's image, and humans can never attain to or fully understand God. The boundary between God and humanity cannot be breached from the human side, but it has been breached by Jesus Christ in the incarnation.

We May Not Like It, but We Need Boundaries

Being is a process of recognizing and establishing some boundaries and of removing others, and life is about negotiating boundaries. Bodies are boundaries and are not to be violated. Parenting is often teaching about boundaries and the process of negotiation of boundaries in transition. Elderly people often become cantankerous because they are trying to

---

2. Mikael Tellbe, "The Prototypical Christ-Believer: Early Christian Identity Formation in Ephesus," in *Exploring Early Christian Identity*, ed. Bengt Holmberg, Wissenschaftliche Untersuchungen zum Neuen Testament 226 (Tübingen: Mohr Siebeck, 2008), 115–38, here 121. See Richard Jenkins, *Social Identity*, 4th ed. (London: Routledge, 2014), 105: "Similarity and difference reflect each other across a shared boundary. At the boundary we discover what we are in what we are not, and *vice versa*."

defend the few boundaries they have left. Marriage and sexual intercourse both are a merging of boundaries. To think one can merge such boundaries with any and every person is as ill-founded as to think one is universal and can merge with any and all gods. All relations involve overlapping or sharing of boundary edges, but that is quite different from boundary merging. With marriage two people invite each other into full sharing of boundaries in a way not accessible to others. Sexual intercourse is a physical and psychic expression of that full sharing of boundaries.

"No boundaries" is a nice slogan[3] but a huge illusion, and the people using the slogan would not want literally to live without boundaries. The slogan, of course, seeks to avoid limitations and life-denying restrictions, but where would we be without proper restrictions? Not just anyone is allowed to practice medicine, administer an MRI, or perform a host of other actions, and we don't want them to. Nor do we want people violating our own boundaries. All of us have a sense of personal space and are offended if someone violates that space. We may welcome people into our homes, but we will be offended if they investigate our closets. Our sense of personal space may be different for family and close friends, but it is still operative.

Even though we imagine we do not like boundaries, we cannot live without them. We need boundaries, and we are better off when they are made explicit. Some boundaries are negative; some are positive; some are set for us; and some we set for ourselves. Relations and commitments create boundaries. In addition, all of us have an innate need to distinguish ourselves from others, to show we are not our parents, our siblings, or our friends. Distinguishing ourselves creates boundaries, and it establishes identity.

Life is about finding where our boundaries are—boundaries between parent and child, boundaries marking danger, boundaries where businesses help or violate each other, and boundaries respecting other people and their property and freedom. People of integrity are people who respect the boundaries of other people. We learn we cannot just do what we want with other people's lives and possessions.

3. The slogan is the name of a clothing company and of various sporting or teaching efforts.

If you do not learn to set and negotiate boundaries, you cannot succeed in life, for life is largely about boundary negotiation. Will boundaries be observed and respected or moved and violated? The Old Testament frequently castigates those who move literal boundary stones (for example, Deut. 19:14), which was an ancient way of cheating your neighbor. Violating boundaries is still a way of cheating our neighbors. Our safety and enjoyment depend on our boundaries being observed. We put boundaries around people we do not trust—either literally in prisons or figuratively in not welcoming them. In the process we also put boundaries around ourselves. One has only to think of the wall separating Israel from the Palestinians to know that walls meant to protect also limit.

Groups to which we belong, some by default and some by choice, are about boundaries and convey identity. We all belong to multiple groups where we live, work, or play. Groups are defined by common geography, common goals or vision, common language, common commitments and practices, common relations, and common experiences. Such shared realities mark boundaries and give a sense of group identity. People are seen as positive or negative representatives of their groups, and leaders especially are to embody the chief characteristics of their groups.

Groups have implicit and explicit rules for admission, and all groups require decisions about boundaries. Who gets in, and what must one do or not do to stay in? What distinguishes this group from another? The more exclusive the group, the more specific the markers indicating the boundaries. Military groups and elite schools seek to establish a corporate sense of identity via codes of conduct, uniforms, songs, teams, and discipline. Where individuals do not identify with the sense of identity and the authority of the institution to shape identity, the positive benefit of the group is diminished.

Boundaries—Christian Style

If this is true, the obvious question is: What does the church do—or fail to do—to establish boundaries that create a corporate sense of identity? Boundaries for the church should allow easy access, but if the church does not have positive boundaries, boundaries that create a difference in identity, the church cannot be effective and has little right to exist. Can the church be the church without an awareness that it communicates an identity marked by boundaries, boundaries that must be maintained but not boundaries that exclude without due cause? All are invited, but staying in will mean a redefinition of identity, and that means a change of boundaries.

As indicated in the chapter entitled "Faith Transforms Identity," much of the Bible is about boundaries—a boundary around one tree in Eden, a boundary around Mount Sinai, boundaries in the tabernacle and temple, boundaries between those who serve God and those who do not. The people of Israel had a clearly defined group identity based in their history, the importance of their land, and their covenant with God. They were to be different, and the boundaries, particularly the ethical boundaries and boundaries of ritual purity and impurity, marked their difference. Scripture focuses on boundaries to indicate what is or is not legitimate, what must be honored, and what must be rejected. Who are the elect? What about the others? Do gentiles belong?

Boundaries are a key focus in the New Testament as well, but the understanding of boundaries is radically different. Every city and religion in the ancient world had a temple or multiple temples with priests and/or priestesses and sacrifices. Temples marked boundaries and had restrictions about access and activities. Temples served not only for worship and sacrifice but also as financial institutions and sanctuaries in which people could find refuge. Temples were not to be violated. The early church must have seemed strange to nonbelievers, for it had no temples, no priests/priestesses, and no sacrifices. The boundaries of place, access to God, and restrictions on who could serve were gone, but ethical boundaries were heightened.

The early church knew it had a common geography—not in *a* place, but because of believers' common existence *in* Christ. Boundaries establish rights and privileges, and being within the boundaries of Christ conveyed to believers adoption into the family of God, salvation, the Spirit, engagement with God and community, and purpose, and it also defined the boundaries within which people were to live. What if we took seriously the point made in the chapter on relations, that we live *in Christ*? What if we had some sense that the character of Christ set the boundaries for our own lives? This is indeed what Christianity is supposed to mean. Conversion is a change of boundaries, so that life is not hemmed in by our own self-centeredness but is set within boundaries that fit the character of Christ.

That new "geography" with its redrawn boundaries gave the early Christians common goals, *some* common commitments and practices, common language about their religious experience, *some* common relations, and *some* common experiences. For all their unity, there were still plenty of differences in their identities. They were one in the body of Christ, but there was still the separate identity of their local group and of their individual identity. As a group they belonged to Christ, but the individual members belonged to other groups as well—families, neighborhoods, work groups or guilds, and many more. Group identity does not obliterate subgroup and individual identities. Gentile Christians in Corinth were not the same as gentile Christians in Rome or Jewish Christians in Jerusalem. Slave Christians were one in Christ with their owners—at least theoretically—but slave Christians belonged to a group the owners did not and vice versa, and Paul was not Apollos. Obviously to speak of boundaries and identity requires that we recognize multiple overlapping boundaries that make up our identity. Which boundaries are really essential to who we are as Christians, and which are incidental and could be changed without real loss, or which are a violation of the character of Christ and must be rejected?

A *Christian* understanding of boundaries involves both *boundaries of inclusion and boundaries of exclusion.* Some things must be embraced, for they are foundational to identity, some realities must be welcomed in, and some things must be excluded. Some boundaries must be obliterated, and some boundaries must be reinforced.

Identity is determined by boundaries that mark our existence and set it off from all other people, and foundational for Christians is a baptismal identity. Baptism is a redrawing of boundaries. In baptism we are given a new identity. An old identity is displaced and a new one forms around a new defining center, Jesus Christ. Baptism is "a ritual setting aside of ordinary identity."[4] Rituals are a way of granting entry into a group and show-

4. Christiaan Mostert, "Christian Identity as Baptismal Identity," in *Christian Identity,*

ing that one belongs. Baptism does that and more. Baptism sets a seal on us (2 Cor. 1:22; Eph. 1:13), indicating that we are God's property, and it sets a boundary around us. Yet, as true as the new baptismal identity is, parts of the old identity still remain, even though they are redefined.

We do not all have, nor do we need, a cataclysmic conversion experience, but we do need experiences that set down boundaries to which we keep returning to remember who we are. A Christian understanding of conversion requires a complete reevaluation of one's previous way of life, not its eradication. Despite what people say, with conversion not everything is new. Many of our boundaries do not change and are not specifically Christian. Even though they may be redefined, your body, relations, history, commitments, and locale may all stay the same in distinguishing you from other people. A Christian understanding of boundaries realizes that one boundary trumps all others, redefines them, recontextualizes them, and may obliterate them or establish them, depending on what the boundary is. The boundary of being "in Christ" is the *salient* reality, the one that redefines and regulates all other boundaries. This is the boundary that really counts. The New Testament spends a great deal of time explaining what does or does not fit in that boundary; this is the focus of the virtue and vice lists in the New Testament (such as Gal. 5:19–23). Sexual sin, anger, and the like do not fit, whereas love, peace, and the like do.[5]

Your body is still the first boundary defining you, but as a Christian your body is recontextualized—boundaried by Christ—and reinterpreted. It is not merely yours, but as a temple of God has a double ownership. It belongs to God and is only secondarily yours, and it requires even stronger boundary care than before. Who is allowed to influence your boundaries, and what is allowed within your boundaries? The materialistic assumptions and sexual practices of our society are an assault on our boundaries, and they lead to disaster and violation of God's intent.

Christ redefines boundaries regarding people as well. Groups seek value and honor for themselves, often claiming that outsiders are inferior and insiders superior, as religion, clanishness, and racism have always

---

ed. Eduardus Van der Borght, Studies in Reformed Theology 16 (Leiden: Brill, 2008), 51–65, here 63, quoting Rowan Williams.

5. There is such a thing as righteous anger, rare though it may be.

done. Being in Christ does not eliminate groups or even seeking value and honor, but it redefines boundaries for groups and redefines value and honor and removes the idea that value and honor are found at the expense of other groups. On the contrary, Christians have an investment in the value and honor of other groups. All such boundaries of identity are reframed.

Language marks a boundary that creates and maintains identity. I may have German ancestry, but since German is not my mother tongue, it is unlikely anyone will believe I am a German. Majority groups throughout history have tried to eliminate the identity of minority groups by eliminating their language or not allowing it to be used in schools or public settings. If you want to crush a group's identity, crush its language. This is most evident in the attempt to delete Native American languages. Some attempts to delete a language are understandable reactions against injustice, such as the attempt of the African National Congress in South Africa to prohibit the use of Afrikaans, the traditional language of the whites, but obliterating a language is not a justifiable way to deal with evil.

Not merely the common language of a group creates boundaries, but specific self-designations or "insider" language—whether professional groups, groups of common interest, or otherwise—are boundary markers as well. Language used for self-designation or group description creates boundaries and therefore identity. We define ourselves by what we say about ourselves—and others. Defining them defines us.

The early Christians had language that marked their new identity. They spoke of "outsiders," people who did not have faith (Col. 4:5; 1 Thess. 4:12). Christians saw themselves as a separate group. Faith created an essential boundary of difference, but not a boundary of exclusion. The term "outsiders" was not used because of fear or rejection but because of awareness of a different identity and the need to influence, attract, and demonstrate a commendable difference. Gentile believers were formerly labeled gentiles, but in Christ they were labeled differently and told not to live like gentiles—even though they were gentiles (Eph. 4:17)!

Other terms in the New Testament for Christians include "brothers and sisters," "the elect," "holy ones," "the Way," and "believers." Such terms are in-group language and were ways early Christians identified them-selves.[6] Such language today sounds archaic and worn out, but most of these terms were quite *novel* expressions in the early church.[7] Family terms like "brothers and sisters" created new boundaries for inclusion, closeness, and belonging. "Believers"/"the ones believing" especially was a technical term for Christians and served as a boundary term for identity. These early Christians knew that their trust in Christ changed their iden-tity. The label "holy ones," which has often been translated misleadingly as "saints," designated *those whom God has set apart for himself.* They are people around whom God has set a boundary, for they belong to God. Such self-designations express a new understanding of identity. What language should Christians today use to create and maintain identity, which at the same time would be clear and inviting and not presumptuous or arrogant?

Early church confessions functioned as boundary markers and indica-tors of identity. In effect people said, "We believe these things, not those things, and that determines who we are. We are not like other people who believe other things. If you are going to be part of us, you need to affirm these essential beliefs and have your identity shaped by such beliefs." See, for example, the emphasis in 1 John on the necessity of affirming Jesus as the Christ, the Son of God who has come in the flesh (2:22–23; 4:2–3, and 15), but note throughout this letter the stronger insistence on action backing up the confession. Designations of boundaries showing commendable difference must not be mere labels or illusions.

A good deal of the discussion in the early church was about boundary markers relating to ethnicity, primarily boundaries between Jews and gentiles. For Jews, being part of the people of God meant being Jewish or becoming a proselyte to Judaism, and boundaries were set up to dif-ferentiate from and negotiate dealings with non-Jews. Detailed regula-

6. See Paul Trebilco, *Self-Designations and Group Identity in the New Testament* (Cam-bridge: Cambridge University Press, 2012).

7. See Trebilco, *Self-Designations and Group Identity*, 65–66, 70–71, 79–80, 89–90, 118–20, 160–61. "The elect," of course, is a term borrowed from Judaism. The others men-tioned are not. Note Trebilco's comment (p. 300): "When early Christians called them-selves 'brothers and sisters,' 'the believers,' or 'the holy ones,' they were creating and shaping their identity and their ongoing life as well as reflecting their experience of what was significant for them."

tions specify what kinds of products could be bought from non-Jews or whether a non-Jewish wet-nurse could be used.[8] In rabbinic material Jews are the elect and other nations are as nothing,[9] and gentile groups are just as disparaging of Jews, both examples showing how horribly group identity can be practiced at the expense of others. It is easy to set restrictions on outsiders or even to have one set of rules for insiders and another for outsiders. Ancient societies were hierarchical, as is ours, and people marked themselves off from those deemed different or beneath them. Texts like Colossians 3:11 with its setting aside of labels like Greek, Jew, barbarian, Scythian, slave, and free are testimony to ancient illegitimate boundaries and the church's rejection of them.

Jewish law-keeping was about boundary maintenance. As we saw earlier, the "new perspective" on Paul argued that his discussion of works was about the boundary markers of circumcision, food laws, and Sabbath keeping that distinguished Jews from gentiles. That is too narrow an understanding of Paul's intent with "works," but at least such boundary markers were classic examples of what he had in mind—any attempt to establish relation with God and distinction from others based on birth, status, effort, or accomplishment. The boundary markers were a way for Jews to say, "We are different, distinguished by our conduct, and not like the sinners of the world."

Illegitimate Boundaries Removed by Christ

With Christ the boundary between Jews and gentiles was set aside. If Christ's death and resurrection had created unity in the body of Christ, then such boundaries could no longer exist. Gentiles were still gentiles and Jews were still Jews, but the boundary between their relations and any ideas of superiority were removed. This conclusion was *not* reached easily, and most New Testament books treat the relation of Jews and gentiles in some way. The book of Acts relates numerous steps along the way as conclusions about ethnicity were drawn, most notably with

8. For example, see Tosefta Abodah Zara, especially 2:5–4:13.
9. For example, Numbers Rabbah 1.4; 4.1; Song of Songs Rabbah 7.8.

Stephen's speech (ch. 7), the account of Peter's forced rethinking with the Cornelius event (chs. 10–11), the Jerusalem Council (ch. 15), and Paul's travels, arrest, and trial (chs. 9, 11, and 13–28).

Paul's letters addressed problems in churches resulting from the failure to understand boundaries. People thought the old boundaries between Jews and gentiles or between honor and shame were still operative. They did not understand the significance of their new, redrawn boundaries in Christ. Especially in Galatians the issues of identity and boundaries are paramount. Is identity established and maintained by the boundary markers of circumcision, food laws, and Sabbath keeping, or is it established by Christ? Can Jews and gentiles eat at the same table? Are gentiles acceptable as gentiles? Paul sought to help people understand that the gospel creates a whole new understanding of boundaries. Nowhere is this more evident than in the conclusion to the baptismal formula in Galatians 3:26–28: "There is neither Jew nor Greek, there is neither slave nor free, there is not male and female, for you all are one in Christ Jesus." The reality of being Jew or Greek, slave or free, male or female remained, but the boundaries and valuations had lost their power to exclude or demean. In Christ these different groups had been united.

The odd thing about this whole discussion is that Paul and other New Testament writers wanted to bring gentiles into relation with the *Jewish* God. For them "Gentile Christians somehow belonged inside Israel while staying outside Judaism."[10] Gentiles did not need to become Jewish proselytes to be included in the promises to Abraham (see Gal. 3:7–14). The Jewish boundary had been leveled, even while Jewish identity remained.

Perhaps no text is so explicitly about boundaries as Ephesians 2:11–22:

Therefore, remember that once you were Gentiles in the flesh, those called "uncircumcision" by those called "the circumcision," but it was merely a circumcision in the flesh and done by human hands. You

10. Bengt Holmberg, "Early Christian Identity—Some Conclusions," in *Exploring Early Christian Identity*, ed. Holmberg, 173–78, here 175. See also William S. Campbell, *Paul and the Creation of Christian Identity*, Library of New Testament Studies 322 (London: T. & T. Clark, 2008), 54: "Paul was seeking to relate gentile Christ followers positively to the traditions of Israel and yet attempting, nevertheless, to prevent them becoming proselytes to Judaism."

were at that time without Christ, alienated from the commonwealth of Israel and strangers of the covenants of promise, not having hope and in the world without God. But now in Christ Jesus you who were once far off have been brought near by the blood of Christ. For he is our peace, the one who made both groups one and destroyed in his own flesh the divisive barrier, the hostility [between the groups]. He nullified the law characterized by commandments with ordinances so that he might create in himself one new being, making peace, and that he might reconcile both groups in one body to God through the cross, by which he eliminated [literally "killed"] the hostility. And when he came, he preached peace to you who were far off and peace to those who were near, because through him we both have access by one Spirit to the Father. Therefore, you are no longer strangers and foreigners, but you are fellow citizens with God's people and members in God's household. You are built on the foundation of the apostles and prophets, of which Christ Jesus himself is the chief cornerstone. On him the whole building is joined together and grows into a holy temple in the Lord, and on him also you are being built by the Spirit into a dwelling of God.

Boundaries dominate the text: the classification as gentiles, the name-calling "uncircumcised" by those who call themselves "the circumcision," the ideas of "alienated," "without God," "far," "divisive barrier, the hostility between the groups," and "foreigners and strangers." Just as present are expressions setting aside the divisions such as "near," "peace," "eliminated the hostility," "access," "reconciliation," "one body," and "members of God's household." This text may allude to the famous barrier in the temple of Jerusalem intended to keep gentiles out of the inner area where the important sacrificial activities took place. Gentiles could frequent the temple area Herod had enlarged, but they could not enter the enclosure that held the temple itself. Warnings in Latin and Greek were placed along the barrier threatening death to gentiles who entered the inner compound. Of course, the temple had other barriers that prevented Jews themselves from proceeding too far, with the holy of holies being accessible only to the high priest on the Day of Atonement. *The point of this and other texts is that the boundaries of exclusion are obliterated, and all are granted access to God and to the family of God, and all are bound together in Christ into a new unity.*

The whole point of the text is that *all* the *illegitimate* boundaries, all the separation and hostility, between people and between people and God have been set aside because of Christ's work. The crucial boundary was the boundary between people and God, but it is removed in Christ. A double reconciliation has taken place—reconciliation vertically with God and reconciliation horizontally with other people. Those distant and outside the boundaries have been brought inside and made one with God and his people, part of the family of God. In both directions access has been granted, hostility has been destroyed, peace has been created, and unity has been established. Those who were foreigners and did not belong have been made family members, people who belong to God and who serve as a dwelling for God. One can no longer live as if boundaries still excluded one from God or from other people in Christ. The unity is lived.

The New Testament's rejection of *ethnic* boundary markers is a major focus and one of its most important teachings. At the same time, ethnicity is an unavoidable identity factor for all of us. In fact, ethnicity is for most *the* largest identity determiner, even though Christianity rejects the dominance of ethnicity. If we do not recognize ethnicity, we may well devalue people, but if we define people in terms of ethnicity, we inevitably set distinctions between insiders and outsiders. Ethnic distinctions may legitimately be recognized, but they must not be allowed to be the basis of denigration and exclusion. Christians must not erect boundaries that diminish and exclude people. They should always be willing to embrace all people, even their enemies.[11]

The issue is what *really* determines your identity and reveals your boundaries—faith in Christ or your nationality and ethnicity? Are you more American—or whatever nationality you are—or Christian? More African American, Latino/a, Asian, white, or Christian? Tragically, for most of us ethnicity trumps faith; we just assume our ethnicity takes priority, but it must not for Christians. The failure of Christians to sub-

11. Language made popular by Miroslav Volf's *Exclusion and Embrace: An Exploration of Identity, Otherness, and Reconciliation* (Nashville: Abingdon, 1996). See the quotation at the beginning of this chapter, p. 176 above.

ordinate ethnicity way down the line is one of the abject failures of the modern church and a basis for continuing racism from all sides. Color of skin and cultural variation are no basis for boundaries and divisions. If you are a Christian, you are a Christian first and foremost, and your ethnicity and that of other people are far less determinative factors. The ultimate defining force in life must be Christ. To say Jesus is Lord is to say he trumps every other determiner in life, including ethnicity.

The Boundaries That Remain

But not *all* boundaries are set aside. Later in Ephesians, in chapters 4–6, the ethical instruction insists on maintaining boundaries between the former life and new life in Christ, between darkness and light, between those who do shameful things and those living in the light, and between evil and righteousness (especially in ch. 5). The discussion of boundaries is not about tolerance and just accepting anything people do or God accepting people unwilling to change. While the boundaries among people, and between people and God, have been obliterated, ethical boundaries remain and are fortified.

This is because positive boundaries have to do with ethics. *The concerns and implications with boundaries involve nearly all aspects of Christian living.* The Torah and much of the Gospels and Letters are discussions of boundaries. Good boundaries are set to guard truth and the well-being of other people and to prevent sin—boundaries of body and sexuality, boundaries of property and truth, boundaries of well-being and time. These boundaries are not to be crossed, and perhaps *the most important among such boundaries are the ones we establish in our own minds* by which we do not allow ourselves mentally to go in the direction of sin. Sin is largely—maybe completely—a violation of boundaries.

Ethical boundaries need serious reflection. Our society used to recognize the importance of ethical boundaries, but now many such boundaries are ignored—unless public figures like politicians and preachers get caught violating them. Sexual boundaries hardly exist anymore, with Christians being derailed here as well, but what have we done to ourselves in the process? Boundaries protecting truth are laughed off, so that lying is not a problem. In fact, some argue that lying is necessary, if one wants to succeed, but for Christians this is absurd.

Jewish rabbis were well aware of boundaries in ethical discussion. They described their efforts interpreting the law as putting a fence around the law so that it would not be violated, just as one puts a fence around a flower garden to prevent damage to the flowers.[12] One of the problems, of course, is that people want to see how close they can come to the boundary without violating it. Often when they get close to the boundary, they throw their mind over, and soon their body follows. This is the way sin occurs.

Boundaries are so important because they have to do with what we let in to shape our identity. Our boundaries should be permeable to grant access to the good but resistant to evil, including *the evil that often is disguised as good*. Sin rarely approaches us as something uninviting and heinous. We need boundaries around the good and what should be so as not to settle for something less.

If sin is a violation of boundaries, ethics has to do with the recognition of and protection of good boundaries. We noted earlier how the Ten Commandments are boundary markers to frame identity and to preserve God's identity, that of other people, and indeed our own. Respect creates boundaries. My daughter is a licensed clinical social worker. Many of her clients are victims of sexual abuse. They are people whose body boundaries have been violated. Many of us have emotional or even physical scars resulting from boundaries being violated. Such events often cause us to erect higher boundaries to avoid further pain, which is understandable, but it may result in our having a fortress mentality. It is difficult to live in healthy relations with a fortress mentality. This relates to the idolatry of security. When danger threatens, we want to protect ourselves, and it is difficult to keep boundaries low. Given the need for security, how large should our boundaries be? It is difficult to love if we can barely see over our boundaries.

The more an ethical boundary is fixed, the less temptation is a factor. If I have precluded theft as something outside my boundaries, I am not

12. Mishnah Avot 1:1.

tempted to steal. Some temptations will still have an allure, but the more that is the case, such as with sexual sin, the more careful one must be about boundary maintenance and distance from the boundary. Like many others, I have had to create distance to make sure sexual boundaries were not violated. Proximity enhances possibility.

Things That Have No Boundaries

Boundaries against sin are mandatory, but no boundaries can be allowed to set the limits of virtue. Yes, virtue must be wise, but it does not have boundaries. Some boundaries are not permitted for Christians, boundaries between races and classes or boundaries that set limits to forgiveness and love. There can be no boundaries of responsibility. One has only to think of Jesus's rejection of Peter's question about how many times he had to forgive (Matt. 18:21–22). Peter sought a boundary for forgiveness, but Jesus says there is none. (Forgiveness does not mean a person can evade responsibility for sin, for forgiveness is about one's own heart more than it is about the other person.) In the parable of the good Samaritan, the legal expert's assumption was that there is a boundary to "neighbor," an assumption Jesus rejected. There can be no "nonneighbor" (Luke 10:25–37).

There can be no boundaries of responsibility because there are no boundaries for the love God calls us to show. (I am not talking about what some *think* is love!) The boundary of your locale can no longer be the extent of your care, for the Great Commission and the nature of love compel a universal vision for God's kingdom and mission in the world. We are defined by our own place but not limited to it. At the same time, no individual can deal with all the needs and problems people have. How will we negotiate boundaries of care wisely so that we are neither immune to the need nor overwhelmed by the responsibility? We can't deal with the whole world, but if we only say, "I will take care of my corner of the world to make sure things here are right," we risk creating a boundary that makes us parochial, diminished, and irresponsible in regard to God's larger mission.

So, what are your boundaries? Which ones do you just assume, whether you should or not? Which need to be reinforced, and which need to be minimized? How do you negotiate boundaries? How fixed or permeable are your boundaries, especially your ethical boundaries? Who gets included in your definitional boundaries and how easily? How do you do boundary maintenance? This is partly the church's responsibility, but the church often seems to have lost its voice. Boundaries are about inclusion and exclusion, so some boundaries are not allowed—those between races or to set the limits of forgiveness—and some boundaries must not be crossed—those that lead you into sin. You are your boundaries.

FACTOR 8

You Are an Ongoing Process of Change

We do not suddenly fall on death, but advance towards it by slight degrees; we die every day. For every day a little of our life is taken from us; even when we are growing, our life is on the wane.

—Seneca, *Moral Letters*, "On Despising Death"

None of us is the same man in old age that he was in youth; nor the same on the morrow as on the day preceding. Our bodies are hurried along like flowing waters; . . . of the things which we see, nothing is fixed. Even I myself, as I comment on this change, am changed myself. . . . Every instant means the death of our previous condition.

—Seneca, *Moral Letters*, "On Being"

You will change. Your humanity is both a gift and a responsibility, but the gift comes only as potential. What will you do with the gift? A meaningful identity—who God says you are—is something that must be attained, and that does not happen without work over time. Identity is a never-accomplished process until death. Change is the only constant. You have changed, and you will continue to do so, but most of us do not reflect much on coming change, nor do we prepare for it. Of course, some

193

change cannot be anticipated and we cannot specifically prepare for it. With such cases we can only prepare for the contingencies of life.

Change comes for all kinds of reasons; some changes such as aging are inevitable. Some change comes because of new experiences, training, success, a new job, and new opportunities; some because of failure, loss of a job, retirement, or conflict; some because of rejection or acceptance; some because of changes in interests; some because of changes in relations and what others say of us; and some because of learning and changes in thinking, religious or otherwise. Every action changes us. Sometimes the change is merely because we got dissatisfied or bored. Country singer Sara Evans has a song entitled "I Keep Looking" that includes the words "Just as soon as I get what I want I get unsatisfied. . . . I keep looking for something more." That is true for many people, and the things we think will satisfy rarely do. Isn't there more to life than what most are chasing?

Some change is incremental and hardly noticeable until one looks at previous stages—like looking at old photographs of oneself. Some change needs immediate and radical implementation. If one is going the wrong direction, continuing in that direction makes no sense, but humans tend to prefer the rut they are in to actually becoming who they should be.

The process and stages of life are well known and have been treated by the psychologist Erik Erikson in his theory of eight stages of development from infancy to old age and the lessons to be learned at each stage.[1] Gail Sheehy's book *Passages* also emphasized the transitions that people go through and the importance of going through each stage well.[2] The issues of identity or failure of identity in one stage do not disappear on moving to another. They still are issues that must be addressed. The identity question "Who am I?" is asked all the way from womb to tomb.[3]

---

1. Erik H. Erikson, *Identity, Youth, and Crisis* (New York: Norton, 1968).

2. Gail Sheehy, *Passages: Predictable Crises of Adult Life* (New York: Bantam, 1977).

3. William Willimon, cited by Christiaan Mostert, "Christian Identity as Baptismal Identity," in *Christian Identity*, ed. Eduardus Van der Borght, Studies in Reformed Theology 16 (Leiden: Brill, 2008), 51–65, here 62.

Life Demands Change

One reason the question "Who am I?" keeps being asked is because we keep changing. Unfortunately, too many people stop—or never start—asking the question in any meaningful way. Their identities seem frozen in an unhealthy place, even though all is changing. Progress and improvement do not happen. People succumb to life's defaults and previous superficial answers, are content with the insignificant, and fail to be truly human. Is that why there are so many zombie movies?

We change, and therefore we have to keep asking the question about our identity and reassessing who we are. If identity is a narrative construct, if it involves a story, change is inevitable. We can most easily watch change take place in children as they move to maturity. Life is a process of continually forming an identity, and late teen and early adult periods are especially important, for there people are taking responsibility for their own lives, making decisions, and having experiences that shape them. The more life experience we have, the more our identity is stamped. The farther we are down the road, the less likely radical change will happen, even if it should. Still, change and process are just as real for adults at all stages of life. Regardless of how far down road we are, radical change may still be needed—and is possible if honesty and humility are present.

In the midst of change there is both continuity and difference. Continuity of self does not mean sameness of self. I am the same person who was once a teenager, but I am vastly different in virtually every respect. What is it that makes me the same when physically and in every other way I am hardly recognizable as the person years ago? There is a me that is rooted in the continuity of my body and memory that is the same though changing. There is a narrative identity of the same person going through this life process, even though the story may have departures or even U-turns. Identity is the result of the continuity of physical body and memory moving through the process *and* the awareness that it is *I* who am on this journey. The worth of the identity—the self that is involved in the process—depends on some understanding of the *values* directing the journey and the goal(s) toward which it moves. Is this process of change headed in the right direction, and is it guided by the right motives?

Change can be positive or negative, of course. A positive process of change is characterized by a long-term conscious effort toward a worthy goal and confidence of attaining it. The whole discussion of process presumes that there is a goal or there are goals, that there are values to be pursued, that life is supposed to go somewhere, that tasks are to be accomplished, and that life is to be productive. From Genesis 1 on, humans are told to be productive; we are supposed to achieve something beyond our own existence. Many in our society have lost all sense of something beyond their own existence.

A negative process of change is characterized by long-term avoidance of reality, no commitment to a worthy goal, and no discipline to move in the right direction. Think of the failures of Saul and even David in the Old Testament. Too many people still seem interested only in survival, holding on to any privilege, self-gratification, and distraction. Surely life is more than that—and not so stultifyingly boring and depressing.

Why are we so passive in watching change just happen? Why do we not evaluate more honestly and effectively the internal and external messages we encounter, testing the truth and validity of the messages, and make wise decisions about the way we want to go to establish a worthwhile identity— or that God wants us to go? Is it again the problems of laziness and pride? Why are we not much more careful and intentional about our identity and its changes, making sure we are moving in the right direction? Much we do not control. We *can* control investment in learning and in monitoring honestly what is happening in our lives. We *can* practice disciplines that keep us in touch with God and assist maturation, but that requires planning and commitment to life both as a gift and as a responsibility.

Everyone plans for something, even if it is as mundane as planning what to do tomorrow. The very fact of planning points to a process. Should we not develop a specific plan with specific steps of implementation to become the person God intends? Such a plan, no doubt, will frequently be adjusted, but without a plan of investment in good practices and determination to follow it, we will not do the journey well.

The truth is, you are more than you presently are, and God wants you to be more than you presently are. There is a summoning self calling us. All of us know sin, failure, and limitation, but you are more than your sin, your failures, and your limitations. Your identity is still in process, and in telling you who you are God calls you past your present to a better and more mature identity. The issue is not merely that we change but how

Christianity focuses on God's continual transformative work in us. Christianity is about transformation. This has nothing to do with attaining an image for show; it is about substance and authenticity of being. This is not about role playing but actually being conformed to the character of God.

Obviously time is important in a process of change. We live based on the past, but we cannot live the past. We live in anticipation of the future, but we cannot live the future. We have to live in the present, fleeting as it is, based on the past and pulled by the future. Jesus called people to live in the present. Too many of his contemporaries wanted to live in their heroic past or in their messianic future, just as people do now, but Jesus had an immediacy that he also expected of his disciples. Jesus called them to live honestly in the present, to be themselves actually *present* in the moment and *present* to the people with them, even while they prepared for and experienced change. Even the present, though, is in process; it cannot be grasped and held.

Sometimes identity changes are mandated by other people, for good or ill. "R-Day," reception day, is the day when new recruits are inducted into the US Military Academy at West Point. They strip to their underwear, their hair is cut off, they put on a uniform, and they learn new rules for saluting, marching, and conduct. As one person put it, "On R-Day you surrender your old self in stages." The rest of the West Point experience is a reconstruction of identity, and the goal toward which recruits are moving is clear. The new identity cannot be achieved without the surrender of the old. That is analogous to what happens with conversion, whether it be a radical reversal or a process over time. To be what one should be requires laying aside what one is.[4] But what can and should be laid aside, and what cannot and should not?

Conversion Is an Ongoing Process

Change may be inevitable for all humans, but Christians especially should be conscious of and focused on the process of change, for Christian-

---

4. Any change in identity, whether positive or negative, is both a setting aside and a new appropriation. Nazis tried to obliterate the identity people had by shaving their head, replacing their clothes with a uniform, and replacing their name with a number. Some rituals of baptism in the early church also involved taking off old clothes and putting on new ones after baptism.

ity, if it is about anything at all, is about conversion and transformation, and *conversion is an ongoing process*, not merely an event. Christianity is about an ongoing transformation of identity, a subverting of who you are by yourself. It involves a death, your death, and new life enabled by God, but you cannot experience new life without being willing to let go of the old and willing to change. Nor is this willingness to die a onetime event; it is the *pattern of life with Christ*. None of this is surprising, for Christianity is about continually dying and rising with Christ, which will be treated later.

The Greek word for "disciple" (*mathētēs*) is from the verb "to learn" (*manthanō*); a disciple is a learner, and discipleship is about continually learning from and continually being shaped by the character of Christ. It is about following Jesus; it is a process, a narrative movement. A disciple of Christ does not graduate; he or she is always a disciple. Being a Christian means laying aside one kind of identity to find true identity in life with Christ—"denying self, taking a cross, and following Jesus." Interestingly, this classic description of discipleship is found seven times in the Gospels (Matt. 10:38–39; 16:24–25; Mark 8:34–35; Luke 9:23–24; 14:27; 17:33; and John 12:25–26), and all but one use the Greek present tense to describe following Jesus.[5] The present tense indicates unfolding action, something ongoing and continual.[6] Luke 9:23 adds *each day*—"take up your cross each day"—to emphasize even more that discipleship is an ongoing process by its very nature. Similarly, Paul often uses "the ones believing"—a participle—to refer to Christians as believers. Fifteen of the seventeen occurrences of this participle use the present tense, again emphasizing that belief is no mere decision but an ongoing commitment to and walk with Christ. Only such a continual believing qualifies as saving faith. Christianity is a process, a walk with God, not merely an emotional decision or a onetime event.

In fact, the most common metaphor in both Old and New Testaments to describe a life of faith is walking. Enoch and Noah walked with God, and Abraham is instructed to walk before God and to be blameless (Gen.

---

5. Luke 17:33 does not use the language of following.
6. There are variations, of course, depending on context.

5:22; 6:9; 17:1). The form of the word for "walk"[7] for all three men (and elsewhere) has the connotation of "walking about with." It is a continual walk, a living with, that is in mind. The Israelites were told "to fear the LORD your God, to *walk* in all his ways, to love him, to serve the LORD your God with all your heart and with all your soul" (Deut. 10:12). The famous words of Micah 6:8 are similar: "What does the LORD require of you but to do justice, and to love kindness, and to *walk* humbly with your God?" One could summarize much of the Old Testament ethic with Isaiah 30:21: "This is the way; walk in it."

Translations sometimes mute this emphasis by translating "walk" as "live" or some other expression, but that is unfortunate. The New Testament has the same metaphorical focus on walking. Obvious examples are 2 Corinthians 5:7 ("for we walk by faith, not by sight") and Galatians 5:16 ("walk by the Spirit"). Ephesians 4 and 5 are virtually framed on this metaphor of walking (see 4:1, 17; 5:2, 8, 15). "The way" is an important metaphor in Jewish thought, but in Acts it becomes a name for the early Christian movement. Only with difficulty can one ignore that biblical faith is an ongoing process, a continual walk with Christ. God's people have always been a pilgrim people, a people on the move who know their real home is elsewhere. Their God is a God on the move, one who chose to manifest his presence in a tent, for he is accompanying his people on their life's journey.

This is not what many think of when they think of Christianity. They think of a decision, asking Jesus into your heart, or believing certain ideas. They are more like the rich young ruler who asked Jesus, "What good thing must I do that I may have eternal life?" (Matt. 19:16/Mark 10:17/Luke 18:18). The young man's question seems to imply "Tell me what I have to do so I can get it over with and get on with my life." Jesus told him to sell his possessions and to come and—again using the present tense—to follow him continually. Life with God is not something to be taken care of, to get over with, so that you can do what you want. Life with God is walking with, following, and being faithful. It is a process over time.

The evangelistic efforts of many churches to achieve a decision—often a superficial one, to get people to say the sinner's prayer, with no sense

7. The hithpa'el.

that trust in Christ means walking with Christ—is a gross distortion of the gospel and the cause of much of the failure of the church. It does not lead to the transformation of identity that the gospel promises. Surely the church must do its evangelism more honestly and more holistically. If conversion is not demonstrated over time, one must seriously question whether it occurred.

No one should doubt that conversion is a process, even if the church has failed to do justice to the idea. The texts using the present tense for believing and following should be sufficient to make the point, but many other texts make the same point in other ways. In 2 Corinthians 3:18 the Christian life is described as a life of growth, a process of continually being transformed—again present tense—from one stage of "glory" to another. In Romans 12:2 Paul told Christians they should be continually transformed—present tense—by the renewing of their minds. He urged them to grow into Christ in every respect (Eph. 4:15) and reminded them that they were taught to put off the old being, to be continually renewed—present tense—in their minds, and to put on the new being (Eph. 4:22–24 and Col. 3:9–11). In Philippians 3:12–14 Paul described himself as straining to pursue the goal of the high calling of God in Christ Jesus. First Peter 2:2 instructs Christians, like newborn babies, to desire the pure spiritual milk so that they may *grow into salvation*. Growth and continual renewal are the assumption of Christian ideas of salvation and conversion. Frozen identities are not allowed. Nor may we legitimately think of initial commitment that grows cold or becomes hardly discernible over time. If conversion is a process, time should lead to an increasing and more informed commitment.

One of the most joy-filled women I know told me that she had been sexually molested when young, so much so that she could hardly talk because of the shame. She had read that God promised to be her counselor, and for *six years*, five days a week when her family was not there, she set an empty chair in front of her to remember God's presence, wept, read her Bible, and prayed. It was a long process, but God restored her honor and filled her with joy. Over time she was transformed by God's Spirit. She was already a Christian, but what happened for her was no less a conversion. Conversion must not be thought of merely as an initial turning from sin, as important as that is. Sometimes conversion is immediate and radical, and sometimes it involves a period of time. Sometimes it involves tearing down and reorientation before rebuilding. Sometimes the tearing down has already happened to us, and conversion is a process of restoration, but it is always a process moving us from thinking our life is our own to the realization that our lives belong to God, and it always brings healing and wholeness in numerous areas as we walk with God.

The reality of the process of faith is evident in other ways. As mentioned before, the New Testament often describes and directs Christians with a blend of the indicative and the imperative. It is within this tension of the indicative and the imperative that we must understand my phrase "who God says you are." This tension in effect instructs people to make real in their lives what the gospel asserts is already true. For example, Romans 6:3 says, "We were baptized into his [Christ's] death," and then 6:11 says, "Thus also consider yourselves dead to sin but living to God in Christ Jesus." This blend of the indicative and the imperative is present throughout the New Testament.[8] These imperatives are "commemorative imperatives," intended to remind people who they really are.[9] But these imperatives have another function as well. They call people to live out their identity and to keep progressing toward the goal of being like Christ. Christian ethical behavior is a *result*, not the origin, of new life, and the combination of indicative and imperative reflects the presence of the new age in the midst of the old. The indicative describes the newness of God's work, and the imperative directs that we take our identity from that new reality. The combination as well points to the relation of God's work, the indicative, and the required human response, the imperative. Action is required, but even human action results from God's work for us and in us.

Dying and rising with Christ is another aspect of the ongoing process of change. This thinking is central to Paul's thought and expresses in his terms what Jesus meant with "deny self, take up a cross, and continually follow me." Dying and rising is what happens in conversion and baptism.

8. The blend of indicative and imperative is frequent in Paul's letters and is in large part the structure of the first half of 1 Peter. Jesus used it in Matt. 5:13–16 and Luke 12:31–32.

9. Troels Engberg-Pedersen, "Galatians in Romans 5–8 and Paul's Construction of the Identity of Christ Believers," in *Texts and Contexts: Biblical Texts in Their Textual and Situational Contexts; Essays in Honor of Lars Hartman*, ed. T. Fornberg and D. Hellholm (Oslo: Scandinavian University Press, 1995), 477–503, here 501.

Romans 6:4 says, "We were buried with him [Christ] through baptism into death, that just as Christ was raised from the dead through the glory of the Father, so also we might walk in newness of life." But dying and rising is the pattern of daily life, something one continually does.[10] Paul asserted, "I am dying every day" (1 Cor. 15:31)—again present tense; his willingness to pattern his life on Christ's death and resurrection exposed him to death daily. Such language only escalates the fact that Christian faith involves an ongoing process of change. To follow Christ means a dying, the willingness to keep rejecting a self-centered existence and the destructive character of sin. Paul directs Christians to put to death practices that do not fit with Christ (for example, Col. 3:5–9). But there is no sense in dying unless resurrection occurs and leads to a higher and better form of living, and this is exactly what Paul thinks happens with faith. The Spirit of God in us, the same God who raised Jesus, both enables dying to sin—in effect turning our backs on sin—and keeps making us alive so that we keep increasing toward the character to which Christ calls us (Rom. 8:11–13). Conversion is a process, so we keep activating the will as the Spirit works in us. In fact, "Faith means *becoming creative with God and his Spirit.*"[11] We keep making choices that conform to life with God, and every day is a process of dying and rising.

Maintaining Identity in the Process of Change

The process of change is part of what gives life value and makes it exciting. Identity is both grounded in the past and open to the future, and this openness enables freedom within the broad boundaries of faith and engages us in work for God. The task of becoming is a dynamic quest, one that requires discipline, if change is to be fruitful. Learning, both from one's own investment and from involvement with others, is essential, and this is one reason the church is so important. Identity maintenance and

10. On dying and rising see Rom. 6:1–2; 7:4; 8:11–12; 1 Cor. 6:14; 10:16; 2 Cor. 4:10–11; 5:14–15; Gal. 2:19–20; 5:24; 6:14; Eph. 2:5–6; Phil. 3:9–10, 21; Col. 2:12–15; 2:20–3:5; 2 Tim. 2:11.

11. Anthony C. Thiselton, *Interpreting God and the Postmodern Self: On Meaning, Manipulation, and Promise* (Grand Rapids: Eerdmans, 1995), 154.

enhancement happen for Christians at least partly in the church's worship and education. People want church to be entertaining and comfortable, but instead it should be formative and instructive, and that requires time and investment. Most churches fail miserably with education, especially adult education. Without continual learning we can never be the person God calls us to be. The gospel *requires* a life of the mind, for the life of the mind is the key to maturity, progress, and productivity. I do not mean Christians must be academics; I do mean Christians must be discerning, analytical, and thoughtful as they decide what living for Christ means in their own situation. If this is true, the church must rethink radically and invest heavily in how it engages and instructs people.

The purpose of the church, as far as it relates to humans, is identity construction and maintenance. The process of identity formation in early Christianity was *communal*.[12] It still is. Identity formation is dialogical. The church is a primary place for the conversation with the external community about who we are, if we are willing to hear each other and be honest with each other. The body image and unity in Christ—again the participationist language—are a necessary focus. This is merely a process of actually understanding the gospel and living it out. The church is an agent of, and the result of, this kind of identity formation. If identity formation is communal and dialogical, we can neither focus on *nor* neglect our individuality. We have to keep doing identity maintenance in our communities, but individually we have to take responsibility for our own learning. What will you do to ensure your learning? You cannot flourish in the ongoing process of change without a serious learning program, and serious learning will involve honesty, deeper thinking, study, and investment in the right kinds of experiences.

But to what end is all this growth and seeking for knowledge? Paul's prayer in Colossians 1:9–10 is instructive. He prays that the Colossians will be *filled with knowledge of God's will* in all wisdom and spiritual understanding so that they might *live lives worthy of the Lord*, pleasing in every respect, with every good work *bearing fruit and increasing in the knowledge of God*. The goal of the prayer is knowledge of and per-

---

12. John K. Riches, *Conflicting Mythologies: Identity Formation in the Gospels of Mark and Matthew* (Edinburgh: T. & T. Clark, 2000), 307.

formance of God's will, which lead to deeper knowledge of God. Performance of knowledge leads to productivity and greater knowledge. Knowledge of God experienced, comprehended, and lived out leads to relational knowledge of God. This in turn leads to being empowered by God and to worship, a worship focused on God's work on our behalf. The goal is increasing conformity to the will of God, productive living, and a deeper relation to God.

Such a process requires humility regarding both knowledge and attainment. There is always an awareness that our knowledge is partial: we see as if through a mirror and with uncertainty (1 Cor. 13:12). If the process is ongoing, there can never be a sense of "I reached the goal." In his description of himself in Philippians 3:12–14, Paul twice asserts that he has no sense that he has achieved the goal, but with his eyes on the prize he continually seeks to lay hold of the high call of God because he *had been laid hold of* by Christ. As with Paul, the grip of Christ on one's life gives an identity and energizes. It does not allow arrogance or preoccupation with the past. The process of change is not haphazard or unsettling due to lack of direction. What makes identity is largely determined by a goal, values worth pursuing, and the degree to which one approaches the goal. This is to take seriously the summoning self, which knows it is created in the image of God and is responsible to God. For Christians life is founded in God and moves toward God. Identity projects a future, and it does so nowhere as much as with Christianity. Christians are pulled by hope in God's future so that all of life is moving in the same direction. There is a faithfulness, a constancy, even in the midst of change or disaster. This constancy creates a moral momentum in the same direction,[13] which makes life easier. When you have committed to a faithful walk with God, many temptations just are no longer temptations.

What does faithfulness mean in a context of change? Faithfulness is a key factor in maintaining identity within a process of change. "Fidelity [gives] unity to lives that otherwise splinter."[14] But to what will we be

---

13. Cf. Stanton Jones, "The Loving Opposition: Speaking the Truth in a Culture of Hate," *Christianity Today*, July 19, 1993, 19–25, here 24: "We build a moral and personal momentum by the choices we make."

14. Vernon White, *Identity* (London: SCM, 2002), 72, quoting Milan Kundera, *The Unbearable Lightness of Being*.

faithful? Tell me to what you are faithful, and I will know who you are. Part of being faithful is being faithful to your own being and commitments, and that is a factor in any person's identity. Paul Ricoeur said character designates the set of lasting dispositions by which a person is recognized. "An element of loyalty is thus incorporated into character and makes it turn toward fidelity, hence toward maintaining the self."[15] Of course, people can be faithful to positive or to negative traits they have developed throughout life. The latter is disastrous. Such people are too proud, too stubborn, or too incapable of change. Yes, there is a need for fidelity to ourselves, but not to the parts that destroy life.

For Christians, however, faithfulness takes on another dimension and a greater specificity. It is faithfulness *to Christ* and life with Christ. The process of change for Christians is rooted in faithfulness to Christ. One has only to think of Jesus's emphasis on being faithful in small things (e.g., Luke 16:10–12; NIV uses "trust" and "trustworthy" to convey the idea). But, even here—or especially here—fidelity must be a creative fidelity, for change is inevitable, and a freedom from self and for life is required. There is always a discerning process by which one honestly determines the will of God, which brings freedom in changing circumstances.

Faithfulness is also crucial in all our relations. People, especially family members, look for faithfulness and fidelity from others. Often people test others to see if they will be faithful; they want to know if they can trust the relation. Children test parents to see if the relation is as substantial as they hope. Perhaps the greatest effectiveness of a Christian witness is the willingness to be faithful, regardless of the circumstances.

Sometimes change comes as a result of tragedy, as a result of sin in the world, or from aging and death. We delude ourselves to think that life is always moving higher and higher. Even when we walk faithfully with God, life is sometimes hard and frustrating, and it includes suffering and death. The simplistic answers many Christians give to life's hardships cannot help. Paul recognizes in 2 Corinthians 4:16–18 that change has two dimensions, one moving toward life and one moving toward death:

15. Paul Ricoeur, *Oneself as Another*, trans. Kathleen Blamey (Chicago: University of Chicago Press, 1992), 121. Also see White, *Identity*, for whom loyalty and faithfulness are major themes.

"Though outwardly we are wasting away, yet inwardly we are being renewed day by day. . . . So we fix our eyes not on what is seen, but on what is unseen, since what is seen is temporary, but what is unseen is eternal." Paul was aware of countervailing tendencies—an ongoing inner positive renewal and an outer process of decay. Our bodies break down, and our minds are part of our bodies. If we live long enough, nearly all of us will experience decline in cognitive ability. We adjust to the changes in life, but sometimes the process is frustrating.

The ongoing process of change has its own end—in death—but is that it? Of course not; being fixed on what is unseen, the eternal, rooted Paul's efforts even more in his expectation of God's future. Identity, at least Christian identity, has a future because of the resurrection, but that implies accountability to God and *assessment by God of the validity of one's identity*. Identity theorists often emphasize that accountability and responsibility are our only criteria for continuity of identity.[16] We have continuity because we are responsible for all our actions and are being pulled toward God by accountability for those actions.

Who will we be in the hard times, and how will we navigate our changing identity even to the point of death? Will we indeed experience continual renewal and the moral momentum of life with God, or will we become a shell of a human wrapped around our own self-centeredness?

Who are you becoming? Are you satisfied with what you have become? If you said yes, you need to be more honest. Is God satisfied with what you have become?

Two things are clear. First, passivity is out, which was already obvious in the chapter on actions. You cannot be the person God calls you to be without focus and effort over time. Second, the ongoing process of change depends on a goal summoning and directing the change, and this leads into the next chapter on the future.

16. For example, Thiselton, *Interpreting God*, 74.

FACTOR 9

You Are Your Future

Consider three things and you will not fall into the hands of transgression. Know from where you come and where you are going and before whom you are about to give account and reckoning . . . before the King of kings of kings, the Holy One, blessed is he.

—Mishnah Avot 3:1

"Eucatastrophe": the turn to hope, the moment of turning from darkness to light, from bad to good, from crucifixion to resurrection. "The Resurrection is the eucatastrophe of the story of the Incarnation—This story begins and ends in joy."

—J. R. R. Tolkien, "On Fairy Stories"

Your identity is shaped by its anticipated future; the self is an anticipated self. Saying "You are your future" may sound strange, but the future pulls us and shapes us. In treating the image of God (in the chapter on factor 1) I made the point that dignity determines destiny. The reverse is also true. Destiny determines dignity. "In the Christian view, the being of humans is bound up . . . with the future to which they are destined."[1] If I have some

1. Wolfhart Pannenberg, *Anthropology in Theological Perspective*, trans. Matthew J. O'Connell (Philadelphia: Westminster, 1985), 273.

sense that my destiny is worthwhile, it elevates my sense of value on the way. If my destiny will give dignity, I live into that dignity. The expectation shapes present action. Of course, if the assumed destiny is misguided or seems negative or unsure, the result for the way we live may be negative as well.

Do remember that no one identity factor by itself determines identity; the nine factors work together to shape who we are, and the future is entwined with *all* other aspects of identity. The future is projected by one's physical and psychological makeup—to say nothing of one's mortality—and by being placed in a narrative history. The future is involved with our relations, for, like it or not, our future is bound with the future of the people to whom we relate. The future is involved in our commitments, for commitments themselves imply a future. The future is involved with our actions and with the internal self-interpreting, self-directing memory, and obviously with the ongoing process of change. The future is limited or enabled by our boundaries. The anticipated future is, therefore, an important part of one's identity. Identity presupposes a future, and all of us live from hope, especially Christians, and especially if life has any meaning at all.

Considering seriously the future implications of our present actions can reorient our lives, but too often we do not take our own futures seriously. We can act like the future does not exist, but it keeps coming. We may act like the future is more of the same, but it will bring change, possibly good and possibly terrible. We can try to hide, but our minds know the risk of the future and the certainty of death. Nothing stays the same. How will you steward your future? What happens to your identity if you are given a diagnosis of three months' life expectancy or if you are being married in three weeks?

Expectation regarding the future includes what we think is possible and what limits or enables life. How large is your vision for the future? Christianity has a *large* vision for the future, the only vision worth having, one that brings meaning, purpose, and hope, for it is about seeing God, knowing God, and unending participation with God.

Why does the future shape identity? We are always living forward. Life is a process, a journey, and we always have a sense of something coming. The future is the fuel that gets us past the present, but even though the future draws us, the future, as far as life on this earth goes, is itself draining away. It is a limited future, even though we try to tell ourselves otherwise. The future is both limited and unknown, which can cause anxiety, but we usually assume that something better is coming. Rarely do we think the future will be worse, but it may well be worse. Estimates of world population growth to eleven billion people by 2100 are scary. Predictions about ice melt and coastal water levels because of global warming create anxiety. The unending violence in our societies and war between nations leave us wondering if there is any place to hide. The economic divide between the haves and the have-nots likely will only get larger, so the future does not seem enticing at all. Individually we may face calamity and heartache. Worse and much more personal is our own death. Can there be hope in the face of death? We deal well with calamity and death *only with some sense that the story is not over.* Death haunts us, but the restlessness of our souls cries out for more than this short life. If this brief life is all there is, life is insane, depressing nonsense, a cosmic accident, and nothing really matters.

An Alternative Future to Live Toward

God offers an alternative future, one beyond our expectation, and Christianity calls for a conversion of our thinking, one driven by expectation, one that slants us into God's future, not as a pious wish but as a conviction based on the promise of God that reorients life.[2] Happiness does not exist without hope, hope for life now and for eternity. Christian hope says life *does* matter, that things can be better in this world, that *we* can be better, that death is not the end, and that life with God will be better. The gospel gives us a vision of an alternative and better identity. Given the promises of God, what possible positive self could you become and how can you get there? The identity question is not just "Who are you?," for that question implies "Who are you becoming?" and "Who can you and should you become?" We do not know who we really are until God's promised future reveals it.

That sense of "something better" presupposes a value system, and all

2. See Richard B. Hays, "The Conversion of the Imagination: Scripture and Eschatology in 1 Corinthians," *New Testament Studies* 45 (1999): 391–412.

of us seek to find value for ourselves. Unfortunately, many in our society assign large value to things that have little value. What will—note the future tense—give real and lasting value? What illusions will we create to impress others or convince ourselves that we are valuable? Most fixate on possessions and enjoyment as marks of success, but you are neither your possessions nor your enjoyment. Possessions are not a sign of success, and especially not if they are gained by cheating or if in the process relations are destroyed. Enjoyment, although important, is fleeting and no sign of real value.

If the self is an acting self looking for something to do, it needs to find something worthwhile, a goal *worth* the effort, which obviously looks to the future.[3] Without direction to a goal, life is meaningless. The question of what we are to pursue is crucial, and surely it should be something beyond our own happiness. What role do self-love, self-preservation, and love of pleasure rightly have? Is desire a good or a bad thing? How does the issue of sin and self-centeredness fit in the discussion of our future? Should we view ourselves as good or as hopelessly sinful? Do we distort the future by poor choices? How do we deal with aging and death? All such questions engage the future. Therefore, a vision of the future determines who we are and how we live, and the better that vision, the more the future shapes our identity and actions in a positive way. Anticipation drives life. Next year will be *better*. I will lose weight, get out of debt, have better relations, go on vacation, move to a better place, do what I know I should.

The goal we are moving toward may or may not be worth it, be it our team winning the championship, getting out of debt, buying a house, retirement, or whatever, but we do live forward, even if it is just toward payday. The brevity of life raises even more the question of purpose. Why are we here? What are we supposed to do? Adam and Eve were told to tend the garden. Abraham was told he would be a blessing. Moses was

3. See the comments of Patrick McNamara, *The Cognitive Neuropsychiatry of Parkinson's Disease* (Cambridge, MA: MIT Press, 2011), 38: "The agentic self is future oriented, goal oriented, and action oriented." On 55–56 he adds, "An ideal, hoped-for self also strongly motivates people and strongly influences decision making. . . . Presumably, the agentic self uses hoped-for and feared possible selves as a system for self-regulation and as a system for goal setting and realization of long-term intentions. Who do I want to become? Who do I fear becoming?"

told to lead a people and form a great nation. Leaders lead people toward a goal, but all of us need goals and seek purpose. We can accomplish *x*, and life will be better. We can acquire *x*, a house, a spouse, children, a job to sustain us, something enjoyable, a trip to somewhere. The future is the reason we go to school, save, and plan.

Most importantly, the summoning self—that ideal self out in front of us—calls us, even if we are unaware of it, and energizes, motivates, and directs our decisions and actions. This ideal self is a basis of hope and possibility because it provides a vision of what can and should be. Unfortunately, our legitimate summoning self, what we should be, is often sacrificed for a cheap substitute that seems more pleasurable at the moment. Failure to live up to our *own* anticipation leads to guilt, cynicism, denial of what should be in favor of a lesser goal, depression, and a diminishing of self.

Still, we are pulled by a sense of what we should be and can become. God seeks to put us on a path to this ideal self, the self God intended with creation. We will not fully know ourselves until we are in the eternal presence of God, but clearly this straining toward the future is a theological and an ethical task. A conscious relation to God now and in the future provides the basis for identity.

Inherently the future involves a sense of *responsibility* to ourselves, to others, and to God; this is at the heart of what it is to be human. But with responsibility comes accountability, and that projects a future too. Did I live up to my responsibilities and the call of my summoning self? To whom are we accountable? Judgment—whether our own, society's, or God's—is an essential aspect of identity, and while Christianity does not neglect accountability to ourselves or society, it will not let us ignore accountability to God. People in our society have little sense of accountability to other people or to God, but this is delusion. If you are not accountable, are you even alive?

Our goals and our accountability are at the heart of identity and of identity being shaped by the future. "What makes the self a self is a 'criterion,' a goal or end by which the self measures itself."[4] Clearly such assessment is very much involved with the self-interpreting, self-directing memory. *Life, therefore, is about both memory and vision.* But, if we are

---

4. C. Stephen Evans, *Kierkegaard on Faith and the Self: Collected Essays* (Waco: Baylor University Press, 2006), 271.

only accountable to ourselves, who cares? Is this life nonsense? Christianity asserts that God thinks life is valuable and will hold us accountable for it. Will judgment largely be God asking, "Who are you and how did you show it?" This is a specifically *individual* question for each of us regarding what we did with the life we were given. Again the realization of Rabbi Zusya is incisive. He realized God would not ask, "Why were you not Moses?" but "Why were you not Zusya?"[5] Each of us will be asked, "Why were *you* not who *you* were created to be?"

Because we have—even if we try to ignore it—some sense of the good we should pursue, and because there is an ideal self in front of us calling us, a vision of the future and what can be or should be is always an identity-shaping factor. Seeing the good empowers. *We live from hope.* A sense of the future provides a vision for what comes next, a hope that things can be better, or a way to avoid danger and catastrophe. We are always looking for something to live into that will make our lives significant or more enjoyable. As Gandolf told Frodo in the first *Lord of the Rings* movie, "All you have to decide is what to do with the time that is given to you." The call of the future shapes who we are.

The importance of an anticipated future is nothing new. Note the following:

The comments from Viktor E. Frankl, a Holocaust survivor: "It is a peculiarity of man that he can only live by looking to the future—*sub specie aeternitatis*" and "The prisoner who had lost faith in the future—his future—was doomed."[6]
The three components of happiness are something to do, someone to love, and something to look forward to.[7]
Søren Kierkegaard: Life can only be understood backwards; but it must be lived forwards.[8]

5. See Martin Buber, *The Way of Man according to the Teachings of the Hasidim* (London: Routledge and Kegan Paul, 1950), 18.
6. Viktor E. Frankl, *Man's Search for Meaning*, rev. ed. (New York: Washington Square, 1984), 94–95.
7. Gordon Livingston, *Too Soon Old, Too Late Smart: Thirty True Things You Need to Know Now* ([Philadelphia]: DaCapo Lifelong, 2004), 9.
8. This is a summary of a longer saying: "Philosophy is perfectly right in saying that life must be understood backwards. But then one forgets the other clause—that it must

Charles Taylor: "In order to have a sense of who we are, we have to have a notion of how we have become, and of where we are going."[9]

Philip Esler: "All this means that groups tell themselves who they are in part by imagining where they are going."[10] The same is true for individuals.

Early in life the future is relatively mapped for us by others as we progress through childhood and school, age-appropriate learning activities, and expectations society places on us. We may think we are in control of our future, but that is partly true at best. Often systems and lack of resources and possibilities limit our choices. We do not even think that things could be different. Further, life brings events and forces into our lives over which we have no control but to which we must respond. Opportunities are missed or grasped, catastrophes disrupt and change possibilities, and new relations or events open new options.

Even if we feel our own future is unimportant, impossible, or unattractive, we still work so that things will be better for our children. Children have been viewed throughout history as "our" future. Even if people had no eschatology—no understanding of the future or life after death—their name lived on in their children, but the Christian hope does not focus on children. It focuses on seeing God and living with God.

Furthermore, our attitudes about life determine what we expect in the future. How pessimistic or optimistic are you about life? Is human history progressing or in such a state that only divine judgment can remedy things? Optimistic attitudes led to the popularity of postmillennialism in the nineteenth century. People expected things to get better and better until God's kingdom was here. Negative attitudes lead to a focus on an apocalyptic intervention; things are so bad that God must come, destroy everything, and start over. What is the basis of your optimism or pessimism?

---

be lived forwards." See *Søren Kierkegaard's Journals and Papers*, ed. Howard V. Hong and Edna H. Hong, 7 vols. (Bloomington: Indiana University Press, 1967), 1:450 (no. 1030).

9. Charles Taylor, *Sources of the Self: The Making of the Modern Identity* (Cambridge, MA: Harvard University Press, 1989), 47.

10. Philip F. Esler, *Conflict and Identity in Romans: The Social Setting of Paul's Letter* (Minneapolis: Fortress, 2003), 337.

From where do we *really* draw our identity? If life is about both memory and vision, do we live out of our past or out of our future? Neither can be neglected, but while the past cannot be changed, the future has the possibility for real growth and change, change that invades the present and shapes the future. Hope for the future determines how we feel about the present, whether we are in a holding action or have some sense of moving toward value and improvement. *We live from hope.* Hope is integral to faith. Romans 4:21 in a classic statement defines Abraham's faith as the conviction that what God promised he is able to do. Faith is a trust in and a commitment to God's future. The gospel by its very nature has an eschatology, a focus on the future, or it is not good news.

Everyone knows that Christianity has a focus on the future, but surprisingly, churches today do not emphasize the future very much. Earlier generations had prophecy conferences and fire and brimstone messages. Such excesses, especially when associated with date setting and a wrong kind of "otherworldliness," are embarrassing, as are some present views about Israel or hell. Vacuous statements about heaven appear, but specifics about the Bible's teaching on the future are rarely given, and judgment is rarely mentioned. Often discussions of eschatology were and are both confusing and divisive. Getting in and staying in seem to be the primary concerns of the church, but why bother getting in if we do not know how being in will change our future?

Further, the assumptions both Christians and non-Christians make are simplistic and unjustified. Bonhoeffer's cheap grace is paralleled by a cheap hope, which should be quickly rejected. The gospel is not "pie in the sky" and does not focus much on going to heaven. People who die, even Christians, do not become angels—or at least there is no biblical basis for such an idea. People who die are not still with us and are not watching us from above, despite what is often said at funerals or events where people of the past are commemorated. At least there is no biblical basis for such ideas—no, not even Hebrews 12:1. Surely churches need to do a better job teaching about God's future.

Vision promotes identity, and the gospel is about a vision for life. You need a vision that does not conclude at a dead end. The reality of aging and death is inescapable. The problem of theodicy—why God permits evil, suffering, and death—lurks behind every eschatological question and answer. We need something beyond this life to make it worthwhile and meaningful. Does God have a plan for creation? What explanation can there possibly be for the suffering in the world? Do we have an identity beyond the grave? Death cannot explain itself, nor can we explain it merely as humans, but we must deal with it honestly. Irenaeus, an early church father, even said, "The business of the Christian is nothing else than to be ever preparing for death."[11] Robert Browning said, "You never know what life means till you die: even throughout life tis death that makes life live."[12] His point is that death gives life its seriousness and fills it with the demand for meaning and significance. As important as that is, ultimately the issue is *the vindication of God*. Will God be shown to be righteous? God needs a future, Jesus needs a future, and so do humans.

A hope for justice is at the heart of any thought of the future. Scripture asserts that God has a plan from Genesis 1 on, and especially from Genesis 12 on. The Old Testament is largely a plea for justice and a condemnation of injustice. Jesus came to establish justice and create disciples who live justly. The gospel is an assertion that in an unjust world God is still for us, seeks us, and loves us, despite what may seem to be the case. The gospel is an assertion that God is indeed righteous, has shown it already with the incarnation and with the death and resurrection of Christ, and will demonstrate it again in the future when justice will reign.

Dealing with Time

The gospel is a weaving together of the past and the future, but humans do not handle time well, understandably so given its complexity. Some try to hold on to the past and fail to do justice to the present and future, but life is always changing. Some assume that their identity can be held at some level they have achieved, but identity cannot be held, even when people do not realize they are changing. Identity can be stunted so that the im-

11. Irenaeus, "Fragments from the Lost Writings of Irenaeus," no. 11, in *Ante-Nicene Fathers*, 1:570.

12. Robert Browning, "The Ring and the Book—Guido," in *The Poetical Works of Robert Browning*, 2 vols. (London: Smith, Elder, 1899), 1:278.

maturity of an earlier age is still present or so that one is locked in the past instead of adapting to a changing situation. Such "frozen identities" are not preserved; they are disabled and thwarted. We cannot hold the past.

Some focus only on the present as if the past and future were irrelevant. The demands of the present, or at least the preoccupation with the present, crowd out any meaningful consideration of the past or future, but both are unavoidable forces. The present does indeed need our focus, but the present cannot be grasped. It is experienced only in process, and it fades quickly.

Some focus on the future and fail to do justice to the present. This "otherworldliness" is escapism and does no justice to God's call on our present lives. We can and should prepare for the future, but we cannot live there. While sometimes we choose our future, sometimes our future chooses us, for which no preparation is possible. Even with the future, part is given and part is chosen.

We can live in neither the past nor the future. Some Jews often tried to live in the past, and some Christians have tried to live in the future. Earlier I pointed out that Jesus encouraged—even forced—people to live in the present, based on the past, and pulled by the future. This triple hold on time deserves reflection, and we must do justice to past, present, and future. How could life be otherwise when viewed as the grand narrative of God's actions in the world?

The Future Is Now

But Christianity inserts a new option for dealing with time, one based on the pouring out of the Spirit, the coming of the kingdom of God, and the resurrection. Jesus and the early church taught that *the future has invaded the present* and determines how life in the present is lived. Christians live in the *presence of the future.*

The good news of the gospel is that the anticipated future of God is already present and at work. Jesus repeatedly asserted the presence of the kingdom, especially in his Nazareth synagogue "sermon" in Luke 4:16–22. Isaiah 61 was a messianically loaded text in first-century Judaism, and Jesus surprised everyone by quoting this text and saying it was fulfilled in his work. As the one anointed by the Spirit, he was fulfilling the promises of God. Things were not as they had been. Sinners were invited to the feast; freedom, forgiveness, and grace were now being dispensed in his ministry; and evil was being confronted. A new age had begun. The time had been fulfilled, and the kingdom had arrived (Mark 1:15). This was Jesus's good news, and this focus on the presence of the kingdom is a major feature of his teaching throughout the Gospels, but he also pointed to a future, final consummation and judgment (for example, Matt. 24–25 and parallels). Judgment is an essential part of the future, or this life makes no sense. Biblical judgment always has a dual focus, on God coming to set things right and on God holding people accountable.

The early church likewise asserted that the "end of the ages" had come upon them (1 Cor. 10:11) because of the resurrection and the Spirit being poured out. According to Joel 2:28–32, the Spirit was to be poured out as an end-time event, but the early Christians knew they had experienced that pouring out at Pentecost. Like Jesus, the early church knew both the presence of the new age and that final fulfillment was still future. They also knew the persistence of the old age. With Jesus, the early church, and still for us, eschatology was and is in the process of being fulfilled. Several texts express this theology clearly: "The hour is coming and now is" (John 4:23); "The kingdom of God is in your midst" (Luke 17:21), but the immediately following verses describe a time of waiting before the coming of the Son of Man; "Since we have been justified . . . we will be saved" (Rom. 5:9); believers "have been transferred from death to life," but resurrection is still future (John 5:24–29). Christian theology is framed on a "now and not yet" dynamic. As 1 John 3:2 has it, "We are *now* children of God, but it has *not yet* been revealed what we will be. We know that when he is revealed we will be like him, for we will see him as he is." With Christianity many of the benefits of God's future are already present and impacting life. Eternal life, new birth, forgiveness, reconciliation, justification/acquittal, the pouring out of the Spirit, and much more—all items belonging to the end of the age—are all present possessions. Yet much is still future, and we await the final fulfillment of promises already at work.

The presence of God's future provides peace, energy, purpose, and new life now, but most significant are the *ethical* consequences. How could one have such convictions about the future without being drastically altered by the expectation? "Everyone who has this hope on him [Christ] purifies himself or herself, just as that one is pure" (1 John 3:3). Ethics can be grounded on several theological foundations—creation, covenant, Christology—but for Christians ethics are framed also and by necessity by the future, by the now and not yet of Christian thought.

Christians live in the overlap of the ages, well aware of the reality of the old age and that they live between the times. While they know the reality of the old age and still have to deal with sin, suffering, and death, they do not take their identity there. They take their identity from the newness Christ brings and the expectation of the fulfillment of God's promises.

But what can we actually know about the future? Most assumptions about the future—even among Christians—are juvenile and do not result from careful reading of biblical texts or from hard thought. Christians and others have too frequently offered sentimentalized and hardly biblical views of the afterlife. They have debated the order and timing of events, even though Scripture does not give details for such conclusions. We know far less than people think, but what we need to know the gospel provides. Death is not the end, and death is not the victor; God is. We will be held responsible for how we lived. God will judge—both establishing justice and holding people accountable. Life with God beyond death is a reality and is available, not because we have immortal souls, but because of resurrection. Only God is immortal. God is the God who creates life in the midst of death, and resurrection is a demonstration of human— bodily—value and dignity. There will be no lack, suffering, sorrow, or tears in new life *with God*. What the New Testament emphasizes is the defeat of death, the certainty of the triumph of God over evil, and the ethical impact of that expectation. *The primary purpose of eschatological texts, texts on the future, is ethical instruction.*

In the end eschatology—like every other theological topic—is a discussion of God. One's understanding of God preconditions and determines what one believes about the future. Each question answered about God determines the options available for answers about the future *and shapes us*. Does God exist? Does God have a relation to this world? Does God—and life—have a purpose? Does God act in this world? Is God a loving God or a judging God? Could God judge eternally? Can God be loving without being just? Does God experience time, or is time a phenomenon that only humans experience? Why be ethical if there is no judgment? What of a doctrine of reward? If the kingdom has come in Jesus, what is the ethical significance of the kingdom?

But eschatology is not merely a discussion of God. Eschatology arises from the clash of what is with what ought to be, if faith in a God of righteousness is to be maintained. This world cannot be God's ultimate intent. Creation itself groans as it waits for God's ultimate redemption (Rom. 8:20–22). This world needs to be set right. Still, the nature of the future hope is determined through and through, both as to its content and as to its manner of realization, by the nature of the God in whom belief is placed. The God presented in the gospel is the God who created, who has a purpose being worked out, who loves the ungodly, who has revealed himself in Jesus, and who will bring his grand story to completion. That is the basis for hope. If God has done the hard thing—loving the ungodly—the easy things will assuredly happen. The completion at Christ's coming will be the ultimate revelation of the love of God. The day of the Lord is not a day first of all for the people but a day of the *revelation and vindication of God's character* of absolute righteousness. God is vindicated before the world by a salvation that comes from him through fulfillment of his promises to Israel in Christ.

No matter what else we say, Christianity is about the future and the future's impact on the present. Note, for example, how substantively and significantly Paul bases his theological, pastoral, and ethical arguments on the future. To take 1 Corinthians as an example, perhaps his most pastoral letter, every chapter except chapters 12 and 14, both of which focus on the church as the body of Christ, have some focus on the future. Christians are those in whom the witness of Christ has been established, those who await the revelation of Christ, who will establish them blameless in the day of the Lord (1:6–8). What God has prepared for his people is unimaginably great (2:9). People will be rewarded for their labor—or not (3:8, 12–15; 9:27). God, knowing people's hearts, will judge all people righteously (4:4–5; 5:5, 12–13). Believers will be involved in judging the world and angels (6:2–3). Those defined by sin will be excluded from the kingdom, and what is temporary will be set aside (6:9–10; 11:32). Because of the future hope and because the present world is passing away, present life is reoriented and lived by different standards (7:29–31). Because of

Christ, believers' lives are oriented to God (8:6). Believers are those for whom God's future has broken in (10:11) and those who in the Lord's Supper proclaim Christ's death until he comes (11:26; cf. 16:22). Again, the temporary will be set aside, and completion ushered in. We will see God face-to-face and we will know God in reality (13:8–12). God will raise believers just as he raised Christ (6:13–14); the kingdom of God will be completed; Christ will reign; evil and death will be defeated forever; and believers will be transformed and given immortality (15:1–57). The significance of such hope is entirely ethical in that it enables endurance and productive work for God (15:58). The same focus can be seen in all of Paul's letters to varying degrees, and in the rest of the New Testament as well.

Quite clearly too, the identity of believers is changed because their *future* has been changed. "Our lives have been hidden with Christ in God," and our thinking should be reoriented accordingly (Col. 3:2–3). Our "citizenship is in heaven" (Phil. 3:20), which is to say our identity, our real being, is determined by our relation to God. We are "travelers and pilgrims" (Heb. 11:13 and 1 Pet. 2:11–12), which is to say that our identity is not determined by this world, our present geography—even though we have responsibilities for it—but by our future geography with God.

The future is important especially for Christian identity because of some sense of being engaged in the ongoing work God is doing, something that is not yet complete but is in process, something that is bigger than we are, and something of significance beyond the grave. Paul even describes believers as "partners" with God (1 Cor. 3:9; 1 Thess. 3:2).[13] This brings us back to where we started—humans engaged with God because they were created in God's image. Once again it is clear: humans take their identity from their God—and they live from hope.

Living from Hope

If we are to live from hope, how should it be understood? Hope is not a wispy dream but a solid conviction based on God's promise. Hope has

---

13. Some shrink from this identification, but the text seems clear to me.

always been undervalued, even in Christian thinking. It certainly was not a fundamental part of religion in the ancient Near East or in Greek and Roman cultures. The Greek word for "hope" was ambiguous and could even refer to negative outcomes, but not for Jews or Christians. "Hope" is crucial in the Old Testament and is a way of speaking about *trust* in God and an assurance about God, especially in the Psalms, where frequently people asserted their hope in the Lord and encouraged others to hope in him as well. (See, for example, Ps. 71:5: "For you are my hope, Lord.") The Lord is "the hope of all the ends of the earth" (Ps. 65:5). Jeremiah even spoke of Yahweh as "the hope of Israel" (Jer. 17:13; see also 14:8).

In the New Testament hope is as foundational as anything. The trilogy of faith, hope, and love appears ten times in the New Testament. Many will remember from 1 Corinthians 13:13 that these three remain when all else has faded, which shows that in eternity we still will hope in God. We will always live in openness to God's future and place our trust in God. Although 1 Corinthians 13 says love is the greatest of the three, in Colossians 1:4–5 hope is given priority as the basis of faith and love. In Romans 8:24 Paul even says, "You were saved by hope," and describes hope as focused on things not seen, very much the same as Hebrews 11:1 says about faith.

What is the difference between faith and hope? Not much. Both are essentially trust, and both have a focus on the unseen future. Faith may emphasize participation with Christ more, and hope may emphasize the future more. The best definition of hope may well be "Hope is faith on tiptoe."[14]

If the gospel is a gospel of hope, what is the content of the hope? First, genuine hope involves the abandonment of all calculations of the future. Hope is not about charts and date setting, and attempts should be abandoned to lay out an order more specific than texts like 1 Corinthians 15:20–28 already give. Hope is the conviction that the promises of God will be accomplished, that God will be revealed as God, that Christ will gather his people and be Lord of all, and that we will be restored to the glory humans should have because we are the image of God. The content of the hope is both about God's ultimate revelation of himself in Christ

---

14. C. F. D. Moule, *The Meaning of Hope* (Philadelphia: Fortress, 1963), 11.

and about humanity's ultimate achievement of God's intent. We live and lead from this hope, and this hope orients and activates life.

Does hope have a prayer in a world filled with hate? As a social worker, my daughter often dealt with sexual abuse cases. My daughter was doing art therapy with a seven-year-old girl, and the little girl wrote, "Have hope for me, please." She had some sense she was not going to make it unless someone redrew her map and offered an avenue to a different future. You cannot be different until you see yourself differently and act on it. The grace of God gives a clear vision and avenue for life to be different. Grace is about a different but very attainable future.

Much of the world similarly is looking for some reason for hope. Napoleon reportedly said, "A leader is a dealer in hope," which is precisely what Christian ministers should be. You cannot lead if you do not know where you are going and that you actually have a goal, if you do not know why you are going, and if you do not know the way to go. The gospel is the answer to all three, and as Christians it is all we have, both in addressing a hurting world and in addressing ourselves.

Perhaps the most important part of the message of hope is that you are more than you presently are. You are called to a higher level of existence, and by God's grace you can be different. That requires, of course, the willingness to move past the present, but that is what dying and rising with Christ and denying self to follow Christ are about.

I do not know the future for your individual identity, but I do know the frame in which your individual future should be lived. With regard to that frame, I have no doubt about the biblical assertion of the presence of the kingdom brought by Jesus's ministry or about the newness brought by the resurrection and by the pouring out of the Spirit. Nor do I have doubt about the reality of future judgment, where we will be held accountable for our lives. But these assertions ring hollow if the newness is not demonstrated in the lives of believers. If there is no evidence of the newness as something lived, should we not be laughed out of sight? The church has the task of demonstrating the presence of the new age in the midst of the old. That means living into one's own God-defined future.

A Final Appeal for Identity—
That You Become a Person

*Until I can tell the story of my self from the vantage of God's
action for me, I have not provided an authentically Christian
narrative of who I am. . . . Ongoing conversion of one's self
to the God who has made us for Himself is the normative
narrative of Christian identity.*

—Christopher J. Thomas, *Christian
Doctrine, Christian Identity*

There you have it, the nine factors of your identity: your physical and psychological makeup; your history; your relations; your self-interpreting, self-directing memory; your commitments; your actions; your boundaries; your ongoing process of change; and your future.

So, who are you? And who are you supposed to be? Perhaps more importantly, who do *you want to be*, and is it anything close to who God says you are? Many have a manufactured identity made to fit an image, but looking good is not good enough. What we all need is authenticity of being, that we live in accord with our true selves, not just the self we think we want to be but the self God calls us to be. Knowing who we are is not something we acquire by ourselves. We know ourselves only by knowing our God. Knowing ourselves is less important than knowing who made us, calls us, goes with us, and *knows us*. Peace cannot be found anywhere else.

How much are you willing to invest in yourself? People think they can look like giant oaks without putting down deep roots. When they realize how much effort it takes to put down deep roots, they settle for being bramble bushes.[1] To be who you really are takes work, but it is good and rewarding work. "To be a human, Augustine argues, is to be the consistent, enduring subject of one's deliberations and actions."[2] Anyone can rebel, and anyone can acquiesce, but it takes real effort to be a person. People often complain that they are not who they should be, but they take no action to change. Will you be yourself, not just any self, but the self you should be, the one you were created to be? Will you give attention to yourself, think about yourself, be honest with yourself, and take action with God's help and in dialogue with others to change?

My friend worried that a focus on identity would lead to self-centeredness and suggested focusing instead on vocation. In a real sense identity *is* a vocation, our one and only vocation. It is the individual's response to become what God has called each of us to be.

Dag Hammarskjöld said,

At every moment you choose yourself. But do you choose *your* self? Body and soul contain a thousand possibilities out of which you can build many *I*'s. But in only one of them is there a congruence of the elector and the elected. Only one—which you will never find until you have excluded all those superficial and fleeting possibilities of being and doing with which you toy, out of curiosity or wonder or greed, and which hinder you from casting anchor in the experience of the mystery of life, and the consciousness of the talent entrusted to you which is your *I*.[3]

At some point you have to take responsibility for yourself. You can blame your parents and your circumstances only so long; *you* are responsible

---

1. I used this analogy in *Stories with Intent: A Comprehensive Guide to the Parables of Jesus* (Grand Rapids: Eerdmans, 2008), 176.

2. Christopher J. Thomas, *Christian Doctrine, Christian Identity: Augustine and the Narratives of Character* (Lanham, MD: University Press of America, 1999), 89.

3. Dag Hammarskjöld, *Markings*, trans. Leif Sjöberg and W. H. Auden (New York: Knopf, 1965), 19.

for who you are. You deserve the chance to make an *honest* and critical analysis of yourself and choose *with an honest executive self* to be who you should be. You deserve to be the real you.

Here is the really crucial point. You do choose yourself, even though it is only in the context of the givens of your life. Yes, there is the huge debate about your ability to choose, the limits to your ability to choose caused by sin, hardwiring, and other people's sins and inabilities, but *you still choose yourself.* You did not choose to be born, your family of origin, or where you were born. *You* do choose if you will stay where you were born and how you will handle relations, even messy family relations. *You* choose whether you will be honest with yourself about yourself and whether you are willing to be displeasing to yourself in order to become what you should be. *You* choose whether you will be honest about and examine the society of which you are a part. *You* choose to accept or reject illusion. *You* choose whether you will live an unexamined life. *You* choose whether you will take responsibility for your actions. *You* choose how you will handle your urges and desires, especially your anger and your sexuality. *You* choose whether you will give attention to and love God and God's will or whether you will ignore God's intent for your life and go your own way. *You* choose how and where you will invest yourself and what interests you will pursue, whether your life will focus on really important issues and relations or on temporary pleasure. *You* choose whether you will be self-centered. *You* choose whether you will invest in your own learning and hold yourself accountable for learning. *You* choose the people you allow to be models and mentors of your life. *You* choose whether you will have good will toward people, even if they do not deserve it. *You* choose how you will react to injustice. *You* choose whether you will live from a sense of entitlement and privilege, so that you do not function from any sense of justice and fairness. *You* choose whether you will blame other people for your failures and all that is wrong in life. *You* choose how you treat people. *You* choose what kinds of attitudes characterize your life. *You* choose how you will steward your body and to what kinds of abuses and dangers you expose it. *You* choose the communities—or at least some of them—that you allow to tell you who you are and that will be formative in shaping you.

Is God present in your choices? Of course, but Madeleine Boucher makes a scary point: God assists people in the choices they make.[4] God helps us choose life with him or lets us go our own way and even ignore him. Why God is so tolerant I do not know, but I do know choosing to ignore God is a disastrous path. Romans 1:24–28 makes the point three times that in response to humans turning from God, "God gave them over." That is not a final giving over, as the rest of Romans makes clear. Despite human rebellion, God still seeks to live with us, nurture us, and participate with us. God still assists our choices to return to him. Even our choices are not ours alone.

Often people are not even aware of the possibilities for choice, but at some level we choose the source of our vision for life. All of us have an image of what life is—some set of assumptions, some ideology, or some theology, however poorly formed. What will give the vision of life that enables the broadest array of good choices? This is precisely what the gospel of Jesus Christ seeks to do. The transfiguration account is instructive. After Jesus is visibly transformed and Peter makes a bumbling statement about building three tabernacles, God says, "This is my beloved Son in whom I take delight. *Listen to him*" (Matt. 17:5). He is the one to whom you should listen to know who God says you are. His vision is the only vision worth having. From where does your vision of life come? Is it a trustworthy vision, and do you commit to it?

While in Hitler's prison Dietrich Bonhoeffer wrote a poem entitled "Who Am I?" in which he described the ambiguity he experienced from what others told him about himself and what he felt about himself, but he closed the poem by saying, "Who am I? They mock me, these lonely questions of mine. Whoever I am, thou knowest, O God, I am thine."[5]

It is indeed only with God's help that we can become ourselves, for we were created for life with God. Even in dire situations and the ambiguity of our own existence, the one true foundation and support for life is that we *belong to God.* That is not a foundation that may be merely presumed or accepted as some "cheap grace." It is the bracing and life-shattering moment of being alone before and with God. It is a foundation from

4. Madeleine Boucher, *The Mysterious Parable* (Washington, DC: Catholic Biblical Association of America, 1977), 54 and 62.

5. *A Testament to Freedom: The Essential Writings of Dietrich Bonhoeffer*, ed. Geffrey B. Kelly and F. Burton Nelson (San Francisco: HarperSanFrancisco, 1990), 539–40.

which we *must* live—honestly—with the full knowledge that grace never comes without cost. Still, even if the cost is high, as it was for Bonhoeffer, there is no other place to live and be one's true self.

In the parable of the prodigal we are told that the prodigal was in dire straits, and then "he came to himself" (Luke 15:17), a stunning assertion that he was not who he should be. All of us need to come to ourselves, but what will make you come to yourself, your *real* self? Why do we so often have to come to the end of our rope before we come to ourselves and realize that we are not living who we really are?

As with the prodigal, being who God says you are involves the rejection of *part* of who you say you are. Which part? The part that does not fit with the character of God, for you were created in God's image. This is not a rejection of self.[6] It is the rejection of self-centeredness and the rejection of an inadequate and misguided self that allows you to reach that summoning self that says you were created in the image of God and should live like it. You do not have to accept the negative voices from others or from within that say you are worthless or of little value. Nor should you accept the deluded voices affirming your superiority. God does not view you negatively or as better than others. God calls you to be your summoning self, and God is eager to walk with you and assist you on the way.

We started with the question, Who are you? So, what is the answer, the honest answer, which *you alone* can give? I have only given the elements at which you must look and some relevant biblical texts. Perhaps the answer should be given while looking at yourself in a mirror, for the person in the mirror knows. If this book has any purpose at all, it is to assist you to come to yourself. Look in the mirror and be conscious of being an individual before God, responsible to God, and energized for life by a God who cares for you, loves you, and calls you to participate in life with God. You will never be yourself anywhere else. How will you show who you are? What will you change to become who God says you are? You deserve to be who God says you are.

6. Again, see Henri J. M. Nouwen's statement, "Self-rejection is the greatest enemy of the spiritual life because it contradicts the sacred voice that calls us the 'Beloved.' Being the Beloved constitutes the core truth of our existence" (*Life of the Beloved: Spiritual Living in a Secular World* [New York: Crossroad, 1992], 33).

Select Bibliography

Akerlof, George A., and Rachel E. Kranton. *Identity Economics: How Our Identities Shape Our Work, Wages, and Well-Being.* Princeton: Princeton University Press, 2010.

Anderson, E. Byron. *Worship and Christian Identity: Practicing Ourselves.* Collegeville, MN: Liturgical Press, 2003.

Asano, Atsuhiro. *Community-Identity Construction in Galatians: Exegetical, Social-Anthropological, and Socio-Historical Studies.* Journal for the Study of the New Testament Supplement Series 285. London: T. & T. Clark International, 2005.

Augustine. *Confessions.* Translated by William Watts. Loeb Classical Library. Cambridge, MA: Harvard University Press, 1977.

Baumgarten, Albert I., Jan Assmann, and Guy G. Stroumsa. *Self, Soul, and Body in Religious Experience.* Studies in the History of Religions 78. Leiden: Brill, 1998.

Benner, David G. *The Gift of Being Yourself: The Sacred Call to Self-Discovery.* Downers Grove: InterVarsity, 2004.

Bevere, Allan R. *Sharing in the Inheritance: Identity and the Moral Life in Colossians.* Journal for the Study of the New Testament Supplement Series 226. London: Sheffield, 2003.

Brawley, Robert L. "Identity and Metaethics: Being Justified and Ethics in Galatians." In *Character Ethics and the New Testament: Moral Dimensions of Scripture,* edited by Robert L. Brawley, 107–26. Louisville: Westminster John Knox, 2007.

Select Bibliography

Bulkeley, Kelly. *The Wondering Brain: Thinking about Religion with and beyond Cognitive Neuroscience.* New York: Routledge, 2005.

Burke, Peter, and Jan E. Stets. *Identity Theory.* New York: Oxford University Press, 2009.

Campbell, William S. *Paul and the Creation of Christian Identity.* Library of New Testament Studies 322. London: T. & T. Clark, 2006.

Cocksworth, Christopher J. *Holding Together: Gospel, Church, and Spirit; The Essentials of Christian Identity.* London: Canterbury Press Norwich, 2008.

Cooper, Terry D. *Sin, Pride, and Self-Acceptance: The Problem of Identity in Theology and Psychology.* Downers Grove: InterVarsity, 2003.

Cromhout, Markus. *Walking in Their Sandals: A Guide to First-Century Israelite Ethnic Identity.* Eugene, OR: Cascade, 2010.

Crook, Zeba A., and Philip A. Harland, eds. *Identity and Interaction in the Ancient Mediterranean: Jews, Christians, and Others; Essays in Honour of Stephen G. Wilson.* New Testament Monographs 18. Sheffield: Sheffield Phoenix, 2001.

Dunning, Benjamin H. *Aliens and Sojourners: Self as Other in Early Christianity.* Philadelphia: University of Pennsylvania Press, 2009.

Duquoc, Christian, Casiano Floristán Samanes, and James Aitken Gardiner, eds. *Christian Identity.* Edinburgh: T. & T. Clark, 1988.

Ehrensperger, Kathy, and J. Brian Tucker, eds. *Reading Paul in Context: Explorations in Identity Formation; Essays in Honour of William S. Campbell.* Library of New Testament Studies 428. London: T. & T. Clark International, 2010.

Engberg-Pedersen, Troels. "Galatians in Romans 5–8 and Paul's Construction of the Identity of Christ Believers. In *Texts and Contexts: Biblical Texts in Their Textual and Situational Contexts; Essays in Honor of Lars Hartman,* edited by T. Fornberg and D. Hellholm, 477–503. Oslo: Scandinavian University Press, 1995.

Erikson, Erik H. *Identity and the Life Cycle.* New York: Norton, 1980.

———. *Identity, Youth, and Crisis.* New York: Norton, 1968.

Esler, Philip F. *Conflict and Identity in Romans: The Social Setting of Paul's Letter.* Minneapolis: Fortress, 2003.

Evans, C. Stephen. *Kierkegaard on Faith and the Self: Collected Essays.* Waco: Baylor University Press, 2006.

Feinberg, Todd E. *Altered Egos: How the Brain Creates the Self.* Oxford: Oxford University Press, 2001.

Frey, Jörg, Daniel R. Schwartz, and Stephanie Gripentrog, eds. *Jewish Identity in the Greco-Roman World = Jüdische Identität in der Griechisch-Römischen Welt*. Leiden: Brill, 2007.

Gallagher, Shaun. *How the Body Shapes the Mind*. Oxford: Clarendon, 2005.

Hakola, Raimo. *Identity Matters: John, the Jews, and Jewishness*. Leiden: Brill, 2005.

Harland, Philip A. *Dynamics and Identity in Early Christianity*. London: T. & T. Clark, 2010.

Holmberg, Bengt, ed. *Exploring Early Christian Identity*. Wissenschaftliche Untersuchungen zum Neuen Testament 226. Tübingen: Mohr Siebeck, 2008.

Holmberg, Bengt, and Mikael Winninge, eds. *Identity Formation in the New Testament*. Wissenschaftliche Untersuchungen zum Neuen Testament 227. Tübingen: Mohr Siebeck, 2008.

Horrell, David G. *Becoming Christian: Essays on 1 Peter and the Making of Christian Identity*. Library of New Testament Studies 394. London: Bloomsbury, 2015.

Hvalvik, Reidar, and Karl Olav Sandnes, eds. *Early Christian Prayer and Identity Formation*. Wissenschaftliche Untersuchungen zum Neuen Testament 336. Tübingen: Mohr Siebeck, 2014.

Jeffrey, David L. *People of the Book: Christian Identity and Literary Culture*. Grand Rapids: Eerdmans, 1996.

Jewish and Christian Self-Definition. Vol. 1, *The Shaping of Christianity in the Second and Third Centuries*, ed. E. P. Sanders. Philadelphia: Fortress, 1980. Vol. 2, *Aspects of Judaism in the Graeco-Roman Period*, ed. E. P. Sanders with A. I. Baumgarten and Alan Mendelson. Philadelphia: Fortress, 1981. Vol. 3, *Self-Definition in the Greco-Roman World*, ed. Ben F. Meyer and E. P. Sanders. Philadelphia: Fortress, 1982.

Jossa, Giorgio. *Jews or Christians? The Followers of Jesus in Search of Their Own Identity*. Translated by Molly Rogers. Wissenschaftliche Untersuchungen zum Neuen Testament 202. Tübingen: Mohr Siebeck, 2006.

Kelsey, David H. *Eccentric Existence: A Theological Anthropology*. 2 vols. Louisville: Westminster John Knox, 2009.

Kilner, John F. *Dignity and Destiny: Humanity in the Image of God*. Grand Rapids: Eerdmans, 2015.

Kocur, Miroslav. *National and Religious Identity: A Study in Galatians 3,23–29 and Romans 10,12–21*. Österreichische Biblische Studien 24. Frankfurt am Main: Peter Lang, 2003.

Larmore, Charles. *The Practices of the Self.* Translated by Sharon Bowman. Chicago: University of Chicago Press, 2010.

LeDoux, Joseph E. *Synaptic Self: How Our Brains Become Who We Are.* New York: Viking, 2002.

Lieu, Judith M. *Christian Identity in the Jewish and Graeco-Roman World.* Oxford: Oxford University Press, 2004.

Lints, Richard, Michael S. Horton, and Mark R. Talbot, eds. *Personal Identity in Theological Perspective.* Grand Rapids: Eerdmans, 2006.

MacIntyre, Alasdair. *After Virtue: A Study in Moral Theory.* 3rd ed. Notre Dame: University of Notre Dame Press, 2007.

Martin, Raymond, and John Barresi. *The Rise and Fall of Soul and Self: An Intellectual History of Personal Identity.* New York: Columbia University Press, 2006.

May, Alistair Scott. *The Body for the Lord: Sex and Identity in 1 Corinthians 5–7.* Journal for the Study of the New Testament Supplement Series 278. London: T. & T. Clark, 2004.

McFarland, Ian A. *Difference and Identity: A Theological Anthropology.* Cleveland: Pilgrim Press, 2001.

McLean, Kate C., and Moin Syed, eds. *The Oxford Handbook of Identity Development.* Oxford: Oxford University Press, 2015.

McNamara, Patrick, *The Neuroscience of Religious Experience.* Cambridge: Cambridge University Press, 2009.

Meyer, Ben F. *The Early Christians: Their World Mission and Self-Discovery.* Wilmington, DE: Michael Glazier, 1986.

Mikoski, Gordon S. *Baptism and Christian Identity: Teaching in the Triune Name.* Grand Rapids: Eerdmans, 2009.

Moxnes, Halvor, ed. *Constructing Early Christian Families: Family as Social Reality and Metaphor.* London: Routledge, 1997.

Pannenberg, Wolfhart. *Anthropology in Theological Perspective.* Translated by Matthew J. O'Connell. Philadelphia: Westminster, 1985.

Pascal, Blaise. *Pensées.* Translated by W. F. Trotter. New York: Modern Library, 1941.

Paul, Ellen Frankel, Fred Dycus Miller, and Jeffrey Paul. *Personal Identity.* Cambridge: Cambridge University Press, 2005.

Perry, John. *Identity, Personal Identity, and the Self.* Indianapolis: Hackett, 2002.
———. *Personal Identity.* Berkeley: University of California Press, 2008.
Riches, John K. *Conflicting Mythologies: Identity Formation in the Gospels of Mark and Matthew.* Edinburgh: T. & T. Clark, 2000.
Ricoeur, Paul. *Oneself as Another.* Translated by Kathleen Blamey. Chicago: University of Chicago Press, 1992.
Rowan, John, and Mick Cooper, eds. *The Plural Self: Multiplicity in Everyday Life.* London: Sage, 1999.
Schwöbel, Christoph, and Colin E. Gunton, eds. *Persons, Divine and Human: King's College Essays in Theological Anthropology.* Edinburgh: T. & T. Clark, 1991.
Seesengood, Robert Paul. *Competing Identities: The Athlete and the Gladiator in Early Christianity.* London: T. & T. Clark, 2006.
Shoemaker, Sydney, and Richard Swinburne. *Personal Identity.* Oxford: Blackwell, 1984.
Siegel, Daniel J. *The Developing Mind: How Relationships and the Brain Interact to Shape Who We Are.* New York: Guilford, 1999.
Sorabji, Richard. *Self: Ancient and Modern Insights about Individuality, Life, and Death.* Chicago: University of Chicago Press, 2006.
Taylor, Charles. *Sources of the Self: The Making of the Modern Identity.* Cambridge, MA: Harvard University Press, 1989.
Tellbe, Mikael. *Christ-Believers in Ephesus: A Textual Analysis of Early Christian Identity Formation in a Local Perspective.* Wissenschaftliche Untersuchungen zum Neuen Testament 242. Tübingen: Mohr-Siebeck, 2009.
Thiselton, Anthony C. *Interpreting God and the Postmodern Self: On Meaning, Manipulation, and Promise.* Grand Rapids: Eerdmans, 1995.
Thomas, Christopher J. *Christian Doctrine, Christian Identity: Augustine and the Narratives of Character.* Lanham, MD: University Press of America, 1999.
Tucker, J. Brian. *Remain in Your Calling: Paul and the Continuation of Social Identities in 1 Corinthians.* Eugene, OR: Pickwick, 2011.
———. *You Belong to Christ: Paul and the Formation of Social Identity in 1 Corinthians 1–4.* Eugene, OR: Pickwick, 2010.
Tucker, J. Brian, and Coleman A. Baker. *T. & T. Clark Handbook to Social Identity in the New Testament.* London: Bloomsbury, 2014.
Udoh, Fabian E., et al., eds. *Redefining First-Century Jewish and Christian Iden-*

tities: Essays in Honor of Ed Parish Sanders. Notre Dame: University of Notre Dame Press, 2008.

Van der Borght, Eduardus, ed. *Christian Identity.* Studies in Reformed Theology 16. Leiden: Brill, 2008.

Van der Watt, J. G., and F. S. Malan. *Identity, Ethics, and Ethos in the New Testament.* Beihefte zur Zeitschrift für die neutestamentliche Wissenschaft und die Kunde der älteren Kirche 141. Berlin: Walter de Gruyter, 2006.

Van Huyssteen, J. Wentzel, and Erik P. Wiebe, eds. *In Search of Self: Interdisciplinary Perspectives on Personhood.* Grand Rapids: Eerdmans, 2011.

Volf, Miroslav. *The End of Memory: Remembering Rightly in a Violent World.* Grand Rapids: Eerdmans, 2006.

———. *Exclusion and Embrace: An Exploration of Identity, Otherness, and Reconciliation.* Nashville: Abingdon, 1996.

Welker, Michael, ed. *The Depth of the Human Person: A Multidisciplinary Approach.* Grand Rapids: Eerdmans, 2014.

White, Vernon. *Identity.* London: SCM, 2002.

Zangenberg, Jürgen, Harold W. Attridge, and Dale B. Martin, eds. *Religion, Ethnicity, and Identity in Ancient Galilee: A Region in Transition.* Wissenschaftliche Untersuchungen zum Neuen Testament 210. Tübingen: Mohr Siebeck, 2007.

Index of Names and Subjects

INDEX OF NAMES AND SUBJECTS

Index of Scripture References

INDEX OF SCRIPTURE REFERENCES